"Why would any sane person . . . alternately boil and freeze on a mountain so high that often only 10 or 15 steps can be taken without sitting down to recover one's breath in the rarefied atmosphere?

"The answer may come as a surprise: because of the tremendous amount of solid evidence that on the mountain the Turks call Agri Dagh—The Mountain of Agony—a substantial vestige of the Ark of Noah—if not the Ark's massive hull itself —remains to this very day, frozen in the glacial ice, but occasionally attaining the surface when the ice cap recedes under the blazing sun.

"... On August 17, 1970, at 1:30 P.M., I attained the incredibly difficult 16,946-foot peak of Ararat...."

JOHN WARWICK MONTGOMERY

Dr. Montgomery is presently Professor of Law and Theology at the International School Of Law in Washington, D.C.

For a number of years he was professor and chairman of the Division of Church History and Christian Thought at Trinity Evangelical Divinity School in Deerfield, Illinois, and was also director of its European program at the University of Strasbourg, France.

He has also been a regular visiting professor of Theology at Concordia Seminary and at De Paul University.

In 1970 he served as Honorary Fellow of Revelle College, University of California, at San Diego.

Dr. Montgomery holds seven earned degrees, including a Doctorate in Philosophy from the University of Chicago and a Doctorate in Theology from the University of Strasbourg.

A frequent contributor to *Christianity Today*, the author has been honored by inclusion in *Who's Who in America, Who's Who in France,* and *The Dictionary of International Biography*.

He is an ordained Lutheran minister and the author of some twenty books in the areas of theology, philosophy, and church history.

THE QUEST
FOR NOAH'S ARK

A Treasury of Documented Accounts from
Ancient Times to the Present Day of Sightings
of the Ark and Explorations of Mount Ararat,
with a Narration of the Author's Successful
Ascent to the Summit of Noah's Mountain

John Warwick Montgomery

SECOND EDITION
REVISED AND EXPANDED

INCLUDING SATELLITE DATA

DIMENSION BOOKS
Bethany Fellowship, Inc.
Minneapolis, Minnesota

THE QUEST FOR NOAH'S ARK

Published by Pyramid Publications for
Bethany Fellowship, Inc.

Dimension Books edition published December, 1974

ISBN: 0-87123-477-7

Printed in the United States of America

DIMENSION BOOKS are published by
Bethany Fellowship, Inc.
6820 Auto Club Road
Minneapolis, Minnesota 55438, U.S.A.

For

NANO CHALFANT
GUY DUERBECK
DORA HILLMAN
ROBERT C. SPROUL

ἄγγελοι

> The mighty Ark
> Rests upon Ararat; but nought around
> Its inmates can behold, save o'er the expanse
> Of boundless waters the sun's orient orb
> Stretching the hull's long shadow, or the moon
> In silence through the silver-curtained clouds
> Sailing, as she herself were lost, and left
> In hollow loneliness.

—William Lisle Bowles, English divine, poet and antiquary (1762-1850)

Preface

A source of added frustration that I have occasionally experienced in an already frustrating world is the suspicion that I myself would not necessarily want to read some of the books I have written. Not (hopefully) because they lack quality or significance, but because they do not always "grab" one at depth level. Strange to say, this book about an exceedingly high mountain does operate in depth; even its author would have difficulty putting it down! Why?

To begin with, the book interrelates high adventure and scholarship. This is not generally the case: as a rule, one must read fiction or journalistic travelogue literature (essentially a species of fiction!) to find excitement; and scholarly tomes, like certain sermons, cause the Eutychus in us to fall asleep, sometimes with disastrous results. The split between scholarship and adventure is unfortunate, for there have been many adventurous scholars. Archaeological literature has often displayed the excitement of scholarship, and so, characteristically, has the literature of mountaineering. Wilfred Noyce's book, *Scholar Mountaineers*,[1] reminds us of the connection as incarnated in Dante, Petrarch, Rousseau, Goethe, Leslie Stephen, and many others. The present volume endeavors to follow this noble tradition, for it offers not only an anthology of the accounts of those who have ascended one of the great mountains of the globe, but also (often translated into English for the very first time from Greek, Latin, and French) every responsible report of sightings of Noah's vessel on Ararat—from the most ancient times to our own day. No single volume in any language can provide the reader with as much primary source information on Greater Ararat and its diluvial secret as this one. Armchair explorers are going to have difficulty escaping from these pages!

---

[1] Wilfrid Noyce, *Scholar Mountaineers: Pioneers of Parnassus* (London: Dennis Dobson, 1950). Cf. Sir Gavin de Beer's *Early Travelers in the Alps* (New York: October House, 1967).

Secondly, this book focuses on a quest. We often complain about the "flatness" of life; its lack of "heights" or "mountain-top experiences." In using such expressions, we are tacitly bearing witness to the need for Ponce de Leon's Cuidad de Oro, Campanella's City of the Sun, James Hilton's Shangri-La.[2] How frequently such longings connect with mountain fastnesses![3] Do we perhaps realize instinctively that our quest for ultimate meaning can only be fulfilled "higher up": in a realm as far above ordinary experience as heaven stands above earth? Does the search become, when carried through consistently, a search for the Grail—a search for religious truth that stands above us?[4]

Perhaps this is one of the reasons why so many key biblical events are associated with mountains (the giving of the Law on Sinai, the Transfiguration of Our Lord, etc., etc.). The line of demarcation between the antediluvian world and our world passes directly through the summit of Greater Ararat, and the quest upon which this book is predicated likewise centers there.

> Back through the dusk
> Of ages Contemplation turns her view,
> To mark, as from its infancy, the world
> Peopled again from that mysterious shrine
> That rested on the top of Ararat.

So are we gripped by the vision: a melody that produces infinite variations even in our own time, from C. Day Lewis' "Noah and the Waters," which turns the Noahic tale into a commentary on the Marxist over-

---

[2] cf. Frederic R. White (ed.) *Famous Utopias of the Renaissance* (New York: Hendricks House; Farrar, Straus, 1946); Elaine Sanceau, *The Land of Prester John* (New York: Alfred A. Knopf, 1944); Michel Massian (ed.), *Les explorateurs* (Paris: Robert Delpire, 1965).

[3] See Henri Bordeaux, "The Call of High Places," in M.A. Michael (ed.), *Traveller's Quest* (London: William Hodge, 1950), pp. 29-52.

[4] cf. *The Quest of the Holy Grail*, trans. P. M. Matarasso (Harmondsworth, Middlesex, Eng.: Penguin Books, 1969); Bernard Blackstone, *The Lost Travellers* (London: Longmans, Green, 1962).

throw of the existing order,[5] to the Danny Kaye-
Richard Rogers lighthearted musical rendition in
Broadway's *Two by Two*.[6] Unsatisfying as such pre-
sentations are, they keep us from forgetting the quest.
Did the great Deluge really occur? Were eight souls
saved by water? Could the very vessel in which the race
survived still await discovery on one of the most awe-
inspiring and numinous mountains on the globe? Could
Scripture really—even in this age of science—convey
not a poetic, demythologized truth which leaves us on
the flatlands of existence, but a factual record of real
happenings, capable of saving us even as Noah was
saved?

This author answers all of these depth questions
about heights with a yes. He had read the travellers and
commentators such as Marco Polo, who wrote:

> In the heart of Greater Armenia is a very high
> mountain, shaped like a cube, on which Noah's
> ark is said to have rested, whence it is called the
> Mountain of Noah's Ark. It is so broad and long
> that it takes more than two days to go round it.
> On the summit the snow lies so deep all the year
> round that no one can ever climb it; this snow
> never entirely melts, but new snow is for ever fall-
> ing on the old.[7]

And he has read Thomas Hartwell Horne, who even
after Parrot's ascend of Ararat in 1928 could speak of
it in these terms:

---

[5] Lewis employs as his prefatory quotation the following passage
(!) from the *Communist Manifesto:* "Finally, when the class war is
about to be fought to a finish, disintegration of the ruling class and
the old order of society becomes so active, so acute, that a small part
of the ruling class breaks away to make common cause with the revolutionary class, the class which holds the future in its hands. . . ."

[6] cf. also David Garnett's novel, *Two by Two: A Story of Survival*
(New York: Atheneum, 1964).

[7] Marco Polo, *The Travels,* ed. and trans. Ronald Latham (London: The Folio Society, 1968), p. 34.

> ARARAT, a celebrated mountain in the Greater
> Armenia, on which Noah's ark rested after the del-
> uge. (Gen. viii.4). It is of stupendous height, and
> inaccessible to the summit, which is covered with
> perpetually frozen snow: and the magnitude of the
> peak is annually increasing in consequence of the
> continual accession of ice.[8]

But having ascended Ararat himself, he knows that it is
indeed accessible. He likewise believes biblical truth is
accessible, and is, in the final analysis, the only truth
that remains accessible forever. With the writer of
Prayers from the Ark, he prays its concluding peti-
tion:[9]

> The Ark waits,
> Lord,
> the Ark waits on Your will,
> and the sign of Your peace.
>
> •
>
> The Ark waits,
> Lord;
> it has endured.
> Let me carry it
> a sprig of hope and joy,
> and put, at the heart of its forsakenness,
> this, in which Your love clothes me,
> Grace immaculate.

JOHN WARWICK MONTGOMERY

23 January 1972
The Festival of the Transfiguration of Our Lord

*   *   *

---

[8] Thomas Hartwell Horne, *An Introduction to the Critical Study and Knowledge of the Holy Scriptures,* III (7th ed.; London: T. Cadell, 1834), p. 548.

[9] Carmen Bernos de Gasztold, *Prayers from the Ark.* trans. Rumer Godden (London: Macmillan, 1963), p. 65. Cf. the same author's *Creatures' Choir* (New York: Viking Press, 1965).

The second edition of *The Quest for Noah's Ark* updates the first by the inclusion of two additional essays, the most extensive of which deals with the existing possibility that satellite photography may offer corroboration of the Ark's survival. The actual photograph corresponding to the "unidentified object" drawing in the first edition has now been substituted for that drawing.

Readers who know Turkish may be interested in the series of seven articles on the survival of the Ark which were based on the present book and appeared under my by-line in *Hürriyet,* the largest newspaper in Turkey ("Nuh'um Gemisini Aradik," *Hürriyet,* November 16-22, 1973).

JOHN WARWICK MONTGOMERY

29 September 1974
The Festival of St. Michael and All Angels

Acknowledgements

The author wishes to express his gratitude to the Newberry Library, Chicago, for its unfailing kindness in providing materials necessary to the historical side of this project. Would that all libraries held so high the ideal of bibliographical service! Thanks also to G. S. Dugdale, Librarian of the Royal Geographical Society, London, for his kind consideration in verifying certain references and in putting photocopies of relevant materials at my disposal.

He likewise wishes publicly to thank his Graduate Research Assistant, Mr. James R. Moore, B.S., M.Div., who aided him in so many ways in the completion of this book. May the angels who keep watch over Research Assistants give Mr. Moore special attention as he proceeds to the University of Manchester, on a Marshall Scholarship, for doctoral study!

Finally, the author's appreciation goes to all holders of copyrighted materials who have graciously allowed passages from their works to appear in this volume.

NOTE TO NOTES

In the first three Parts of this book, square brackets surrounding material in notes to the text distinguish our editorial comments from notes which were a part of the original selection quoted. In brief, [ ] = Montgomery.

16

Contents

Part Four: Ark Fever: Today's Endeavor To Find Noah's Ark

Appendices

Genesis 6:13–16

וַיֹּאמֶר אֱלֹהִים לְנֹחַ קֵץ כָּל־בָּשָׂר בָּא לְפָנַי כִּי־מָלְאָה
הָאָרֶץ חָמָס מִפְּנֵיהֶם וְהִנְנִי מַשְׁחִיתָם אֶת־הָאָרֶץ׃ עֲשֵׂה
לְךָ תֵּבַת עֲצֵי־גֹפֶר קִנִּים תַּעֲשֶׂה אֶת־הַתֵּבָה וְכָפַרְתָּ אֹתָהּ
מִבַּיִת וּמִחוּץ בַּכֹּפֶר׃ וְזֶה אֲשֶׁר תַּעֲשֶׂה אֹתָהּ שְׁלֹשׁ מֵאוֹת
אַמָּה אֹרֶךְ הַתֵּבָה חֲמִשִּׁים אַמָּה רָחְבָּהּ וּשְׁלֹשִׁים אַמָּה
קוֹמָתָהּ׃ צֹהַר תַּעֲשֶׂה לַתֵּבָה וְאֶל־אַמָּה תְּכַלֶּנָּה מִלְמַעְלָה
וּפֶתַח הַתֵּבָה בְּצִדָּהּ תָּשִׂים תַּחְתִּיִּם שְׁנִיִּם וּשְׁלִשִׁים
תַּעֲשֶׂהָ׃

13 And God said unto Noah, The end of all flesh is come before me; for the earth is filled with violence through them; and, behold, I will destroy them with the earth.

14 ¶ Make thee an ark of gopher wood; rooms shalt thou make in the ark, and shalt pitch it within and without with pitch.

15 And this is the fashion which thou shalt make it of: The length of the ark shall be three hundred cubits, the breadth of it fifty cubits, and the height of it thirty cubits.

16 A window shalt thou make to the ark, and in a cubit shalt thou finish it above; and the door of the ark shalt thou set in the side thereof; with lower, second, and third stories shalt thou make it.

- - - - - - - - - - - - - - - - -

Genesis 7:11–20

וּבִשְׁנַת שֵׁשׁ־מֵאוֹת שָׁנָה לְחַיֵּי־
נֹחַ בַּחֹדֶשׁ הַשֵּׁנִי בְּשִׁבְעָה־עָשָׂר יוֹם לַחֹדֶשׁ בַּיּוֹם הַזֶּה
נִבְקְעוּ כָּל־מַעְיְנֹת תְּהוֹם רַבָּה וַאֲרֻבֹּת הַשָּׁמַיִם נִפְתָּחוּ׃
וַיְהִי הַגֶּשֶׁם עַל־הָאָרֶץ אַרְבָּעִים יוֹם וְאַרְבָּעִים לָיְלָה׃
בְּעֶצֶם הַיּוֹם הַזֶּה בָּא נֹחַ וְשֵׁם־וְחָם וָיֶפֶת בְּנֵי־נֹחַ וְאֵשֶׁת
נֹחַ וּשְׁלֹשֶׁת נְשֵׁי־בָנָיו אִתָּם אֶל־הַתֵּבָה׃ הֵמָּה וְכָל־הַחַיָּה
לְמִינָהּ וְכָל־הַבְּהֵמָה לְמִינָהּ וְכָל־הָרֶמֶשׂ הָרֹמֵשׂ עַל־
הָאָרֶץ לְמִינֵהוּ וְכָל־הָעוֹף לְמִינֵהוּ כֹּל צִפּוֹר כָּל־כָּנָף׃
וַיָּבֹאוּ אֶל־נֹחַ אֶל־הַתֵּבָה שְׁנַיִם שְׁנַיִם מִכָּל־הַבָּשָׂר אֲשֶׁר־
בּוֹ רוּחַ חַיִּים׃ וְהַבָּאִים זָכָר וּנְקֵבָה מִכָּל־בָּשָׂר בָּאוּ
כַּאֲשֶׁר צִוָּה אֹתוֹ אֱלֹהִים וַיִּסְגֹּר יְהוָה בַּעֲדוֹ׃ וַיְהִי הַמַּבּוּל
אַרְבָּעִים יוֹם עַל־הָאָרֶץ וַיִּרְבּוּ הַמַּיִם וַיִּשְׂאוּ אֶת־הַתֵּבָה
וַתָּרָם מֵעַל הָאָרֶץ׃ וַיִּגְבְּרוּ הַמַּיִם וַיִּרְבּוּ מְאֹד עַל־הָאָרֶץ
וַתֵּלֶךְ הַתֵּבָה עַל־פְּנֵי הַמָּיִם׃ וְהַמַּיִם גָּבְרוּ מְאֹד מְאֹד
עַל־הָאָרֶץ וַיְכֻסּוּ כָּל־הֶהָרִים הַגְּבֹהִים אֲשֶׁר־תַּחַת כָּל־
הַשָּׁמָיִם׃ חֲמֵשׁ עֶשְׂרֵה אַמָּה מִלְמַעְלָה גָּבְרוּ הַמָּיִם וַיְכֻסּוּ
הֶהָרִים׃

11 ¶ In the six hundredth year of Noah's life, in the second month, the seventeenth day of the month, the same day were all the fountains of the great deep broken up, and the windows of heaven were opened.

12 And the rain was upon the earth forty days and forty nights.

13 In the selfsame day entered Noah, and Shem, and Ham, and Japheth, the sons of Noah, and Noah's wife, and the three wives of his sons with them, into the ark;

14 They, and every beast after his kind, and all the cattle after their kind, and every creeping thing that creepeth upon the earth after his kind, and every fowl after his kind, every bird of every sort.

15 And they went in unto Noah into the ark, two and two of all flesh, wherein is the breath of life.

16 And they that went in, went in male and female of all flesh, as God had commanded him: and the LORD shut him in.

17 And the flood was forty days upon the earth; and the waters increased, and bare up the ark, and it was lift up above the earth.

18 And the waters prevailed, and were increased greatly upon the earth; and the ark went upon the face of the waters.

19 And the waters prevailed exceedingly upon the earth; and all the high hills, that were under the whole heaven, were covered.

20 Fifteen cubits upward did the waters prevail; and the mountains were covered.

- - - - - - - - - - - - - - - - -

Genesis 8:1

וַיִּזְכֹּר אֱלֹהִים אֶת־נֹחַ וְאֵת כָּל־הַחַיָּה וְאֶת־כָּל־הַבְּהֵמָה
אֲשֶׁר אִתּוֹ בַּתֵּבָה וַיַּעֲבֵר אֱלֹהִים רוּחַ עַל־הָאָרֶץ וַיָּשֹׁכּוּ

AND God remembered Noah, and every living thing, and all the cattle that was with him in the ark: and God made a wind

דָּמִים: וַיִּסָּכְרוּ מַעְיְנֹת תְּהוֹם וַאֲרֻבֹּת הַשָּׁמָיִם וַיִּכָּלֵא 2

הַגֶּשֶׁם מִן־הַשָּׁמָיִם: וַיָּשֻׁבוּ הַמַּיִם מֵעַל הָאָרֶץ הָלוֹךְ וָשׁוֹב 3

וַיַּחְסְרוּ הַמַּיִם מִקְצֵה חֲמִשִּׁים וּמְאַת יוֹם: וַתָּנַח הַתֵּבָה 4

בַּחֹדֶשׁ הַשְּׁבִיעִי בְּשִׁבְעָה־עָשָׂר יוֹם לַחֹדֶשׁ עַל הָרֵי אֲרָרָט:

to pass over the earth, and the waters assuaged;

2 The fountains also of the deep and the windows of heaven were stopped, and the rain from heaven was restrained;

3 And the waters returned from off the earth continually: and after the end of the hundred and fifty days the waters were abated.

4 And the ark rested in the seventh month, on the seventeenth day of the month, upon the mountains of Ararat.

PART ONE

The Deluge and the Ark

1

The Flood in Universal Tradition

*Hugh Miller (1802-1856) "was a remarkably inter-
esting person. . . . It is unfortunate that he is so forgotten, for lyrical geologists are not common phenomena,"
remarks Princeton University Professor C. C. Gillispie
(Genesis and Geology [1951], p. 170). The following
passage from Miller's immensely popular* Testimony of
the Rocks ([1857], pp. 268-75) *bears this out. Miller
stresses the strength and universality of a tradition that
"well nigh the whole human race, in an early age of the
world's history," was destroyed by a great deluge. (We
shall not arbitrate between his limited flood theory and
Morris' universal theory given below in "The Design of
the Ark.") In addition to being one of the greatest
harmonizers of Genesis and geology that the church has
ever known, Miller was "an accomplished essayist, . . .
a crusading editor, political commentator, and religious
reformer" whose influence on Scottish opinion was
commonly reported to be second only to that of Thomas Chalmers, with whom he led the Free Church
movement which left the Church of Scotland in 1843
(Gillispie, pp. 170ff; see the article on him in the* Dictionary of National Biography).

The destruction of well nigh the whole human race,
in an early age of the world's history, by a great deluge,
appears to have so impressed the minds of the few survivors, and seems to have been handed down to their
children, in consequence, with such terror-struck im-
pressiveness, that their remote descendants of the present day have not even yet forgotten it. It appears in almost every mythology, and lives in the most distant
countries, and among the most barbarous tribes. It was

25

the laudable ambition of Humboldt,[1]—first entertained at a very early period of life,—to penetrate into distant regions, unknown to the natives of Europe at the time, that he might acquaint himself, in fields of research altogether fresh and new, with men and with nature in their most primitive conditions. In carrying out his design, he journeyed far into the woody wilderness that surrounds the Orinoco, and found himself among tribes of wild Indians whose very names were unknown to the civilized world. And yet among even these forgotten races of the human family he found the tradition of the deluge still fresh and distinct; not confined to single tribes, but general among the scattered nations of that great region, and intertwined with curious additions, suggestive of the inventions of classic mythology in the Old World. "The belief in a great deluge," we find him saying, "is not confined to one nation singly,—the Tamanacs: it makes part of a system of historical tradition, of which we find scattered notions among the Maypures of the great cataracts; among the Indians of the Rio Erevato, which runs into the Caura; and among almost all the tribes of the Upper Orinoco. When the Tamanacs are asked how the human race survived this great deluge—'the *age of water'* of the Mexicans,— they say, a man and a woman saved themselves on a high mountain called Tamanacu, situated on the banks of the Asiveru, and, *casting behind them over their heads* the fruits of the mauritia palm-tree, they saw the seeds contained in these fruits produce men and women, who re-peopled the earth. Thus," adds the philosophic traveller, "we find in all simplicity, among nations now in a savage state, a tradition which the Greeks embellished with all the charms of imagination." The resem-

---

[1] [Baron F. H. Alexander von Humboldt (1769-1859), the great German naturalist and traveller. His *Voyage aux régions équinoxiales du Nouveau Continent, fait en 1799-1804* (Paris, 1870ff.) was published in thirty folio and quarto volumes; included is his *Vues des Cordilieres et monuments des peuples indigenes de l'Amérique* (English translation, 1814), which contains flood accounts to which Miller refers. Professor Karl Bruhns' detailed and reliable biography of Humboldt (3 vols.; Leipzig, 1872) is available in an English version (1873).]

blance is certainly very striking. "Quit the temple," said the Oracle to Deucalion and Pyrrha, when they had consulted it, after the great deluge, regarding the mode in which the earth was to be re-peopled,—"veil your heads, unloose your girdles, and throw behind your backs the bones of your grandmother." Rightly interpreting what seemed darkest and most obscure in the reply, they took "stones of the earth," and, casting them behind them, the stones flung by Deucalion became men, and those by Pyrrha became women, and thus the disfurnished world was peopled anew. The navigator always regards himself as sure of his position when he has *two* landmarks to determine it by, or when in the open ocean he can ascertain, not only his latitude, but his longitude also. And this curious American tradition seems to have its two such marks,—its two bisecting lines of determination,—to identify it with the classic tradition of the Old World that refers evidently to the same great event.

There are other portions of America in which the tradition of the Flood is still more distinct than among the forests of the Orinoco. It is related by Herrera, one of the Spanish historians of America,[2] that even the most barbarous of the Brazilians had some knowledge of a general deluge; that in Peru the ancient Indians reported, that many years before there were any Incas, all the people were drowned by a great flood, save six persons, the progenitors of the existing races, who were saved on a float; that among the Mechoachans it was believed that a single family was preserved, during the outburst of the waters, in an ark with a sufficient number of animals to replenish the new world; and, more curious still, that it used to be told by the original inhabitants of Cuba, that "an old man, knowing the deluge was to come, built a great ship, and went into it with his family and abundance of animals; and that,

---

[2] [Antonio de Herrera y Tordesillas (1549-1625), author of the *Historia general de los hechos de los Castellanos en las islas y tierra firme del Mar Oceano* (4 vols.; Madrid, 1601-1615), an indispensable work for the study of the customs of western hemisphere aborigines. The work was translated into English in the 18th century.]

wearying during the continuance of the flood, he sent
out a crow, which at first did not return, staying to feed
on the dead bodies, but afterwards returned bearing
with it a green branch." The resemblance borne by this
last tradition to the Mosaic narrative is so close as to
awaken a doubt whether it may not have been but a
mere recollection of the teaching of some early missionary. Nor can its genuineness now be tested, seeing
that the race which cherished it has been long since extinct. It may be stated, however, that a similar suspicion crossed the mind of Humboldt when he was
engaged in collecting the traditions of the Indians of
the Orinoco; but that on further reflection and inquiry
he dismissed the doubt as groundless. He even set himself to examine whether the district was not a fossili-
ferous one, and whether beds of sea-shells, or deposits
charged with the petrified remains of corals or of fishes,
might not have originated among the aborigines some
mere myth of a great inundation sufficient to account for
the appearances in the rocks. But he found that the region was mainly a primary one, in which he could de-
tect only a single patch of sedimentary rock, existing as
an unfossiliferous sandstone. And so, though little pre-
judiced in favour of the Mosaic record, he could not
avoid arriving at the conclusion, simply in his character
as a philosophic inquirer, who had no other object than
to attain to the real and the true, that the legend of the
wild Maypures and Tamanacs regarding a great destructive deluge was simply one of the many forms of
the oldest of traditions which appears to be well-nigh
co-extensive with the human family, and which, in all
its varied editions, seems to point at one and the same
signal event. Very varied some of these editions are.
The inhabitants of Tahiti tell, for instance, that the Supreme God, a long time ago, being angry, dragged the
earth through the sea, but that by a happy accident
their island broke off and was preserved; the Indians of
Terra Firma believe, that when the great deluge took
place, one man, with his wife and children, escaped in
a canoe; and the Indians of the North American lakes

hold, that the father of all their tribes being warned in a dream that a flood was coming, built a raft, on which he preserved his family, and pairs of all the animals, and which drifted about for many months, until at length a new earth was made for their reception by the "Mighty Man above."

In that widely-extended portion of the Old World over which Christianity has spread in its three great types,—Greek, Romish, and Protestant,—and in the scarce less extended portion occupied by the followers of Mohammed, the Scriptural account of the deluge, or the imperfect reflection of it borrowed by the Koran, has, of course, supplanted the old traditions. But outside these regions we find the traditions existing still. One of the sacred books of the Parsees (representatives of the ancient Persians) records, that "the world having been corrupted by Ahriman the Evil One, it was thought necessary to bring over it a universal flood of waters, that all impurity might be washed away. Accordingly the rain came down in drops as large as the head of a bull, until the earth was wholly covered with water, and all the creatures of the Evil One perished. And then the flood gradually subsided, and first the mountains, and next the plains, appeared once more." In the Scandinavian Edda, between whose wild fables and those of the sacred books of the Parsees there has been a resemblance traced by accomplished antiquaries such as Mallet, the tradition of the deluge takes a singularly monstrous form. On the death of the great giant Ymir, whose flesh and bones form the rocks and soils of the earth, and who was slain by the early gods, his blood, which now constitutes the ocean, rushed so copiously out of his wounds, that all the old race of the lesser giants, his offspring, were drowned in the flood which it occasioned, save one; and he, by escaping on board his bark with his wife, outlived the deluge. The tradition here is evidently allegorized, but it is by no means lost in the allegory.

Sir William Jones, perhaps the most learned and accomplished man of his age (such at least was the estimate of Johnson),[3] and the first who fairly opened up the great storehouse of eastern antiquities, describes the tradition of the Deluge as prevalent also in the vast Chinese empire, with its three hundred millions of people. He states that it was there believed that, just ere the appearance of Fohi in the mountains, a mighty flood, which first "flowed abundantly, and then subsided, covered for a time the whole earth, and separated the higher from the lower age of mankind." The Hindu tradition, as related by Sir William, though disfigured by strange additions, is still more explicit. An evil demon having purloined the sacred books from Brahma, the whole race of men became corrupt except the seven Nishis, and in especial the holy Satyavrata, the prince of a maritime region, who, when one day bathing in a river, was visited by the God Vishnu in the shape of a fish, and thus addressed by him:—"In seven days all creatures who have offended me shall be destroyed by a deluge; but thou shalt be secured in a capacious vessel, miraculously formed. Take, therefore, all kinds of medicinal herbs and esculent grain for food, and, together with the seven holy men, your respective wives, and pairs of all animals, enter the ark without fear: then shalt thou know God face to face, and all thy questions shall be answered". The god then disappeared; and after seven days, during which Satyavrata had conformed in all respects to the instructions given him, the ocean began to overflow the coasts, and the earth to be flooded by constant rains, when a large vessel was seen coming floating shorewards on the rising waters; into which the Prince and the seven virtuous Nishis entered, with their wives, all laden with plants and grain, and accompanied by the animals. During the deluge Vishnu preserved the ark by again taking the form of a fish, and tying it fast to himself;

---

[3] [Sir William Jones (1746-1794), linguist (knew 13 languages well and was moderately acquainted with 28 others), founder of the Asiatic Society, and eminent British orientalist. Monuments to his memory were erected in St. Paul's, London, and in Calcutta. His prolific works appeared in a collected edition, with memoir of his life by Teignmouth, in 1804.]

and when the waters had subsided, he communicated
the contents of the sacred books to the holy Satyavrata,
after first slaying the demon who had stolen them. It is
added, however, that the good man having, one occasion long after, by "the act of destiny," drunk mead,
he became senseless, and lay asleep naked, and that
Charma, one of three sons who had been born to him,
finding him in that sad state, called on his two brothers
to witness the shame of their father, and said to them,
What has now befallen? In what state is this our sire?
But by the two brothers,—more dutiful than Charma,
—he was hidden with clothes, and recalled to his
senses; and, having recovered his intellect, and perfectly knowing what had passed, he cursed Charma, saying,
"Thou shalt be a servant of servants." It would be difficult certainly to produce a more curious legend, or
one more strikingly illustrative of the mixture of truth
and fable which must ever be looked for in that tradition which some are content to accept even in religion
as a trustworthy guide. In ever varying tradition, as in
those difficult problems in physical science which have
to be wrought out from a multitude of differing observations, it is, if I may so express myself, the mean result of the whole that must be accepted as approximately the true one. And the mean result of those dim
and distorted recollections of the various tribes of men
which refer to the Flood as a result which bears simply
to this effect,—that in some early age of the world a
great deluge took place, in which well nigh the whole
human family was destroyed.

*   *   *

*We have seen that Flood stories appear in the tradi-
tions of peoples throughout the world. Many of them
include the provision of a boat to escape the waters.
The chart below shows the representation of the principal ideas of the biblical account of the Deluge in but
a small portion of non-biblical traditions. The more
important larger collections of Flood stories are:*

A. Catcott, A Treatise on the Deluge (1761), pp. 55-98.

A. Bedin, Les traditions messianiques (1851), pp. 199-225.

F. Lenormant, Les origines de l'histoire (1880).

R. Andree, Die Flutensagen (1891).

J. G. Frazer, Folklore in the Old Testament (1918).

J. Riem, Die Sintflut in Sage und Wissenschaft (1925).

E. Sykes, Dictionary of Non-Classical Mythology (1961).

The schematic summary on the following page is taken from Byron C. Nelson's Deluge Story in Stone, first published in 1931 and reprinted by Bethany Fellowship in 1968.

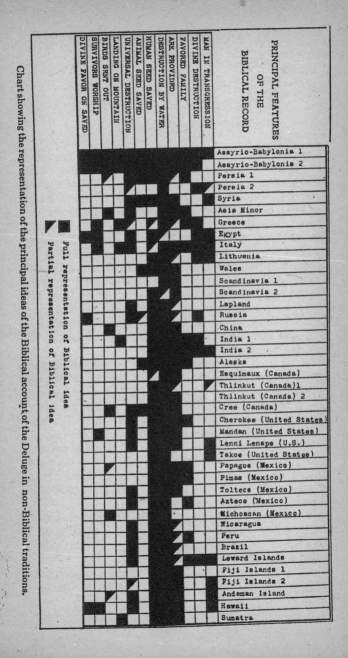

Chart showing the representation of the principal ideas of the Biblical account of the Deluge in non-Biblical traditions.

2
The Deluge Viewed Archaeologically

Archaeologists have unearthed what many consider to be literary and geological evidences of the Noachian Deluge. The passage below summarizes the most important of these finds and relates them to the biblical account. Its author, Dr. Edwin M. Yamauchi, formerly of the Department of History at Rutgers University, now serves as Associate Professor of History at Miami University, Oxford, Ohio. His prolific writings include: Greece and Babylon, Mandaean Incantation Texts, *and* Composition and Corroboration in Classical and Biblical Studies. *The following passage is taken from his forthcoming volume in Lippincott's "Evangelical Perspectives" series (edited by John Warwick Montgomery),* The Stones and the Scriptures.

A sensation was created in 1872 by the publication of the 11th Gilgamesh tablet, as it contained striking Babylonian parallels to the biblical flood story. George Smith, an erstwhile banknote engraver, made the exciting discovery while studying tablets in the British Museum. Some of the lines of the text were missing. A London newspaper, *The Daily Telegraph,* provided funds for George Smith to go to Nineveh to find the missing portions. Hunting in the midst of hundreds of cuneiform tablets, Smith was with incredible luck able to find the missing pieces.

In 1929 in excavating Abraham's city of Ur in southern Mesopotamia Leonard Woolley came upon a thick layer of water-borne sediment 8-10 feet thick, which he claimed as evidence for *the* flood: "Taking into consideration all the facts, there could be no doubt that the flood of which we had thus found the only possible evidence was the Flood of Sumerian history and legend, the Flood on which is based the story of Noah."[1] Later study, however, has shown that there were other flood deposits at Kish, Fara, and Nineveh, which were not identical with the flood deposit at Ur, dated c. 4000 B.C. A recent study by Max Mallowan suggests that the flood of the Gilgamesh Epic should be identified with the flood deposit at Tell Fara (ancient Shuruppak, the home of Ziusudra—hero of the Sumerian story of the flood), and dated c. 2700 B.C.[2] One of the arguments for a date of 2700 B.C. would be the link with Gilgamesh who must have lived about this time. The flood episode, however, is not integrally bonded to the Gilgamesh story and may come from a much older period. The numerous flood stories, collected by James Frazer from the Near East, from Greece, from South Asia, from the Pacific, from the Americas, etc. seem to point to a deluge of an even greater antiquity. Albright has argued recently:

It is very difficult to separate a myth found all over the world, even as far away as pre-Columbian South America, from the tremendous floods which must have accompanied successive retreats of the glaciers in the closing phases of the Pleistocene Age. In other words, the Flood story presumably goes back, in one form or another, at least ten or twelve thousand years and, for all we know, much further.[3]

In 1965 the full text of an important Babylonian work including both a creation and a flood account— the Atrahasis Epic—was published. Before 1965 only

[1] Leonard Woolley, *Ur of the Chaldees,* p. 29.
[2] M. Mallowan, "Noah's Flood Reconsidered," *Iraq,* XXVI (1964), 62-82. R. Raikes, "The Physical Evidence for Noah's Flood," *Iraq,* XXVIII (1966), 52-63, suggests that further soundings are necessary to settle the question.
[3] W. F. Albright, *Yahweh and the Gods of Canaan,* pp. 98-99; cf. G. Ernest Wright, *Biblical Archaeology,* p. 33.

one-fifth of the story had been known. The new tablets were discovered by Alan Millard stuffed away in a drawer of the British Museum. Whereas the *Enuma elish* traces the conflict between the older gods led by Tiamat and the younger gods led by Marduk to the boisterous behavior of the latter which kept their elders from sleeping, the new texts point to the refusal of the younger gods to continue their toil. It was in order to relieve the gods from labor that man was created. The flood was sent, according to the Atrahasis Epic, because men became too noisy for any of the gods to sleep. The overall plot of Creation—Rebellion—Flood found in the Atrahasis Epic is thus similar to the biblical story, though the ethical and theological contrasts are striking. On the question of whether or not there was borrowing, Millard concludes:

> In that the patriarch Abraham lived in Babylonia, it could be said that the stories were borrowed from there, but not that they were borrowed from any text now known to us. Granted that the Flood took place, knowledge of it must have survived to form the available accounts; while the Babylonians could only conceive of the event in their own polytheistic language, the Hebrews, or their ancestors, understood the action of God in it.[4]

Whereas in the Bible God sends the flood because of men's wickedness, the Babylonian gods send the flood because of their own annoyance at not being able to sleep. When the flood is over, Jehovah smells the sweet savour of Noah's sacrifice and blesses him (Gen. 8:21-9:1). When Utnapishtim, the hero of the Babylonian account, pours out a libation, "The gods smelled the sweet savor. The gods gathered like flies over the sacri-

---

[4] A. R. Millard, "A New Babylonian 'Genesis' Story," *Tyndale Bulletin*, XVIII (1967), 18.

ficer," inasmuch as they had not received any nourishing sacrifices for a week.[5]

[5] Alexander Heidel, *The Gilgamesh Epic and Old Testament Parallels*, p. 87. The daily cult in pagan temples was essentially the provision of food for the gods. In the Hittite Kumarbi Myth the god Ea warns Kumarbi that if he should destroy mankind, no one would remain to feed the gods with offerings. In the Babylonian *Pessimistic Dialogue* a servant suggests to his master that he should be able to coerce the gods by refusing to offer sacrifices. Cf. Edwin M. Yamauchi,, "Anthropomorphism in Ancient Religions," *Bibliotheca Sacra*, CXXV (1968), 29-44.

3
Genesis and Gilgamesh

Now that we have been introduced to the archaeological background of Noah's Flood, it is fitting that we focus our attention on its most significant literary parallel to the biblical account, the Gilgamesh Epic. In his exceedingly important volume, The Gilgamesh Epic and Old Testament Parallels,* *Alexander Heidel, late member of the research staff of the University of Chicago's Oriental Institute, discusses the Ark and its landing-place as related in the two accounts. At the end of the book he underscores the incomparably greater dignity and ethical quality of the biblical record and asserts that it is obvious from these and other differences that "the arguments which have been advanced in support of the contention that the biblical account rests on Babylonian material are quite indecisive" (p. 267).*

The Ark

Another interesting point of comparison is the ark which the hero of the flood constructed. Like the hero himself, the ark is known by a number of different terms in the various flood stories. The Sumerian recension designates it as a *magurgur*, which means "a very great ship," "a giant boat."' This word occurs also in the Semitic Babylonian deluge fragment from Nippur, where it corresponds to the Semitic phrase *elippu rabî-tu*, used two lines previously in that text and signifying "a great ship or boat."

The Gilgamesh Epic calls this craft by the general term *elippu*, "vessel," "ship," "boat." Once it also uses

---

* 2d ed. (1949), pp. 232-37, 250-51.
[1] A. Poebel, *Historical Texts* (Philadelphia, 1914), p. 58.

êkallu (Tablet XI:95), a word which, derived from the Sumerian language, literally means "a great house" and occurs in reference to palaces and temples. This term is employed as a poetic designation for the ark, giving "an indication of its large size, with its many stories and compartments."[2] In the passage under discussion I have translated it somewhat freely with "the mighty structure."[3] Berossus refers to the deluge boat as *skaphos, ploion,* and *naus,* all three of which mean "ship," or "boat."

The Old Testament word for the ark is *tēbâ.* Outside of the biblical flood story, this term occurs only in Exod. 2:3-5, where it is applied to the reed vessel in which the infant Moses was saved. The Hebrew *tēbâ* is hardly related, as has been suggested, to the Babylonian *tebîtu,* denoting a deep-drawing freight ship (for in that case we should expect *ṭēbâ* instead of the actual *tēbâ,* but rather to the Egyptian *db't,* meaning "chest," "box," "coffin."[4] In the Septuagint and the New Ttestament, Noah's ark is kalled *kiōbtos,* "box," "chest," "coffer"; this term is applied also to the chest (Hebrew *'ărōn*) placed at the entrance of the temple by Jehoiada, the priest (II Kings 12:10-11), and to the ark of the covenant (cf., e.g., Exod. 25:10 ff. and Heb. 9:4).

These comparisons show that as there is no etymological connection between the name of Noah and the Babylonian names for the hero of the flood, so there is none between the Hebrew term for the ark and the Babylonian designations for the same vessel.

The Old Testament deluge ark was made of *gōfer*

---

[2] Morris Jastrow, Jr., *Hebrew and Babylonian Traditions* (New York, 1914), p. 330, n. 1.

[3] The term *bîtu,* "house," as a name for the ark, does not occur in the Babylonian versions of the deluge, contrary to the opinion formerly held by some scholars, whose view was based on an erroneous interpretation of Tablet XI:24, which they rendered: "Construct a house, build a ship!" The corresponding passage in the Atrahasis Epic (Fragment II) has very plainly: *ú-bu-ut bi-ta bi-ni e-li-ip-pa.* This can mean only: "Destroy (thy) house, build a ship."

[4] For references see A. Salonen, *Die Wasserfahrzeuge in Babylonien* (Helsinki, 1939), p. 48, n. 2.

wood. The meaning of this expression, found only in
Gen. 6:14, is quite uncertain, although it is generally
held to refer to some kind of resinous wood, such as
pine or cypress. The Hebrew *gōfer* is hardly derived
from the Babylonian and Assyrian *gipâru,* which in
some passages appears to denote some kind of tree or
shrub. *Gipâru* is a loan-word from Sumerian. Consequently, if *gōfer* were etymologically related to *gipâru,*
it would likewise have to be a loan-word, either from
Sumerian directly or from Babylono-Assyrian. In that
case, however, we should expect a form something like
gifar in Hebrew. As a loan-word from Babylonian, the
term *gōfer* would presuppose a form like *gupru* (cf.
Babylonian *kupru* and Hebrew *kōfer*), which has actually been found in two or three passages, but in the
sense of "table."[5] In the preserved portions of the Babylonian deluge traditions nothing is said about the
kind of wood that was used for the construction of the
boat.

Utnapishtim's vessel had seven stories and was divided vertically into nine sections, thus having sixty-
three compartments (Tablet XI:60-62). Its roof was
like that of "the subterranean waters," i.e., it was as
strong as the earth, which holds the subterranean
waters in their place (Tablet XI:31).[6] According to
the Semitic Nippur fragment, the boat was topped with
"a strong cover." It had a door (Tablet XI:88.93) and
at least one window (XI:135). Noah's ark, on the
other hand, had three stories and consisted of numerous unspecified cells, or compartments. It had a
door in its side and an opening for light below the roof
(Gen. 6:16). The Hebrew term used to designate the
opening for light is *ṣōhar*. This word has been equated
with Arabic *ẓahrun* and Babylonian *ṣîru,* both meaning
"back," and has been taken to refer to the roof of the

---

[5] Once it occurs in the Gilgamesh Epic, Tablet II, col. ii. 33 (Old
Babylonian version).

[6] H. V. Hilprecht, *The Babylonian Expedition of the University
of Pennsylvania,* Series D, Vol. V, Fasc. 1 (Philadelphia, 1910), p. 54.

ark.[7] But if ṣōhar really meant "roof," the addition "above" or "from above," in Gen. 6:16, would be quite superfluous, inasmuch as it is self-evident that the roof is "above." Moreover, the specification "to a cubit" world be meaningless.[8] From these considerations and the references to a window in Gen. 8:6' and the main Babylonian account of the flood, it is reasonably certain that the term in question denotes an opening for light. This opening was one cubit in height and, according to the prevalent explanation, extended all around the ark, interrupted only by the posts supporting the roof. This interpretation seems to be favored by the wording of the text: "Thou shalt make an opening for light for the ark and to a cubit shalt thou make it complete from above." This passage seems to indicate that Noah is to construct an opening for light completely around the ark.[10]

The Old Testament ark was coated inside and out with pitch, or bitumen, to make it watertight. Bituminous materials figure more prominently in the main Babylonian account than they do in the biblical. Utnapishtim poured six (var.: three) shar of pitch into the furnace, or pitch pot, and three shar of asphalt. The purpose is not stated, but there can be no doubt about it—he melted these substances and then calked the boat therewith. This is quite clear from Berossus' statement: "Some get pitch from the ship by scraping (it) off." The word for pitch, as we shall see later on, is the same both in Genesis and in the Gilgamesh Epic.

---

[7] Wilhelm Gesenius, Hebräisches und aramäisches Handwörterbuch über das Alte Testament, ed. Frants Buhl (Leipzig, 1915), pp. 675-76; Hermann Gunkel, Genesis (Göttingen, 1910), p. 142; Otto Procksch, Die Genesis (Leipzig, 1913), pp. 447-48

[8] See Eduard König, Die Genesis (Gütersloh, 1919), pp. 344-45, and Hebräisches und aramäisches Wörterbuch zum Alten Testament (Leipzig, 1931), p. 383.

[9] I take hallon to denote either the same thing as the ṣōhar or a part thereof.

[10] A. Dillmann, Genesis, trans. W. B. Stevenson, I (Edinburgh, 1897), 272; Franz Delitzsch, Neuer Commentar über die Genesis (Leipzig, 1887), p. 171; S. R. Driver, The Book of Genesis (New York and London, 1904), p. 88.

In addition to these materials, Utnapshtim used three *shar* of oil, which the basket-carriers brought. Of this oil, one *shar* was used presumably to saturate the water-stoppers; the other two *shar* the boatman stowed away, for unspecified purposes (Tablet XI:65-69). The use of oil is not mentioned in the biblical narrative.

Noah's ark, as evidenced by its dimensions and the names by which it is designated in Greek and Hebrew, was of flat-bottomed, rectangular construction, square on both ends and straight up on the sides. Such a craft is represented on bronze coins from the Phrygian city Apameia, which already at the time of Caesar Augustus bore the cognomen *kibōtos,* distinguishing it from other cities of the same name in Bithynia and Syria. To the right these coins, dating from the reign of Septimius Severus (A.D. 146-211) on down and betraying doubtless Jewish influence, picture an open chest swimming in the water and bearing the inscription *NOÊ* or simply *NÔ.* In the chest are seen the deluge hero and his wife, both appearing from the waist upward. On the raised lid of the ark a dove is perched, while another comes flying toward the ark with a twig in its claws. To the left the same pair of human beings are seen but standing on dry ground and raising their right hands in adoration.[11]

The length of Noah's ark was "three hundred cubits, its breadth fifty cubits, and its height thirty cubits" (Gen. 6:15). Since the cubit is here given without any qualifying addition, it probably represents the ordinary Hebrew cubit, which supposedly corresponded to the distance from the tip of the middle finger to the elbow and measured about 18 inches. According to this standard, the ark was 450 feet long, 75 feet wide, and 45 feet high, and had a displacement of approximately 43,300 tons.[12]

---

[11] H. Usener, *Die Sintfluthsagen* (Bonn, 1899), pp. 48-50; Sir J. G. Frazer, *Folk-lore in the Old Testament,* I (London, 1918), 156-57.

[12] [i.e., 96,992,000 pounds total displacement on the basis of long tons. Morris' figure of 48,600,000 pounds (below, in "The Design of the Ark") gives the weight of the loaded Ark based on a partial displacement of 15 cubits, the draft implied by Gen. 7:20: "the waters

Utnapishtim's boat, on the contrary, was an exact cube, the length, width, and height each being 120 cubits. Since the Babylonian cubits was equal to about 20 inches, 120 cubits correspond to about 200 feet. The Babylonian vessel, accordingly, had a displacement of about 228,500 tons. The shape and manner of construction of Utnapishtim's boat are strongly reminiscent of the *guffa*, a kind of coracle made of wickerwork and coated inside and out with bitumen. But, contrary to the view expressed by King,[13] it is by no means identical with this circular craft, which is still in constant use on the lower Tigris and Euphrates. Tablet XI:30 and 57-58, which instructs Utnapishtim that the length and the width of the boat should be equal and which then gives the exact height of its walls and the exact length of each side of its deck, refers to a quadrangular craft. King's argument that the boat's interior division of each story into nine vertical sections "is only suitable to a circular craft in which the interior walls would radiate from the center" overlooks the possibilities that the compartments may have extended from side to side,[14] or that Utnapishtim may have built in four walls, two of which ran in one direction and two in another, crossing at right angles to make nine square rooms on each floor.[15]

Berossus speaks of a boat over 3,000 feet long and more than 1,200 feet wide. The height of this fabulous vessel is not given.

There is thus a decided variance between the dimensions of the boat as contained in the Babylonian traditions and those given in Genesis. But all accounts agree that the hero of the deluge was divinely ordered to construct the vessel in which—to borrow a phrase from the Babylonian versions—"the seed of all living crea-

prevailed above the mountains covering them fifteen cubits deep." Since 15 cubits was half of the Ark's height, Morris' figure is approximately half of Heidel's. Filby's figures *(The Flood Reconsidered* [1971], p. 88) should be considered less accurate.]

[13] [L. W. King,] *Legends . . . .*, pp. 80-81.
[14] Paul Haupt in *Beiträge zur Assyriologie*, X, Heft 2 (1927), 8.
[15] A. Schott in *Zeitschrift für Assyriologie*, XL (1931), 16.

tures" was saved from the waters of the great flood that covered the earth. Moreover, the Atrahasis Epic (Fragment III) would seem to indicate that the god who disclosed the imminent calamity even drew a plan of the boat. The detailed instructions which Noah received amounted to about the same thing. According to Tablet XI, Utnapishtim himself appears to have drawn up the necessary plans.

The Landing-Place of the Ark

The place on which Utnapishtim's boat came to rest is given in the Gilgamesh Epic as Mount Nisir, which signifies the "Mount of Salvation," if our reading is correct and if the name is of Semitic origin. Such a mountain, or mountain range, is recorded in the annals of King Ashurnasirpal II of Assyria (883-859 B.C.), according to which it was situated to the south of the Lower Zab and is probably to be identified with Pir Omar Gudrun, having an altitude of about 9,000 feet.[16] Berossus names the mountains of the Gordyaeans, or the Kurds, as the landing-place of the boat of Xisuthros. These mountains, corresponding to Jebel Jûdî, where also Syriac and Arabic traditions localize the landing-place, are in the southwestern part of Armenia. The Genesis account is quite indefinite on the point under consideration, stating merely that the ark grounded "on (one of) the mountains of Ararat." The name Ararat is identical with the Assyrian Urartu, which, broadly speaking, embraced the territory of Armenia. In three of the four Old Testament passages where the word Ararat occurs, the Septuagint has simply transliterated it (Gen. 8:4; II Kings 19:37; Jer.

---

[16] See E. A. Wallis Budge and L. W. King, *Annals of the Kings of Assyria*, I (London, 1902), 305 ff.; M. Streck in *Zeitschrift für Assyriologie*, XV (1900). ff.; and E. A. Speiser in the *Annual of the American Schools of Oriental Research*, VIII (1928), esp. 18 and 31.

51:27 [28:27 in the Septuagint]), while in the remaining passage the translators have rendered it with "Armenia" (Isa. 37:38). Since it is believed that the ark rested on the highest peak in the country, it has long been customary to identify the landing-place with Mount Massis (or Agridagh), situated a little northeast of Lake Van and rising to approximately 17,000 feet above sea-level. Evidently through a misunderstanding of Gen. 8:4, this elevation has traditionally been called Mount Ararat."

4

The Design of the Ark

Henry M. Morris, former Professor of Hydraulic Engineering and Chairman of the Department of Civil Engineering at Virginia Polytechnic Institute, offers proof that the Ark was eminently suitable for preserving man and beast during the year of the great Flood ("The Ark of Noah," Creation Research Society Quarterly, VIII [1971], 142-44). *It should be emphasized that inclusion of this revealing article does not necessarily commit us to Morris and Whitcomb's universal Flood theory or to their extremely late dating of Creation. Readers who wish to pursue these questions should consult Whitcomb and Morris'* The Genesis Flood *(1961) and such responses as the articles by J. R. Van de Fliert (*"Fundamentalism and the Fundamentals of Geology," International Reformed Bulletin, XXXII-XXIII [1968]) *and James R. Moore (*"Charles Lyell and the Noachian Deluge," *Journal of the American Scientific Affiliation, XIII [1970]).*

The Biblical record of the great Flood is quite explicit in describing it as a world-wide cataclysm. Its purpose and effect were, in God's own words, to:

destroy man whom I have created from the face of the earth; both man, and beast, and the creeping thing, and the fowls of the air (Genesis 6:7).

The destruction was universal, so far as land animals were concerned. "All in whose nostrils was the breath of life, of all that was in the dry land, died." (Genesis 7:22).

46

However, in order to preserve two of each kind of animal, with which to re-populate the earth after the Flood, as well as Noah and his family, God gave directions for the building of the Ark.

"Make thee an Ark of gopher wood," He said, "rooms shalt thou make in the Ark, and shalt pitch it within and without with pitch. And this is the fashion which thou shalt make it of: The length of the Ark shall be three hundred cubits, the breadth of it fifty cubits, and the height of it thirty cubits. A window shalt thou make to the Ark, and in a cubit shalt thou finish it above; and the door of the Ark shalt thou set in the side thereof; with lower, second and third stories shalt thou make it" (Genesis 6:14-16).

Size of the Ark

The Ark was thus to be essentially a huge box (the Hebrew word itself implies this), designed essentially for stability in the waters of the Flood rather than for movement through the waters. Assuming the cubit to be 1.5 ft., which is the most likely value, the dimensions of the Ark were 45 ft. x 75 ft. x 450 ft., as sketched in Figure 1, to a scale of $1'' = 100'$.

The Ark was obviously a very large structure, taller than a normal three-story building and half again as long as a football field. The total volumetric capacity was 450 x 45 x 75=1,518,750 cubic feet, or 56,361 cubic yards. Since the standard railroad stock car contains 2,670 cubic feet effective capacity, the Ark had a volumetric capacity equal to that of 569 standard stock cars. It obviously could have carried a tremendous number of animals, and was clearly designed to hold representatives from all kinds of animals throughout the entire world.

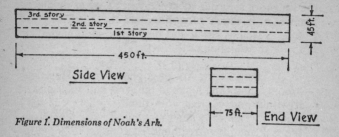

Figure 1. Dimensions of Noah's Ark.

Stability of the Ark

In the complex of hydrodynamic and aerodynamic forces unleashed in the Flood, it was necessary that the Ark remain afloat for a whole year. The gopher wood of which it was constructed was no doubt extremely strong and durable.

Timbers forming the sides and bottom, as well as the floors of the intermediate decks, were probably cut and shaped from great trees that had been growing since the world began, over 1600 years earlier.* The "pitch" (Hebrew *kaphar,* meaning simply "covering") was evidently an excellent waterproofing material, though we do not now know what it was.

In addition to floating it must not capsize under the impact of the great waves and winds which might beat against it. The Scripture says the floodwaters rose at least 15 cubits above the highest mountains (Genesis 7:20), evidently to point out that the Ark was floating freely wherever the waters might propel it. The height of the Ark was 30 cubits, so it seems probable that the 15 cubit figure represents the draft of the Ark when loaded.

When the Ark was floating at this depth, Archimedes' principle tells us that its weight must have equalled the force of buoyancy, which in turn equals

---

* [But cf. W. H. Green, "Primeval Chronology," *Bibliotheca Sacra* (1890), 285-303.]

the weight of the equivalent amount of water displaced. The weight of the Ark therefore was

$$W = 450(75) \left(\frac{45}{2} \right) (w)$$

where w is the weight of each cubic foot of water.

Fresh water weighs 62.4 lbs. and sea water 64 lbs. per cubic foot. Because of the minerals and sediments in the water, its density may well have been at least that of sea water, in which case the weight of the Ark would be calculated at 48,600,000 pounds; this is close enough for practical purposes.

The average unit weight of the Ark must then be half that of the water, or 32 lbs. per cubic foot. The center of gravity of the Ark and its contents presumably would be close to its geometric center, with the framework, the animals, and other contents more or less uniformly and symmetrically dispersed throughout the structure.

Two Tests of Stability

The Ark as designed would have been an exceptionally stable structure. Its cross-section of 30 cubits height by 50 cubits breadth, with a draft of 15 cubits, made it almost impossible to capsize, even in the midst of heavy waves and violent winds.

To illustrate this, assume the Ark tipped through an angle such that the roof was actually touching the water's edge, as sketched in Figure 2. This is an angle of approximately 31°, that is the angle whose tangent is 30/50. Since the weight of the Ark continues unchanged, it must still displace an amount of water equal to half its cross-section. Thus the water surface coincides with the diagonal. The buoyant force B continues to equal W, the weight of the Ark.

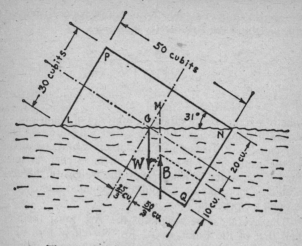

Figure 2. Stability of Ark at 31° angle of tilt.

However, the two forces are not now acting in the
same line. The weight W acts vertically downward
through the center of the Ark's cross-section. The
force B acts vertically upward through the centroid of
the triangle LQN, since this is the location of the center
of gravity of the volume of water that has been displaced by the Ark. The two forces W and B, equal in
magnitude but opposite in direction, form a *couple,* of
intensity equal to the product of either force times the
distance between them.

As long as the line of action of B is outside that of
W, in the direction toward the submerged side of the
Ark, the couple is a "righting couple" and would act to
restore the vessel to its upright position. The magnitude
of the couple is of no particular interest, but the location of M, the *metacenter,* is significant. As long as M
is above G (the centroid of the entire vessel cross-
section) on the axis of symmetry of the vessel, then the
ship is stable.

For the condition shown, M can be calculated to be

8.9 cubits above G on the axis of symmetry (calculated, from dimensions shown on the sketch, as

$$\frac{25/3}{\tan 31^0} - 5 = \frac{125}{9} - 5 = \frac{80}{9} \text{ cu.).}$$

This is almost 13.5 ft. above the centroid and indicates the Ark was extremely stable, even under such a strong angle of listing. The righting couple is then equal to 8.9 (sin 31°) (W)=

$$\left[\frac{80}{(3\ \sqrt{34}\ )}\right] (48,600,000) = 222,000,000 \text{ ft.-lbs.}$$

As a matter of fact, the *metacentric height,* as the distance GM is known, is positive for this cross-section even for much higher angles. Suppose the boat, for example, were tilted through a 60° angle, as shown in Figure 3. The centroid of the immersed area is obviously to the right of the line of action of G, and thus there is a righting couple and the metacentric height GM is positive.

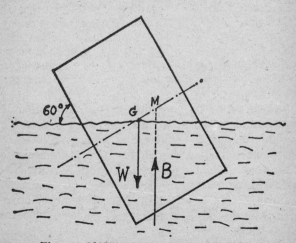

Figure 3. Stability of Ark at 60° angle of tilt.

As a matter of fact, the Ark would have to be turned completely vertical before M would coincide with G. Thus, for any angle up to 90°, the Ark would right itself.

Furthermore its relatively great length (six times its width) would tend to keep it from being subjected to wave forces of equal magnitude through its whole length, since wave fields tend to occur in broken and varying patterns, rather than in a series of long uniform crest-trough sequences, and this would be particularly true in the chaotic hydrodynamic phenomena of the Flood. Any vortex action to which it might occasionally be subjected would also tend to be resisted and broken up by its large length-width ratio.

The Ark would, in fact, tend to be lined up by the spectrum of hydrodynamic forces and currents in such a direction that its long axis would be parallel to the predominant direction of wave and current movement. Thus it would act as a semi-streamlined body, and the net drag forces would usually be minimal.

In every way, therefore, the Ark as designed was highly stable, admirably suited for its purpose of riding out the storms of the year of the great Flood.

5

The Ark's Construction

The Ark as it is described in the biblical text was a uniquely seaworthy vessel. But was it possible that such a vessel could be built? If so, are there any indications that its construction corresponded to its function of preserving many lives? Frederick A. Filby, who received his doctor of philosophy degree from University College, London, and who is a member of the Palestine and Egypt Exploration Societies, has long been a student of the biblical Flood. He answers these important questions in the following excerpt from his book, The Flood Reconsidered *([1971], pp. 92-96).*

Some may feel that the Ark was too large for early man to have attempted. A survey of the ancient world shows in fact the very reverse. One is constantly amazed at the enormous tasks which our ancestors attempted. The Great Pyramid was not the work of the later Pharaohs; it was the work of the 4th Dynasty—long before Abraham! This pyramid contained over two million blocks of stone each weighing about 2 1/2 tons. Its vast sides, 756 feet long,[1] are set to the points of the compass to an accuracy of a small fraction of one degree! The so-called Colossi of Memnon again are not of recent times—they belong to the 18th Dynasty of Egypt. Cut from blocks of sandstone they weigh 400 tons each and were brought 600 miles to their present position. Among the remains of that most ancient Empire in Greece—Mycenae—is the 'Treasury of Atreus'. Above its entrance rests a huge stone lintel 28 feet across. It weighs 120 tons! The Temple of Ju-

---

[1] The difference between the longest side and the shortest side of the Great Pyramid is 8 inches—the sides are 756 feet long, so that the maximum error is 8 in 9072 or 0.09 percent. The maximum error in direction is 5'30" on the east side, an eleventh of a degree!

piter at Baalbek is later, but it is staggering to find in
the retaining wall three great blocks of stone each
weighing about 700 tons. In a quarry nearby is a partly
cut block that would have weighed 1000 tons! As our
thoughts go back to the Colossus of Rhodes, the
Pharos Lighthouse,[2] the Hanging Gardens, the Ziggurats, the Step Pyramid—or even in our own land, to
Stonehenge[3]—we have no reason to suppose that early
man was afraid to tackle great tasks.

To look at this same question again in a somewhat
different light we can find in modern times an example
of a tremendous leap in shipbuilding by a single de-
signer. In 1853 the largest vessel of her type in the
world was the P. & O. liner *Himalaya,* 240 feet by 35
feet with a tonnage of 3438 gross. Yet at the same time
Isambard K. Brunel was planning, and in 1858 produced, the *Leviathan,* later called the *Great Eastern,*
692 feet by 83 feet by 30 feet of approximately 19,000
tons . . . five times the tonnage of any ship then afloat.
So vast was Brunel's leap that even forty years later in
an age of fierce competition the largest liners being
built were still smaller than the *Great Eastern.*[4]

The Ark was, according to the specifications laid
down, to be 300 cubits long by 50 cubits wide by 30
cubits high. The ratios of these numbers are very interesting. They obviously reflect an advanced knowledge
of shipbuilding. The Babylonian account which speaks
of the Ark as a cube betrays complete ignorance.[5]
Such a vessel would spin slowly round. But the Biblical

---

[2] The Pharos lighthouse was 400 feet high.

[3] The large blocks at Stonehenge weigh 50 tons.

[4] For example the crack Cunard liners *Campania* and *Lucania*
(1893) were 13,000 tons and the German *Kaiser Wilhelm der Grosse*
(1897) 14,350 tons. The 36-ton propeller of the *Great Eastern* remains the largest single propeller ever cast. There has been a similar
leap in our own times. In 1960 the largest tankers were of about
80,000 tons; by 1968 the Japanese has built a 312,000-ton tanker. A
Tyneside firm speaks of building vessels of 1,000,000 tons.

[5] Berossus gives the ratio of length to breadth as 5 to 2 i.e. 2½
to 1.

ratios leave nothing to be desired.⁶ These ratios are important from the point of view of stability, of pitching and of rolling. The ratio of length to breadth, 300 to 50, is 6 to 1. Taking the mean of six present-day ships approximately the same size, selected from six different shipping lines, we obtain, as an example, a ratio of 8.1 to 1. The giant liner *Queen Elizabeth* has a ratio 8.6 to 1 while the *Canberra* has 8.2 to 1. But these vessels were designed for speed; the ark was not. Some of the giant tankers have ratios around 7 to 1. Still more interesting are the figures for the *Great Britain* designed by I. K. Brunel in 1844. Her dimensions were 322 feet by 51 feet by 32 1/2 feet so that the ratios are almost exactly those of the Ark. Brunel had the accumulated knowledge of generations of shipbuilders to draw upon. The Ark was the first of its kind!

The height of the Ark, 45 feet, was to be divided into three stories⁷ or decks giving an average of 14 feet each if we allow for the thickness of the floors and assume only a slight slope on the roof. The Ark was also evidently divided longways and crossways into compartments or bulkheads. The AV speaks of 'rooms' which Knox calls 'cabins.'* It would be reasonable to assume at least two long dividing walls running the length of the ship making a central passage with rooms on either side. The Babylonian account suggests nine cross-walls, but as it also claims six decks and a cubic overall shape, this number, while possibly based on some tradition, is not to be taken as certain. It will be

---

⁶ In 1604 a Dutch merchant, Peter Jansen, had a boat built at Hoorn, 120 feet x 20 feet x 12 feet, i.e. exactly the same ratios as the Ark. The vessel proved to be admirably suited for carrying freight. It is said that several vessels with the same proportions were built in Denmark.

⁷ The suggestion (*New Bible Dictionary* [London, 1962], Article 'Ark') that this might possibly mean 'three layers of logs laid crosswise' is most unlikely. This would leave the Ark a great empty box 45 feet high inside! The decks and cross-walls were obviously essential to make the 'rooms' and also to give rigidity to the whole structure. In the Babylonian account the Ark had six stories.

* [On the translation of the Hebrew *KNM*, see Edward Ullendorff's short note, "The Construction of Noah's Ark," *Vetus Testamentum*, IV (1954), 95-96.]

seen, however, that with a central passage of 15 feet
the side rooms could be about 30 feet wide, and if
there were 9 divisions giving 10 rooms in the 450 feet
length each would be 45 feet. We have, of course, no
real idea as to how Noah planned out these rooms
which were probably not all equal in size, but the
average of 20 rooms, 30 feet x 45 feet, on each floor
gives some indication of the space available to him.
These walls would, of course, give the necessary
strength to the whole structure, a fact to which Josephus seems to refer in his account.[8]

There would be doors of some kind to these rooms
in addition to the main door of the Ark which we are
told was in its side.[9] We have already seen from the
very early Egyptian granaries that there was no difficulty in constructing a flight of wooden steps 15 feet
high, so that Noah and his family could easily go from
one deck to another. A sloping ramp would have been
equally easy for Noah to construct if it were required
for moving animals from one deck to another.

One important detail in the text has occasioned some
difficulty in translation and interpretation—the 'window'. That all living creatures in the Ark would require
air and light is obvious, and while the Babylonian account quite overlooks this the Bible makes provisions
for both. The Hebrew text of Genesis 6:16 as translated in the AV reads: 'A window shalt thou make to
the ark and in a cubit shalt thou finish it above'. The
word used here for window, *TSOHAR,* is never again
used in this sense in the Old Testament, and it is quite
different from the word *CHALLON* used in Genesis
8:6 where Noah opened 'the window which he had
made' to release the birds. It is also different from the
word *ARUBBAH* used in Genesis 7:11 for the 'windows of heaven'. Obviously this unusual word *TSO-
HAR* requires further investigation. Brown, Driver and

---

[8] 'Now this ark had firm walls and a roof, and was braced with
cross beams.' Josephus, *Antiquities* I.3.2.
[9] Snofru speaks of making great cedar doors for his palace in his
fourteenth year. W. Flinders Petrie, *History of Egypt* (London,
1903), Vol. I, p. 34.

Briggs[10] give the word as meaning 'noon' but later[11] they say that they prefer the meaning 'roof' to 'light' in Genesis 6:16 although admitting that the latter is a possible translation. Now the word comes from a root meaning to 'mount (in the sky) mid-day, or to shine'. Its cognates mean 'glitter, glisten or shine', and one similar word means 'oil' which is used to give light or to make things shine. The fact that it is equivalent to an Assyrian word for 'back' or even 'roof' seems of less importance—despite Brown, Driver and Briggs. But surely conclusive is the fact that on every one of the other 23 occasions in the Old Testament where *TSO-HAR* occurs it means noon, mid-day. The word plainly means light, as of the mid-day sun, and is given by other authorities as 'brilliance'. Dean Alford[12] translates the passage 'Light shalt thou make for the ark'. As there was no glass available in such early times it is obvious that this space was open and would admit air. Thus God made provision for light and air, two essentials for the living creatures in the ark. If these living creatures—including Noah and his family—being the lightest part of the cargo were on the top deck or floor, then the window would have to provide light and air for the greater part of the length of the top deck.[13] It would seem that the 'window' or 'light' was an open space running possibly nearly the full length of both sides just below the roof which would doubtless be slightly sloping and overhang by a sufficient amount for the rain to fall clear of the walls. This space or light may have been a cubit in height or possibly the text means that the roof was a cubit above the windows: the meaning of the verse is uncertain. The 'window' would be divided at intervals by the main beams either of the cross-walls or of additional 'ribs' used to

---

[10] F. Brown, S. R. Driver and C. A. Briggs, *Hebrew and English* Lexicon (Oxford 1955), p. 843.

[11] *Ibid.*, p. 844.

[12] H. Alford, *Genesis* (London, 1872), p. 32.

[13] A later Jewish work *Pirqe Rabbi Eliezer,* probably ninth century A.D. puts all the beasts on the lowest floor, the birds on the middle and creeping things and Noah's family on the upper deck.

strengthen the whole structure. The 'light' would, in fact, consist of many rectangular windows. These could be closed by sliding wooden panels in exactly the same way that we have already seen that the apertures of the granaries were closed. Further, those which came opposite any rooms in which birds were housed would require a lighter, open, lattice work to prevent the escape of these creatures and it is for this reason that the writer in Genesis 8:6 uses the other word, which in the Old Testament always means a lattice type window. Such a lattice, as we see from Old Testament references, could be slid aside or opened, just as we are told Noah did, for the release of birds.

The arrangements within the Ark seem to be as follows. Noah, his family and the living creatures—a total weight maybe of a hundred or so tons—lived on the top floor where there was ample provision of light and air, and with provision for closing the window spaces when necessary. On the two lower decks the food and water for these creatures, perhaps weighing some thousands of tons, was stored in bins or containers. Thus by far the greater part of the weight was well down in the hold as would be required in the safe loading of any ship and once again we can only marvel at the care and design revealed by the Biblical account of the Ark when contrasted with the crude cubic vessel of the Gilgamesh Epic. There can be no doubt as to which is the original, firsthand description!

PART TWO

The Survival of the Ark

1

The Most Ancient Witnesses

i. Berossus*

The latest known Babylonian deluge version is that of Berossus, a priest of Marduk at Babylon. It is taken from the history of Babylonia which he compiled from native documents and published in Greek about 275 B.C. His writings have perished, but extracts from his history have survived to our day. Of his account of the flood we have two excerpts, both of which are, in turn, based upon an excerpt made by Alexander Polyhistor (last century B.C.) The first and more important of the two reads as follows:[1]

After the death of Ardatās,[2] his son Xisuthros reigned for 64,800 years; under him a great deluge took place; the story has been recorded as follows: Kronos[3] appeared to him in (his) sleep and revealed (to him) that on the fifteenth of the month Daisios[4] mankind would be destroyed by a deluge. He therefore commanded (him) to set down in writing the beginning, middle, and end of all things, to bury (these writ-

---

* [From Alexander Heidel, *The Gilgamesh Epic and Old Testament Parallels* (2d ed. [1949], pp. 116-19).]

[1] Text in *Eusebi chronicorum libri duo*, ed. Alfred Schoene, Vol. I (Berlin, 1875), cols. 20-24. Translated by A. M. Harmon in A .T. Clay, *A Hebrew Deluge Story in Cuneiform* (New Haven, 1922), pp. 82-83; R. W. Rogers, *Cuneiform Parallels to the Old Testament* (New York and Cincinnati, 1926), pp. 109-12; Ebeling in Hugo Gressmann, *Altorientalische Texte zum Alten Testament* (Berlin and Leipzig, 1926), pp. 200-201; and others.

[2] On column 10 of the work from which we have taken the present story, Eusebius calls the king Otìartēs, which is a corruption of Ōpartēs, corresponding to the Babylonian Ubara-Tutu. Both Ardatēs and Ōpartēs may go back to a form Ōpardatēs, or the like (cf. Thorkild Jacobsen, *The Sumerian King List* [Chicago, 1939], p. 75, n. 32).

[3] Corresponding to the Babylonian Ea.

[4] Corresponding roughly to the month of May.

ings) in Sippar,[5] the city of the sun (-god); to build a
boat, and to go aboard it with his relatives and close
friends; to store up in it food and drink, to put into it
also living creatures, winged and four-footed, and,
when all was made ready, to set sail. If asked whither
he was sailing, he should say: "To the gods, in order to
pray that it may be well with mankind!" He obeyed
and built a boat, five stadia[6] in length and two stadia in
width; all these orders he carried out and embarked
with (his) wife and children and his close friends.

After the deluge had occurred, Xisuthros let go some
birds as soon as it ceased; but as they found no food
nor a place to alight, they returned to the ship. After
certain days Xisuthros again let the birds go; these
again returned to the ship, but with their feet stained
with mud. But, when they were let go for the third
time, they did not again return to the ship. Xisuthros
concluded that land had appeared; and, unstopping a
part of the seams of the ship and perceiving that the
ship had grounded upon a certain mountain, he disembarked with (his) wife, (his) daughter, and the pilot;
and after he had prostrated himself to the ground, had
built an altar, and had sacrificed to the gods, he disappeared with those who had disembarked from the ship.
Those who had remained on the ship disembarked
when Xisuthros and his companions did not return,
and sought him, calling (him) by name; but Xisuthros
himself never appeared to them; however, a voice came
from the air, commanding them to be god-fearing, as
was proper; for because of his piety he had gone to
dwell with the gods, and his wife and (his) daughter
and the pilot had received a share in the same honor.
(The voice) told them also that they should go back to
Babylon and, as had been decreed unto them by fate,
that they should recover the writings at Sippar and pass

---

[5] A town in northern Babylonia. The text has Sispara throughout.

[6] The Armenian version has "fifteen stadia." This is probably a
scribal error, which may be due to the preceding date "on the fifteenth of the month Daisios" (so Paul Haupt in *Beiträge Zur
Assyriologie*, X. Heft [1927], 26).

(them) on to men; also that the land where they were belonged to Armenia.

When they had heard these things, they sacrificed to the gods and went on foot[7] to Babylon. But of this ship that grounded in Armenia some part still remains in the mountains of the Gordyaeans in Armenia, and some get pitch from the ship by scraping (it) off, and use it for amulets. These, then, went to Babylon, dug up the writings at Sippar, founded many cities, erected temples, and rebuilt Babylon.

The second excerpt, which Abydenus (probably second century A.D.) made on the basis of Polyhistor's epitome,[8] runs thus:

After him reigned others, (among them) also Sisithros,[9] to whom Kronos foretold that on the fifteenth of Daisios there would occur copious rains; (wherefore) he commanded (him) to hide all available writings in Sippar, the city of the sun(-god). As soon as Sisithros had carried out these commands, he sailed for Armenia, and immediately the rainstorms sent by the god came upon him.[10] The third day, after the rain had

---

[7] Thus the Armenian version. The Greek has "by a roundabout way" (*perix*).

[8] See P. Schnabel, *Berossos und die babylonisch-hellenistische Literatur* (Leipzig and Berlin, 1923), p.p. 164 ff. Text in *Eusebi chronicorum libri duo*, ed. Schoene, Vol. I, cols. 32-34. Translated by H. Usener, *Die Sintfluthsagen* (Bonn, 1899), p. 15, and B. Bonkamp, *Die Bibel im Lichte der Keilschriftforschung* (Recklinghausèn, 1939), pp. 131-32. [Abydenus' fragments are collected in Felix Jacoby, *Die Fragmente der Griechischen Historiker* (F GR HIST), Vol. III/C (Leiden: E. J. Brill, 1958), 685 F. The pertinent fragment is 685 F 3 on pp. 401-402. This fragment is quoted by Eusebius of Caesarea, *Praeparatio Evangelica*, Bk. IX, chap. 12, and by Cyril of Alexandria, *Contra Julianum*, Bk. I, chaps. 8-9. Moses of Chorene (5th century) mentions the fragment in his *Histoire d'Arménie*, Bk. I, chap. 4; however, he says nothing about the survival of the Ark.]

[9] Identical with Xisuthros. A few lines preceding our text, Abydenus calls him Sisuthros.

[10] *Lit.:* and immediately the things from the god came upon him. The god referred to evidently is the chief god of the pantheon, and not Kronos (i.e., not Ea).

subsided, he sent forth (some) of the birds to determine whether they could see land emerging somewhere
from the water; but (the birds,) greeted by an un-
bounded sea (and) at a loss where they should alight,
returned to Sisithros, and others after them (did likewise.) But when upon the third trial he succeeded—for
they returned with their feet full of mud—the gods removed him from the ken of man. But the vessel in Armenia furnished the inhabitants with wooden amulets
to ward off evil.

ii. Josephus and his Sources

*Flavius Josephus (A.D. 37-ca. 100), son of a dis-
tinguished priestly family, Pharisee, and later a turn-
coat historian under Titus, produced four exceedingly
important works at about the same time as the books
of the New Testament were being written:* The Wars of
the Jews, Jewish Antiquities, Against Apion, *and his*
Life of Flavius Josephus. *Three times he mentions the
remains of Noah's Ark. In* Against Apion *he calls to
witness the account of Berossus the Chaldean which we
have reproduced immediately above. "This author,"
says Josephus, "following the most ancient records,
has, like Moses, described the flood and the destruction
of mankind thereby, and told of the ark in which Noah,
the founder of our race, was saved when it landed on
the heights of the mountains of Armenia" (I. 128-
130) The two remaining references, both of which
occur in the* Antiquities, *appear below with notes elu-
cidating the sources on which Josephus depends. We
have not reproduced here the earlier and less accurate
translation by William Whiston but the translation of
H. St. John Thackeray, Ralph Marcus, and Louis H.
Feldman accompanying a text based on the standard
critical editions of Niese and Naber, published in
the Loeb Classical Library (Harvard University Press,
1926-1955). Though his accuracy is not always above
reproach, Josephus saw clearly the need for truthful-
ness in relating historical events. "He was so sure of the*

accuracy of his reporting," observes A. W. Mosley, "that he presented copies of his works to Vespasian, to Titus, to Julius Archelaus, to Herod (king of Chalcis) and to King Agrippa—'all these men bore testimony to me', he wrote, 'that I had the strictest regard to truth'. . . ." Mosley also shows that Josephus saw the need for consulting eyewitnesses and primary sources when composing his accounts, for carefully sifting the traditions that came to him, and for criticizing other historians who had not maintained such high standards.*

The following passage is taken from the Jewish Antiquities *I. 89-95 as translated in Volume IV of the Loeb edition, pp. 43-47.*

When God gave the signal and caused the rainfall to begin, the water poured down for forty entire days, insomuch that it rose to fifteen cubits above the surface of the earth. That was the reason why no more escaped, since they had no place of refuge. When the rain at length ceased, for 150 days the water scarcely began to sink, until at the opening of the seventh month, from the seventh day, it little by little subsided as the month drew to a close. Then the ark settled on a mountain-top in Armenia: observing this, Noah opened the ark and, seeing a little land surrounding it, with hopes now revived, remained where he was. But a few days later, the water continuing to sink, he let loose a raven, to learn whether any other portion of the earth had emerged from the flood and would now make it safe to disembark; but the bird found the whole land inundated and returned to Noah. Seven days after he sent forth a dove to explore the condition of the earth; it returned bearing the marks of clay and an olive-branch in its mouth. Noah, thus learning that the earth was delivered from the flood, waited yet seven days, and then let the animals out of the ark, went forth himself with his family, sacrificed to God and feasted

---

* A. W. Mosley, "Historical Reporting in the Ancient World," *New Testament Studies*, XII (1966), 10-26.

with his household. The Armenians call that spot the Landing-place [*apobatērion . . . ton topon*]*, for it was there that the ark came safe to land, and they show the relics of it to this day.

This flood and the ark are mentioned by all who have written histories of the barbarians. Among these is Berossus the Chaldaean, who in his description of the events of the flood writes somewhere as follows: "It is said, moreover, that a portion of the vessel still survives in Armenia on the mountain of the Cordyaeans,[1] and that persons carry off pieces of the bitumen, which they use as talismans." These matters are also mentioned by Hieronymus the Egyptian,[2] author of the ancient history of Phoenicia, by Mnaseas[3] and by many others. Nicolaus of Damascus[4] in his ninety-sixth book relates

---

* [William Whiston comments at this point: "This *Apobatērion*, or *Place of Descent*, is the proper rendering of the Armenian name of this very city. It is called in Ptolemy Naxuana, and by Moses Chorenensis, the Armenian historian, *Idsheuan;* but at the place itself *Nachidsheuan*, which signifies *The first place of descent*, and is a lasting monument of the preservation of Noah in the ark, upon the top of that mountain, at whose foot it was built, as the first city or town after the flood. See Moses Chorenensis [Moses of Chorene, 5th(?) C., whose *History of Armenia* "remains a work of the first importance for the primitive history of Armenia, not least through its incorporation of many literary remains of the pre-Christian period" (*Oxford Dictionary of the Christian Church*); Whiston himself translated Moses' *History* into Latin], who also says elsewhere, that another town was related by tradition to have been called Seron, or, *The Place of Dispersion*, on account of the dispersion of Xisuthrus's or Noah's sons, from thence first made. Whether any remains of this ark be still preserved, as the people of the country suppose, I cannot certainly tell. Mons. Tournefort [French botanist, d. 1708] had, not very long since, a mind to see the place himself, but met with too great dangers and difficulties to venture through them."]

[1] *Alias* Gordyaeans.

[2] Otherwise unknown (to be distinguished from Hieronymus of Cardia, historian of the Diadochi.) [See his collected fragments in Felix Jacoby, *Die Fragmente der Grieschischen Historiker (F GR HIST)*, Vol. III/C (Leiden: E. J. Brill, 1958), 787 F (pp. 799-800).

[3] Of Patara in Lycia, antiquary and disciple of Eratosthenes, end of third cent. B.C. [The *Oxford Classical Dictionary* (1949) claims that he "published geographical and antiquarian details uncritically."]

the story as follows: "There is above the country of Minyas[5] in Armenia a great mountain called Baris, where, as the story goes, many refugees found safety at the time of the flood, and one man, transported upon an ark grounded upon the summit; and relics of the timber were for long preserved; this might well be the same man of whom Moses, the Jewish legislator, wrote."

* * *

The next passage is to be found in the Antiquities *XX. 24-25 (Loeb edition, volume IX, pp. 402-403).*

A district called Carron[1]. . . . has excellent soil for the production of amomum[2] in the greatest abundance; it also possesses the remains of the ark in which report

---

[4] Friend and biographer of Herod the Great and author of a Universal History which was one of the main sources of Josephus. Here Nicolaus is the last name in a list of authorities; and Josephus perhaps takes over the other names from him. [Ben Zion Wacholder, author of a scholarly and comprehensive treatment of Nicolaus, writes as follows: "Nicolaus' *Histories* was a true universal history. Its scheme may properly be compard to the *Histories* of Ephorus, the first universal historian. But Nicolaus' history was much wider in scope. . . . Even if we credit the broader vision of Nicolaus to the knowledge acquired since the days of Ephorus, the organization of the *Histories* is commendable. Here was neither a mere collection of national histories nor a synchronous account of generations . . . It might . . . be assumed that Nicolaus' claim that he put an immense amount of labor into his history is correct . . . It is evident that he had access to remarkable library resources" *(Nicolaus of Damascus* [1962], pp. 66, 68). See his collected fragments in Felix Jacoby, *Die Fragmente der Griechischen Historiker (F GR HIST)*, Vol. II/A (Berlin: Weidmann, 1926). The one above is fragment 90 F 72 (pp. (376-77).]

[5] The Minni of the O.T. (Jer. 1i. 27), like the *Mannu* of Assyrian inscriptions, are mentioned in close connexion with Ararat.

[1] The location of Carron presents considerable difficulties. It is not Carrhae, which is in northern Mesopotamia. The emendation to Gordyene *(cf. Ant.* i. 93), on the Armenian border east of the sources of the Tigris, is more acceptable geographically, since it is closer to Ararat, the Biblical site where Noah's ark rested. Hence, the reading proposed by J. Macquart, *Osteuropäische und ostasiatische Streifzüge*, 1903, p. 289 n. 4, is *Kardou.*

[2] An aromatic plant of the ginger family, though its exact identity is unknown.

has it that Noah was saved from the flood—remains
which to this day are shown to those who are curious
to see them.

2
The Patristic Testimony

The fathers of the church speak of the Ark's survival on Mount Ararat as common knowledge. They appeal to a well-known fact; for them, there was no need to build a case for its survival. Though the fathers refer often to Noah and the Deluge we have restricted ourselves to those independent patristic testimonies to the survival of Noah's ship.

*   *   *

i. Theophilus of Antioch

Theophilus (ca. 115-185), the sixth bishop of Syrian Antioch, left his pagan upbringing to become an outstanding apologist for the Christian faith. Of his several writings only three books of his Ad Autolycum *are extant. Composed shortly after the year 180, they show Theophilus to be "well versed in contemporary literature and philosophy" and thus to be the possessor of "a comprehensive education and knowledge" (Quasten,* Patrology *[1950], I, 239). The entire treatise was well fitted to lead an intelligent pagan to acceptance of Christianity. The first book deals with the absurdities of idolatry and the difference between honoring the emperor and worshiping God. In his second book Theophilus contrasts the teachings of the prophets with the foolishness of pagan religion and with the theology and cosmogony of the Greek poets. Book three, which includes an account of the Ark's survival (chap. 19), demonstrates the moral superiority of Christianity and the greater antiquity of its doctrine than that of all other religions. The passage below is taken from Marcus Dods' translation in the* Ante-Nicene Fathers *([1885], II, 117). Standard editions of*

Ad Autolycum *are available in J. C. Th. Otto,* Corpus
apologetarum christianorum saeculi secundi *(9 vols;
Jena, 1847-72) and in the separate work of S. Frasca,*
Theophilus Antiochenus, Gli tre libri ad Autolico.
Testo, versione, introd. *(Turin, 1938).*

Moses showed that the flood lasted forty days and forty
nights, torrents pouring from heaven, and from the
fountains of the deep breaking up, so that the water
overtopped every high hill 15 cubits. And thus the race
of all the men that then were was destroyed, and those
only who were protected in the ark were saved; and
these, we have already said, were eight. And of the ark,
the remains are to this day to be seen in the Arabian
mountains.

ii. Faustus of Byzantium

*Very little is known of this 4th-century historian of
Armenia, beyond the fact that he was of Greek origin
a native of Byzantium—and that he wrote his* Historical Library *in Greek. It appears that the work was
translated into Armenian in the first half of the 5th
century, soon after the introduction of the Armenian
national alphabet. The original Greek text has been
lost, and we translate from the French version of Jean-
Baptiste Emine, printed in volume one of Victor Langlois'* great Collection des historiens anciens et modernes
de l'Arménie *([1881], pp. 218-19). Though Faustus'
work has received much criticism from Armenian writers (particularly owing to their chauvinistic suspicions
of a non-Armenian historian of Armenia), Emine
rightly notes that "Faustus' history is, with that of
Moses of Chorene, the capital source for our extant
knowledge of the annals of Armenia during the first
two centuries after the conversion of that land to
Christianity." Indeed, adds Emine: "We find in Faustus' work precious and exact data which one would
search for in vain in the writings of his contemporaries.
. . . In his book he appears to us as a learned and*

weighty historian well acquainted with the events he narrates" (pp. 203-204). It is of more than passing interest that Moses of Chorene and numerous later historians of Armenia borrow from Faustus' work without acknowledgement, thus attesting indirectly to its usefulness.

Bk. III, chap. 10 of Faustus' Historical Library is devoted to St. Jacob of Nisibis (early 4th century), the "Moses of Mesopotamia," one of the prominent figures at the Council of Nicaea (325) and a stalwart opponent of the Arian heresy.* The story about him narrated here by Faustus is of considerable importance, for it appears—either in this form or with variations—in many subsequent writings concerning the Ark's survival. The original source of the story, it must be emphasized, is Faustus—not the later writers to whom it is almost universally attributed. Thus the story reaches us from Jacob's own century.

About this time, the great bishop of Medzpin,[1] a man of Persian origin, Jacob by name, who was an admirable and venerable saint of God, indefatigable in the cause of Christian truth, left his city and betook himself to the mountains of Armenia, that is to say, to Mount Ararat[2] in the principality of Ararat and the canton of Gortouk.[3] He was full of graces of Christ and had the power to do miracles and prodigies.[4] Ar-

---

* On Jacob, see Canon E. Venables' detailed article in *A Dictionary of Christian Biography and Literature to the End of the Sixth Century,* ed. Wace and Piercy (London: John Murray, 1911), pp. 549-50.

[1] [i.e., Nisibis, a powerful fortress city of ancient Mesopotamia. The modern name is Nasibin or Nesib(in), but the town today has little to remind one of its former importance.]

[2] [The text reads "Sararat." Emine, the French editor, comments: "The spelling of the name 'Sararat' given by Faustus appears to me to be a transcriptional error, for it is found only in his writings."]

[3] [Gortouk corresponds to Ptolemy's "Cortaea"—see his *Geography,* V. 13.]

[4] [Numerous supernatural events are connected with Jacob's life, including his miraculous deliverance of Nisibis from Persian attacks. See P. Peeters, "La Légende de saint Jacques de Nisibe," *Analecta Bollandiana,* XXXVIII (1920), 285-373.]

riving at his destination, he prayed God most fervently
to allow him to see the Ark of deliverance built by
Noah—the Ark which had come to rest on that mountain at the time of the Deluge. Now Jacob was accustomed to obtain from God all that he asked of Him.

While he was climbing the rocky face of the inaccessible and arid Mount Ararat,[5] he and those who accompanied him became thirsty from fatigue. Then the
great Jacob[5] dropped to his knees and offered up
prayers before the Lord. At the place where he laid his
head, a spring of water broke forth by which he and his
companions quenched their thirst. It is for this reason
that to this day that spring is called "Jacob's well."[6]

---

[5] [In his *Religiosa historia* or *Vitae patrum*, Theodoret regularly
calls Jacob *ho megas*, "the great," and assigns him the first place
among the Fathers.]

[6] [Parrot, the first explorer in modern times to reach the summit
of Ararat (1829), saw this well near a little deserted chapel some two
thousand feet above the monastery of St. James (i.e., St. Jacob),
"upon the edge of the great glen" (*Journey to Ararat* [1845], p.
227). The monastery was totally destroyed in the blow-out of June,
1840. Parrot wrote of the well as follows (pp. 144-45):

"The fountain which springs out of a rock, at this spot, affords
a clear drinkable water, of a pure natural taste, and is therefore
an object deserving of general estimation; for there cannot be
many perennial springs upon mount Ararat, as I have proved,
to my vexation; since, in all my excursions upon it, I never
either found or heard of any other.

"It is possible that it may have originally induced some devout
monk to establish himself in that locality, whose reputed sanctity
procured for the spring also the reputation of miraculous virtues,
until, in the course of centuries, and the storm of political
events, the peaceful inhabitant was frightened away, and the
miraculous spring alone remained, as the object of universal
veneration among the Armenians, wherever they may be scattered round the world.

"The tradition respecting the wondrous virtue of the water
is this, that the flights of locusts which occasionally traverse
the country on this side, and beyond Caucasus, in countless
numbers, and as a kind of field plague, often laying waste an
entire province in a single day, cannot be expelled otherwise
than by means of a certain bird, which I have never been able
to see; but infer, from the description given of it, to be a kind
of thrush, though the Russians settled in this country call it a
starling. Not very large, it is dark-colored, yellowish white on the
breast and back, and is said to resort in flocks to the Araxes,
when the mulberries are ripe,—though why they do so, is not
well explained,—and to do much damage, by destroying the

But he did not neglect to apply himself zealously to catch sight of the object of his desire, nor did he cease to pray for it to the Lord God.

Already he had arrived near the summit of the mountain, and thoroughly exhausted as he was, he fell asleep. Then the angel of God came and said to him: "Jacob! Jacob!" He answered, "Here am I, Lord." And the angel said: "The Lord gives ear to your prayer and brings to pass what you desire. That which you find on your pallet is wood from the Ark. There it is: I

---

mulberries. Its Armenian name is Tarm; it is also called Tetägush, (*guch*, in the Tatar language, means *bird*, and *tut* is the Armenian for *mulberry*,) the Tatars call it Gasyrtshakh. Should it make its appearance in a tract infested by the locusts, then the fields are soon saved, for it pursues the locusts with implacable enmity. For the purpose of enticing this serviceable bird, the water of the holy well is brought into requisition; and, for this purpose, it is sufficient just to fill a pitcher or a bottle with it, and to set it down in the neighborhood of the locusts, taking care, however, not to let the vessel touch the ground anywhere on the way; for, in that case, the water immediately disappears; but set in the open air, and in the proper place, it never fails to attract to the spot a flock of the tetägush, which soon rid the district of the devouring plague. Not merely the common people and Armenians, but some even of the educated classes, and not the Armenian creed, have sought to convince me of the truth of this story, and related as a proof, that a few years before, the country round Kislyar, on the northern side of Caucasus, being attacked by locusts, was saved through the virtue of a bottle of water fetched in the greatest haste from the holy well, and which immediately brought together a flock of the birds. At Ararat, and in Tiflis, every one knew that the water was brought, and as to the success attending the use of it, that might be easily learned in Kislyar, where the bottle, with some of the miraculous water, was still lying in the church!"

The blowout which destroyed the town of Arguri in 1840 did not affect St. Jacob's well; Lynch say it in 1893 (*Armenia: Travels and Studies* [1901], I, 194):

"At two o'clock we arrived at the famous rose bush and the holy well. The path has been worn by the feet of pilgrims, who journey hither from the plains. The water issues from a recess in the side of the mountain which has been levelled with a masonry of hewn stone. The overflow nourishes the rose-tree, on the twigs of which are attached countless little ribbons of rag, shreds from the garments of the devout. Just beyond these sacred objects you are shown a level site, overhanging the ravine. Rows of stones are interlaced upon its surface, a sign for pious wayfarers. Here was placed the little shrine which during the great earthquake must have tumbled headlong into the chasm."]

bring it to you: it comes from the Ark itself. From this moment on you shall cease desiring to see the Ark, for such is the will of the Lord." Jacob awoke with the greatest joy, praising and thanking the Lord. He saw the plank, which seemed to have been sliced from a great piece of wood with the blow of an axe. Taking up what had been vouchsafed to him, he retraced his steps, followed by his companions in the quest.

The joy felt by the great prophet Moses, that man who had seen God, could not have been greater than Jacob's—and perhaps was even less—when after receiving the commandments written by the finger of God and with them in his very hands, he descended Mt. Sinai with the tablets for a rebel people—that people who, having turned their faces from the holy places to the earth, departed from the Lord's pathway, worshipped a metal calf, and deeply grieved the bearer of the Law, as the broken tablets so well evidenced. But in the case of the blessed Jacob, the object of our narration, it was not the same, for, full of spiritual consolation, he returned bringing to all the nations of earth the good news bestowed by the Almighty God from his treasures of things hidden and things revealed.

While this man of God was approaching with the wood of the deliverance—that relic of the Ark built by our father Noah, that eternal symbol of the great punishment inflicted by God on man and beast—the inhabitants of the city and the surrounding countryside came forth to meet him with boundless joy and happiness. From the moment they laid their eyes upon the holy man, they pressed in upon him as an envoy from Christ or an angel from heaven; they looked upon the valiant pastor as the prophet who had seen God; they embraced him and kissed the calluses on his weary feet. The people eagerly accepted the gracious gift of the wood, and it is preserved to this day among them as the visible sign of the Ark of the patriarch Noah.[7]

---

[7] [By tradition at the monastery of Echmiadzin, where Parrot in 1829 and Wells in 1932 saw a relic of the Ark. (Whether the same relic, we must leave to the reader to judge!) Parrot, the distinguished explorer who made the first modern recorded ascent of

iii Epiphanius of Salamis

This Palestine-born monk and Bishop of Constantia (Salamis) (ca. 315-403) was a "sleuth-hound of heresy. ... It was the dream of his life to defend ortho- doxy by detecting and refuting heresy in all its

Ararat, relates his experience in the following terms (*Journey to Ararat* [1845], p.p. 101-102):

"The most precious ornaments—the real treasures of this monastery, and to which it is indebted for no small share of the veneration with which it is regarded by all Armenians, are the holy relics which are preserved in the cathedral, deposited each in its own chest. They are never exhibited but on some particular occasions, as at consecrations . . . The object re- specting which I obtained any specific information I shall men- tion somewhat in detail, as contradictory statements upon these matters are to be found in Chardin and Tournefort: and, in some instances, I shall be found to differ from both . . . The hand of St. James, enclosed in a hand of the natural shape, with an arm, of silver gilt: the thumb and fore-finger are bent towards each other, and between them hangs a fragment of the ark of Noah, by a little chain: it is a small, dark-coloured, quadrangular piece of wood, in good preservation, and carved upon one surface. It came into the possession of a monk [St. Jacob of Nisibis], whose legend I shall take another opportunity of giving, by a miracle, which was the cause of his being canonised."

Wells, an American journalist. tells his story thus (*Kapoot* [1933], pp. 223-29:

' "We have come all the way from Chicago on purpose to visit Echmiazin. We are looking for Noah's Ark or what is left of it!" I continued with a smile.

The old man's eyes twinkled. "We have the remains of the Ark here in the church!"

"May we see it?" we all said eagerly.

. . . "I must explain to you, that it is the most prized posses- sion of the monastery. Do not misunderstand me; we do not class it as merely a relic. We have many relics; we even have the iron spear which was thrust into the side of Jesus at his crucifixion; we have the nails and a piece of the Cross, but," he continued with a merry twinkle in his eye, "there are many such relics in other churches. This piece of Noah's Ark is in quite a different category, and no other church in the world possesses or even claims to possess such a thing."

. . . .

He then introduced himself to us.

"I am Archbishop Mesrop. Our Katholikos has recently died and until his successor is elected, I am in charge of Echmiazin!"

. . . .

forms." Epiphanius has left us two great polemical
treatises, the* Ancoratus *and, most important of all his
works, the* Panarion. *The* Panarion *is literally a "medicine chest" of remedies for all forms of erroneous belief. It deals with eighty heresies, twenty of which belong to the pre-Christian period.*

The following passage is taken from the Panarion,
*I.i 18 (the chapter refuting the beliefs of the Naz-
arenes, which Epiphanius classes as the fifth variety of
Judaizing heresy). In this chapter the Bishop roundly
criticizes the Nazarenic Christians for denying the rev-*

The Archbishop . . . told us that, although he himself would
have no objection to our seeing and photographing the portion
of the Ark which had been in the church for centuries, it had
never been shown to a layman.

. . . .

Slowly and reverently the monks filed out of the church and
stood in a line outside, followed by two very old men. Each man
was carrying in his arms a heavy golden casket covered with
precious stones that glittered and sparkled in the bright sunlight,
a sure sign that they were genuine.

. . . .

"You may open the caskets," said the Archbishop, addressing
me.

. . . .

. . . I opened the last casket, which looked very much like an
ordinary ikon from the outside, but on opening the two doors of
the casket, instead of finding the usual painting of Jesus or the
Holy Family, there was a piece of reddish-colored petrified wood,
measuring about twelve inches by nine and about an inch thick.
"You may examine it as much as you like," said the Archbishop. "This is the portion of Noah's Ark which was brought
down from Ararat by one of our monks named Jacob, St.
Jacob."
It was obviously petrified wood, as the grain was clearly
visible, but having expected to see a piece of wood that was
curved like the side of a boat, I remarked that I was surprised
to find it was flat.
Archbishop Mesrop had a sense of humor. He instantly
remarked, "You have forgotten the rudder. Mr. Wells!"
So this was the piece of wood I had come so far to see,
and the thing that so many other travelers, including Lord Bryce,
had been unsuccessful in seeing.'
Cf. with these accounts the description of the relic obtained by
Struys in section 6 below.]

* Henry Barclay Swete, *Patristic Study,* ed. by Arthur W. Robinson
(London: Longmans, Green, 1902), p. 86.

*elational content of such material in the Pentateuch as
the sacrificial system while honoring the patriarchs and
Moses (he levels at them the argument which equally
well applies to religious liberals of the present day:
how can you rely on the Scripture at one point and re-
ject it at another? "Did not the Savior say that a good
tree cannot bear bad fruit?") To refute the Pentateu-
chal criticism of the Nazarenes, he cites instances
where sacrificial events in the Pentateuch had such factual impact on history that the very places where they
occurred still attest to them—as Mt. Zion, where
Abraham offered Isaac. This leads him to mention
Noah and the Deluge.*

*We translate from F. Oehler's critical edition of the
Greek text, with accompanying Latin version by Denis
Petau (1583-1652)—whose rendering of the passage
is not entirely satisfactory and has required correction
on the basis of the Greek. See Oehler's* Corpus haereseologicum, *II/1 (Berlin, 1859), 94-95 (and cf. pp.
32-33) and Karl Holl,* Die Handschriftliche Überlieferung des Epiphanius *(Leipzig, 1910).*

Do you seriously suppose that we are unable to
prove our point, when even to this day the remains[1] of
Noah's Ark are shown in the country of the Kurds?[2]
Why, were one to search diligently, doubtless one
would also find at the foot of the mountain the remnants[1] of the altar where Noah, on leaving the Ark,
tarried to offer clean and fatly animals as a sacrifice to
the Lord God, when he heard God say: "Behold, every
moving thing that liveth shall be meat for you; even as
the green herb have I given you all things."[3]

---

[1] [Gk., *leipsana:* "remains, remnants, pieces, relics."]

[2] ["A region of vague boundaries in Eastern Asiatic Turkey and
western Persia, about lat. 34° - 39 N., long. 38° - 47 E. The surface is mountainous. The inhabitants (the ancient Carduchi) belong
to the Aryan race, but are Mohammedans in creed. They have a
quasi independence under their chiefs, and are noted for their
robberies" (*Century Cyclopedia of Names* [1904], p. 580). The Kurds
remain today the semi-nomadic inhabitants of the Ararat region.]

[3] [Gen. 9:3.]

iv. Chrysostom

*John Chrysostom ("John the Golden-mouthed")
ca. 345-407, patriarch of Constantinople, was the
greatest preacher of the ancient church. Concerning his
sermon "On Perfect Charity," Sir Henry Savile
(1549-1622), the great 17th-century editor of Chrysostom's works in eight folio volumes, wrote: "It is
worthy of the highest note and of Chrysostom himself."
The Migne editor adds: "I heartily concur with Savile's
judgment. The sermon is indeed worthy of Chrysostom,
and is to the greatest degree valuable for instruction in
righteousness." Internal evidence does not permit us to
say whether Chrysostom delivered it in Antioch or at
Constantinople. Our rendering follows the Greek text,
with accompanying Latin translation, as given in
Migne,* Patrologiae cursus completus . . . series graeca,
LVI, cols. 287-88.*

Let us therefore ask them [the unbelieving]: Have
you heard of the Flood—of that universal destruction?
That was not just a threat, was it? Did it not really
come to pass—was not this mighty work carried out?
Do not the mountains of Armenia testify to it, where
the Ark rested? And are not the remains* of the Ark
preserved there to this very day for our admonition?

---

* [Gk., *leipsana:* "remains, remnants, pieces, relics." The same
word is used by Epiphanius, but it is clear from the Greek of the
two writers that Chrysostom is not copying Epiphanius.]

3

Encyclopedists of the Early Middle Ages

i. Isidore of Seville

Isidore (ca. 560-636) was the first Christian writer to undertake the compilation of a summa of universal knowledge. This work, though subject to the limitations of its time, marked its author as one of the most learned men of his age and extended his influence for nearly a millennium; it remains today "among the most important sources for the history of intellectual culture in the early middle ages." Isidore's Etymologies, *continues* Ernest Bréhaut, *"is strikingly complete. . . . Few writers of any period cover the intellectual interests of their time so completely"* (An Encyclopedist of the Dark Ages [1912], p 16). *Moreover, "so hospitable an attitude toward profane learning as Isidore displayed was unparalleled in his own period, and was never surpassed throughout the middle ages" (p. 31).*

We translate from Vol. II of W. M. Lindsay's critical edition of the Latin text of Isidore's Etymologies, *as published in the "Scriptorum Classicorum Bibliotheca Oxoniensis" (1911); the passage, in the section "On Mountains," is designated XIV, 8, 5, and a collateral reference to the landing of the Ark in the mountains of Armenia occurs at XIV, 3, 35. Vincent of Beauvais reproduces verbatim the following passage in his* Speculum naturale, *Bk. VI, chap. 21. As for Isidore, we cannot be sure where he derived his information, but it is interesting that in the composite list presented by Bréhaut (pp. 46-47) none of the sources we have cited in previous sections is included. Thus it may not be presumptuous of us to say that Isidore is not simply culling from the earlier accounts of the Ark's survival.*

Ararat is a mountain in Armenia, where the historians testify[1] that the Ark came to rest after the Flood.
So even to this day wood remains of it[2] are to be seen
there.[3]

ii. Vincent of Beauvais

*Another important mediaeval encyclopedist who
transmitted the tradition of the Ark's survival on
Ararat was Vincent of Beauvais (ca. 1184-1264).
Manifesting "the critical spirit of a modern scholar,"
Vincent was careful to screen his authorities and divide
his references into great, mediocre, little, and of no authority as he penned his massive Speculum quadruplex
(1256-1259)[1] There he reproduces verbatim the
above passage from Isidore (specifying his source, as
was characteristic of this careful compiler).[2] Elsewhere
in the same work[3] he presents the following account of
a monk's ascent of Ararat and his successful acquisition of a piece of the Ark. This narrative appears almost certainly to depend upon the account of Faustus
of Byzantium which has been related above in section
II; however, in Faustus Jacob does not return to his
starting point when he falls asleep, nor does he attain
the summit. Our translation renders the appropriate
section on p. 1266 of the 1624 Douai edition of the
Speculum. Two studies of Vincent are noteworthy:
Desbarreaux-Bernard's Étude bibliographique sur
l'édition du Speculum quadruplex de Vincent de Beauvais (Paris, 1872) and J.-B. Bourgeat's Études sur
Vincent de Beauvais (Paris, 1856).*

---

[1] [Variant reading: "where history testifies."]

[2] [Lat., "lignorum eius vestigia."]

[3] [A 9th-10th century manuscript omits the word "there."]

[1] Astrik L. Gabriel, *The Educational Ideas of Vincent of Beauvais,*
Texts and Studies in the History of Mediaeval Education, No. IV, ed.
by A. L. Gabriel and J. N. Garvin (Notre Dame, Ind.: The Mediaeval Institute, University of Notre Dame, 1956), p. 11.

[2] Book VI, chap. 21 ("Speculum naturale").

[3] Book XXX, chap. 97 ("Speculum historiale").

In Armenia there is a noble city called Ani[1] where a thousand churches and a hundred thousand families or households are to be found. The Tartars captured this city in twelve days. Near it is Mount Ararat, where Noah's Ark rests, and at the foot of that mountain is the first city which Noah built, called Laudume.[2] Close by the city flows the river Arathosi,[3] which traverses the plain of Mongan where the Tartars winter, and empties into the Caspian Sea.[4] But as for that most excellent Mount Ararat, it is said that no man has ever ascended it, except for one monk. They say that this monk, impelled by the ardor of his devotion for Noah's Ark which landed there, tried many times, with all the energy he could muster, to ascend the mountain. When he had climbed part of the way, he would fall asleep on account of his tired limbs, and on waking he would always find himself at the foot of the mountain. Finally, however, the Lord gave in to his persistence: He hearkened to the monk's vow and prayers and so instructed him by His Angel that he might ascend the mountain on one occasion—but for the future would not ever seek to do so again. Thus he safely made the ascent, and when he returned he brought one of the beams[5] from the Ark back with him. At the foot of the mountain he then built a monastery[6] in which he faithfully placed this same beam as (so to speak) a holy relic.

---

[1] [Lat., *Am.* Marginal rubric: "Ani, the noblest city of Armenia." This once populous city, known traditionally as "the city of the 1,001 churches" was repeatedly besieged and captured from 1064 to 1239; sixty years after Vincent wrote this passage, the ruin of the city was completed by an earthquake (1319). Cf. M. F. Brosset, *Les ruines d'Ani* (1860-61).]

[2] [Probably the source of Mandeville's "city of Dayne, which was founded by Noah."]

[3] [The Araxes river.]

[4] [*Mare Sarmaticum* (The Black Sea) should read *Mare Servanicum* (the Caspian Sea); the error may well be transcriptional or typographical.]

[5] [Lat., *asser:* beam, pole, stake, post. The word does not necessarily suggest a large piece of wood.]

[6] [By tradition, the monastery of Echmiadzin. See note 7 to the account of Faustus of Byzantium in section 2.]

4

An Eastern Prince

Brother Jehan Haithon (Hayton), a 13th century Armenian prince who became a Premonstratensian monk in France and wrote an account of the "marvels of the thirteen kingdoms of Asia" has unfortunately been confused with his relative, King Haithon I, and with the narrator of King Haithon's Mongolian travels. Writes E. Bretschneider in his Mediaeval Researches from Eastern Asiatic Sources *([1910], I, 165, n. 450):*

King Haithon I, is not to be confounded with his kinsman, Haithon, prince of Gorhigos, who also became a monk, and spent the latter part of his life in a monastery in Poitiers, in France. He is the author of a History (and Geography) of the Eastern Kingdoms, written in 1307 by Nicholas Falcon in French, from the dictation of Haithon (Bergeron's 'Voyages en Asie'). Falcon afterwards translated this account into Latin ('Historia Orientalis'). Falcon's original French manuscript, which bears the title 'Merveilles des XIII. Royaulmes d'Aise,' was published in 1877 by L. de Backer in his 'Extrême Orient au Moyen-âge.' But Backer is egregiously mistaken in asserting that this Haithon, prince of Gorhigos, was the same as Kirakos, who wrote the account of King Haithon's journey to Mongolia.

Our translation has been made from Backer's French text: L'Extrême Orient au Moyen-âge *[1877], p. 145). In speaking of "the kingdom of Armenia, of its wonders and its power," Haithon declares:*

In Armenia there is a very high mountain—the highest in existence—and its name is Ararat. On that mountain

Noah's Ark landed after the Flood. No one can climb
this mountain because of the great quantity of snow on
it winter and summer. But at the summit a great black
object[1] is always[2] visible, which is said to be the Ark
of Noah.

---

[1] [Old fr., "une grant chose noire."]
[2] [Old fr., "tout adès."]

5

Monks, Merchants, and Knights of the Later Middle Ages

This section contains only the most reliable testimonies to the survival of Noah's Ark in the later middle ages. We have omitted uncritical traveler's accounts such as that of Rabbi Benjamin of Tudela (A.D. 1163): "Two days to Jezireh Ben Omar, an island in the Tigris, at the foot of Mount Ararat, and four miles distant from the spot where the ark of Noah rested; Omar Ben al-Khatab removed the ark from the summit of two mountains and made a mosque of it. There still exists in the vicinity of the ark a synagogue of Esra the scribe."[1] Here Benjamin does not even refer to the true Ararat; he speaks of the mountain Jebel Judi, where, according to Muslim tradition, the Ark landed. However, the location of this landing site is based upon a misinterpretation of the Koran (11:44) in which "Al Judi" was taken as a place name, instead of simply an epithet—the "excellent" or "approved" mountain.[2] In actuality, the Koran does not name the particular mountain on which the Ark landed. Similarly, we pass over the related accounts of Al-Mas'udi, Ibn Haukal, and Elmacin[3] in order to hear the witness of three monks, a merchant, and two knights.

---

[1] "The travels of Rabbi Benjamin of Tudela, A.D. 1160-1173," in *Early Travels in Palestine*, ed. by Thomas Wright (London: Henry G. Bohn, 1848), pp. 93-94.

[2] "The word as it stands in Arabic may simply be a derivative of *júd*, meaning *excellence* or *approval*, the *yá* being added to denote the relation" (*The Holy Qur-án*, ed. and trans. by Muhammad Ali [Lahore, Punjab. India: Ahmadiyya Anjuman-J-Isháat-I-Islam, 1955], p. 462). Cf. John Warwick Montgomery, "The Apologetic Approach of Muhammad Ali and its Implications for Christian Apologetics," *Muslim World*, LI (April, 1961), 111-22, and author's "Corrigendum" in the July, 1961 issue.

[3] See Appendix A for these texts.

*   *   *

i. William of Roubruck

In 1252 a Franciscan called William, a native of the village of Rubruck in French Flanders, was sent by King Louis IX of France on a secret mission to the court of the Mongol Emperor. His Itinerarium *records the experiences he underwent during the next three years and 10,000 miles of journeyings. It is an account to which geographical science, natural history, ethnology, and the history of religions have subsequently been greatly indebted. Sir Henry Yule, the greatest authority on mediaeval geography of the past century, calls it "one of the best narratives of travel in existence" and its author "an honest, pious, stouthearted, acute and most intelligent observer, keen in the acquisition of knowledge"* (Encyclopaedia Britannica, *11th ed.* XXIII, 811). *In his translation of the* Itinerarium, *under the title,* The Journey of William of Rubruck to the Eastern Parts of the World, 1253-55 *([1900], p. xxxvi), William Woodville Rockhill says of Rubruck "that not only was he keen and intelligent, but conscientious and thorough in a high degree. Study of his narrative shows his careful preparation for his work as an explorer." The following passage, taken from pp. 269-70 of Rockhill's translation, was recorded by William between December 23, 1254 and January 13, 1255. His account of the monk who acquired a piece of the Ark agrees with Faustus of Byzantium; it is not the variant version of Vincent of Beauvais. William's monk does not attain the summit of the mountain; he is given a fragment of the Ark.*

Near this city [of Naxua] are mountains in which they say that Noah's ark rests; and there are two mountains, the one greater than the other; and the Araxes flows at their base; and there is a town there called Cemanum, which interpreted means "eight," and

they say that it was thus called from the eight persons
who came out of the ark, and who built it on the
greater mountain.[1] Many have tried to climb it, but
none has been able. This bishop told me that there has
been a monk who was most desirous (of climbing it),
but that an angel appeared to him bearing a piece of
the wood of the ark, and told him to try no more. They
had this piece of wood in his church, they told me.[2]
This mountain did not seem to me so very high, that
men could not ascend it. An old man gave me quite a
good reason why one ought not to try to climb it. They
call the mountain Massis, and it is of the feminine
gender in their language. "No one," he said, "ought to
climb up Massis; it is the mother of the world."[3]

ii. Jordanus

*Friar Jordanus (fl. 1321-1330), a French Domini-
can missionary-explorer and bishop of Colombum in
India, recorded his wide-range experiences in Asia in*
Mirabilia Descripta *(ca. 1329-1338). Its account of
India was "the best . . . given by any European in the
Middle Ages—superior even to Marco Polo's."
"Jordanus' Mirabilia," continues C. R. Beazley, author*

---

[1] The MSS. write this name in different ways—*Cemanium, Cemau-
rum,* and *Cemanum.* I have adopted the last form, as it approximates
more closely the Arabic *Temanin,* the name given by early Moham-
medan writers to the town built here by Noah. Ibn Haukal says that
at the foot of the mountain on which Noah's ark rested is a village
called *Themabim,* "and they say that the companions of Noah descended here from the ark and built this village." Masudi has it that
Noah and his family, in all eighty persons, on coming out of the ark
built a town which they called *Temanin* (eighty), a name which it retained to Masudi's time.

[2] I am told that a piece of the ark is still shown in the monastery
of Nadjivan. Bryce says it is in the treasury of Etchmiadzin. [See note
6 to our selection from Vincent of Beauvais.]

[3] *Massis* is the Armenian name of Ararat, and the monks on the
mountains still tell travellers that the mountain cannot be scaled because it is the cradle of the human race, so a man can no more reach
its top than re-enter his mother's womb. Maundevile speaks of "Arar-
athe which the Jewes clepen Tanuz." Rubruck was misinformed
about the gender of this word, as inanimate objects have no gender
in Armenian.

of the three-volume classic, The Dawn of Modern Geography, *"contains the earliest clear African identification of Prester John, and what is perhaps the first notice of the Black Sea under that name"* (Encyclopaedia Britannica, *11th ed., XV, 512). The passage below is taken from the Hakluyt Society edition of the* Mirabilia, *whose commentary was contributed by Sir Henry Yule.**

In Armenia the Greater I saw one great marvel. This is it: a mountain of excessive height and immense extent, on which Noah's ark is said to have rested. This mountain is never without snow, and seldom or never without clouds, which rarely rise higher than three parts up. The mountain is inaccessible, and there never has been anybody who could get farther than the edge of the snow. And (marvellous indeed!) even the beasts chased by the huntsmen, when they come to the snow, will liefer turn, will liefer yield them into the huntsman's hands, then go farther up that mountain. This mountain hath a compass of more than three days journey for a man on horseback going without halt. There be serpents of a great size, which swallow hares alive and whole, as I heard from a certain trustworthy gentleman who saw the fact, and shot an arrow at the serpent with a hare in his mouth, but scathed it not.[1] In a certain part of the mountain is a dwelling which Noah is to have built on leaving the ark; and there, too, is said to be that original vine which Noah planted, and whereby he got drunk; and it giveth such huge branches of grapes as you would scarce believe. This I heard from a certain Catholic archbishop of ours, a

---

* *Mirabilia Descripta. The Wonders of the East by Friar Jordanus* (London, 1863), pp. 3-4, translated from the Latin text published in 1839 in the Paris Geographical Society's *Recueil de voyages et de mémoires*, IV, 1-68.

[1] Stories of serpents seem to be rife in Armenia. On the Araxes, south of Nakhcheván (see note below), is a mountain called the Serpent Mountain, where serpents are said to collect in such numbers at certain times, that no man or beast dare approach. (See *Haxthausen's Transcaucasia*, pp. 144, 181, 353, etc.)

great man and a powerful, and trustworthy to boot, the lord of that land; and, indeed, I believe I have been at the place myself, but it was in the winter season.[2]

iii. Odoric of Pordenone

Odoric, a Bohemian of Friuli near Pordenone in northern Italy (ca. 1286-1331), was a Franciscan monk who is remembered chiefly for a narrative of his wanderings in the Far East. Beginning sometime between 1316 and 1318, he proceeded via Constantinople and Baghdad to India, Sumatra, Java, and China before finding his way back to Venice where he had begun the journey. Weakened by the hardship of his travel, Odoric stayed briefly in Padua where he dictated the account of his wanderings before setting out for the papal court at Avignon to make a report of the affairs of the church in the Far East and to secure recruits for missions he had visited. The journey was cut short, however, by a serious illness that caused him to be transported to his home province where he spent the few remaining days of his life. The account Odoric dictated lacks the moral and intellectual refinement characteristic of testimonies to the Ark's survival we have already related. Perhaps this may be explained by Odoric's lack of academic sophistication and by the

---

[2] The name of the province and town of *Nakhchevān*, east of Ararat, signifies "first place of descent, or of lodging." The antiquity of the tradition is proved by the fact, that Josephus affirms that the Armenians call the place where the Ark rested "*the place of descent;*" whilst Ptolemy supplies the name of *Naxuana.*

The place alluded to by Jordanus appears to be Arguri, the only village upon Ararat. Here Noah is said to have built his altar on the exact spot now occupied by the church, and it is of the vineyards of Arguri that the Scripture is believed to speak when it is said that "Noah began to be an husbandman, and planted a vineyard." The church is of unascertained but remote date; and the name of the place signifies (*Argh-urri*) "He planted the vine." At Nakhchevān "the grapes were almost unequalled in excellence, and seemed to deserve the honour of growing on the spot." (Smith and Dwight, *Researches in Armenia*, p. 256.) Arguri was buried by an earthquake, accompanied by volcanic indications, July 2nd, 1840 [June 20th, Old Style].

fact that his account was dictated in illness to a friar of probably even less education than his own. Nonetheless, Sir Henry Yule is convinced that the notes he has attached to his translation of Odoric's narrative show "how certainly they are the footsteps of a genuine traveller that we are following." Yule then proceeds to summarize only "a few of those passages which stamp Odoric as a genuine and original traveller" (Cathay and the Way Thither [1913], 24, 25-26). Odoric's testimony to the survival of the Ark is found on pp. 100-102 of Yule's translation.

Departing thence, I came into Armenia the Greater, to a certain city which is called ARZIRON,[1] which in time long past was a fine and most wealthy city, and it would have been so unto this day but for the Tartars and the Saracens, who have done it much damage. It aboundeth greatly in bread and flesh, and many other kinds of victual, but not in wine or fruits. For the city is mighty cold, and folk say that it is the highest city that is at this day inhabited on the whole face of the earth. But it hath most excellent water, the reason whereof seems to be that the springs of this water are derived from the River Euphrates, which floweth at

---

[1] Erzrum, corrupted from *Arzan-al-Rum*, or Roman Arzan, was taken with pillage and havoc by Chinghiz Khan and Timur, but neither kept it long. It was named *Garine*, then *Theodosiopolis*, in honour of Theodosius the Great; the present name was given by the Seljukid Turks, and it means "Roman Country." Even in Tournefort's [1656-1708, French botanist and traveller] time the Franks commonly pronounced the name Erzeron. Though not the highest city, even of the old world, it stands at a height of some 7,000 feet above the sea, and is noted for the severity of its winters, insomuch that a late Italian traveller calls it the Siberia of the Ottoman Empire. In 1855-56 the centigrade thermometer sank to 35° below 0°. Sir J. Sheil saw a heavy snowstorm at Erzrum in July. "The weather as a general rule," says Curzon, "may be considered as on the way from bad to worse." Fruit does not grow, but great quantities of "victual," *i.e.*, of corn and meal, are brought from more genial regions, as it is the place where the great caravans between Persia and Turkey recruit their stores. The Franciscans at this time had a convent at Erzrum, in the custodia of Kars, known in their Annals under the name of *Alzarome* or *Alcarone*.

about one day's journey from the city,[2] and this city is just midway to Tauris.

Departing from it, I came to a certain hill which is called SARBISACALO;[3] and in that country is the mountain whereon is Noah's Ark. And I would fain have ascended it, if my companions would have waited for me. But the folk of the country told us that no one ever could ascend the mountain, for this, as it is said, hath seemed not to be the pleasure of the Most High.[4]

iv. Pegolotti

Francesco Balducci Pegolotti, a merchant in the service of the Company of the Bardi in Florence, prepared a handbook of international trade and commerce in about the year 1340. Titled the "Book of Descriptions of Countries and of measures employed in business, and of other things needful to be known by merchants of different parts of the world . . . ," it has rested undisturbed on the shelves of the Florentine libraries as an appendix to A Treatise on the Decima *by Pagnini and also in original manuscript before two German geographers made use of it in their works at the end of the 18th century. Subsequent references to Pegolotti's handbook all appear to have depended on these secondary scources until Sir Henry Yule was able to translate, edit, and abridge the original manuscript in the Hakluyt Society volume* Cathay and the Way

---

[2] "The town . . . is on a sort of peninsula formed by the sources of Euphrates. The first of these flows at a day's journey from the city" (Tournefort).

[3] This puzzling name occurs also in Balducci Pegolotti's detail of stages on the road to Tauris, under the form of *Sermessacolo*. I can only suggest that these Italian corruptions contain the name of the station of *Hassan-Kala'a*, some twenty-four miles from Erzrum, near where the roads to Kars and Tabriz separate, perhaps under some such form as *Serai-Hassan-Kala'a*. It was once a considerable place, and the site of one of the Genoese castles which protected the road from Trebizond. There are also hot springs at the place. The name *may* however contain the Armenian *Surp* or *Surpazan,* holy.

[4] [Variant reading:] "For the mountain is most holy, and moreover is inaccessible on account of the deep snow that covers at least two-thirds of it."

Thither (Vol. III [1914], pp 137ff.). Chapter 6 of Pegolotti's handbook, "Of the expenses which usually attend the transport of merchandise from Ajazzo of Erminia to Torissi by land," preserves a short but telling reference to the tradition of the Ark's survival on Ararat in a list of what must have been toll stations in the Armenian country. Here, for the first time in a work dealing with the survival of the Ark, we offer this citation as collateral evidence. It shows that the Ark's presence on Ararat was a matter of such common opinion in the medieval period that merchants could use the expression "under Noah's Ark" as a synonym for Ararat, without even mentioning the latter. The passage below is found on pp.. 162-64 of the second edition of Yule's work, revised by Henri Cordier.

At the Caravanserai outside ARZERONE[1]	2	aspers.
At Arzerone, at the Baths	1	"
Ditto, inside the city	9	"
Ditto, as a present to the lord	2	"
Ditto, at the Baths towards Tauris[2]	1	"
At POLORBECH[3]	3	"
At ditto	0 1/2	"
At SERMESSACALO[4] for *tantaullagio*	0 1/2	"
At AGGIA, for the whole journey	0 1/2	"
At the middle of the plain of Aggia, for duty	3	"
At ditto for *tant*	0 1/2	"
At CALACRESTI,[5] ditto	0 1/2	"

[1] Erzrum.

[2] In connexion with these baths at the entrance and exit from the city we read that Ghazan Khan, in building New Tabriz, caused to be erected at each gate of the city a great caravanserai, a market, and a set of baths, so that the merchants, from whatever quarter they came, found a serai and baths adjoining the custom-house where their wares were examined.

[3] *Polorbech*, in Armenian *Polorabahag*, "the round fortress," at nine hours from Erzrum on the Araxes, crossed there to-day by a bridge of seven arches called Choban-Keupri.

[4] I have no doubt that this is the Sarbisacalo of Odoric. [See note 3 to Odoric's account above.]

[5] Probably the place called *Kara-Kilisse* (the Black Church). Kara-Kilisse, on the road from Erzrum to the Persian frontier, is situated 165 kil. to the east of Erzrum, 66 kil. to the N.E. of Diadin, and 99 kil. from Bayazid, on a tributary of the Murad Su.

At the THREE CHURCHES,[6] for *tant*	0 1/2	"
Under Noah's Ark[7], for duty	3	"
Ditto ditto for *tant*	0 1/2	"

And you may reckon that the exactions of the Moccols or Tartar troopers along the road, will amount to something like fifty aspers a load. So that the cost on account of a load of merchandize going by land from Ajazzo of Armenia to Tauris in Cataria[8] will be, as appears by the above details, 209 aspers a load, and the same back again.[9]

v. Sir John Mandeville

The English knight, John Mandeville (d. 1372), wrote a much-debated account (ca. 1360) of the world travels he claimed to have made between 1322 and 1356. The enigmatic Mandeville poses two problems for the historian. First, the question of his identity: he is associated with Jean de Bourgogne or Jean à

---

[6] I presume that this route from Erzrum to Tabriz follows the old Genoese line between Trebizond and Tabriz, which passed to the *south* of Ararat. The *Three Churches* are not therefore those of Echmiazin, but the *Uchkilisi* of the maps in the position just mentioned.

Tre Chiese. "This name (Tre Chiese)," writes Dulaurier, *Hist. des Croisades, Doc. arméniens*, i, Int., p. ci, "is but a translation of the Turkish name *Uch Kiliceh*, which is still given to the convent and church of Echmiazin, with the two-other churches on the right and the left, under the invocation of Saint Hr'ipsimê and Saint Kaïnê." At Uch-Kilisse, there is a monastery supposed to possess the tomb of the patriarch Noah, and with a magnificent church of the 3rd century; during the last war it was pillaged by the Kurds who destroyed the fine library. Not far from the Three Churches is Diadin, on the Murad Su (Eastern Euphrates), and on the road from Trebizond to the frontier, 33 kilom. from Bayazid.

[7] "*Sotto Larcanöe!*" Probably at Bayazid [i.e., Dogubayazit; see our Part Four, "Ark Fever"]. I do not see any good reason to think with Kiepert that Pegolotti's route does not pass through Bayazid and runs along lake Urmiah, instead of passing by Marand. Bayazid is on the road from Trebizond to the Persian frontier, at 264 kil. from Erzrum.

[8] Tartaria?

[9] It is really 203 aspers (about £2. 8s. *od.*).

la Barbe who lived in Liège, France. He is identified with the tombstone inscription in the Church of the Guillelmites near Liège: "Here lies the noble lord Sir John of Mandeville, knight, otherwise named with the beard." Drawing together such lines of evidence, Malcolm Letts argues convincingly that the two individuals are the same person: "The more the problem is studied the clearer it becomes . . . that Mandeville was a man of flesh and blood, born, as he says, at St. Albans, that he practised medicine and was known to his contemporaries as the man with the beard, that he fled the country, and that de Bourgogne was a name invented or borrowed by Mandeville to conceal his identity" (Sir John Mandeville [1949], pp. 20-21). In the second place, there is the accusation that Mandeville's Travels is wholesale fabrication. Granted that Mandeville culled vast quantities of information from Vincent and Odoric and related quite fabulous and imaginative experiences; one must nonetheless reckon with Mandeville's own testimony to his travels at the outset of his narrative, with the death-bed testimony of Jean de Bourgogne recorded by Outremeuse (Letts, pp. 14-15) as to Bourgogne's being obliged "to traverse the three parts of the world," and with Letts' own clever observation that "the English have always loved a good liar and that satire is a two-edged weapon" (p. 40). For those interested in pursuing the question of Mandeville's reliability at greater depth, we would recommend a Retrospective Review *article of 1821 (III/2, 269ff.) which seeks to justify Mandeville by arguing that the charges of falsehood so often brought against him should be directed to his lack of judgment. The account of the Ark reproduced below is taken from chapter 13 of* The Travels *as it appears in the collection edited by Thomas Wright,* Early Travels in Palestine *[1848], 203-204).*

From that city of Artyroun[1] men go to a mountain

---

[1] [i.e. Erzurum.]

called Sabissocolle²; and there beside is another mountain called Ararat, but the Jews call it Taneez, where Noah's ship rested, and still is upon that mountain; and men many see it afar in clear weather. That mountain is full seven miles high³; and some men say that they have seen and touched the ship, and put their fingers in the parts where the devil went out, when Noah said "Benedicte."⁴ But they that say so speak without knowledge; for no one can go up the mountain for the great abundance of snow which is always on that mountain, both summer and winter, so that no man ever went up since the time of Noah, except a monk, who, by God's grace, brought one of the planks down, which is yet in the monastery at the foot of the mountain. And beside is the city of Dayne,⁵ which was founded by Noah, near which is the city of Any,⁶ in which were one thousand churches. This monk had great desire to go up that mountain; and so upon a day he went up; and when he ascended the third part of the

---

² [See above, note 3 to Odoric's account and note 4 to Pegolotti's list.]

³ [Seemingly, an obvious exaggeration. But perhaps Mandeville is giving the total distance to the summit from a nearby location in the foothills, as does Struys (see our notes 2 and 6 to his account). The land distance from Sardar Bulak to the summit does not greatly exceed seven miles.]

⁴ [Letts says that he has "not been able to trace this reference, but the Devil was certainly a passenger.... How he escaped is a mystery" (*Sir John Mandeville* [1949], p. 53, n. 1). Baring-Gould tells how the Devil came to be in the Ark (*Legends of the Patriarchs and Prophets*, p. 115):

"The animals that were brought into the ark were collected and wafted to it by the wind. When the ass was about to enter, Eblis (Satan) caught hold of its tail. The ass came on slowly; Noah was impatient, and exclaimed. 'You cursed one, come in quick.'

When Eblis was within, Noah saw him, and said, 'What right have you in here?'

'I have entered at your invitation,' answered the Evil One. 'You said, "Cursed one, come in;" I am the accursed one.' "]

⁵ [Cf. Vincent of Beauvais' mention of the city of "Laudume."]

⁶ An account of the remarkable ruins, both ecclesiastical and palatial, that are met with at Anni, which was the capital of the Pakradian branch of Armenian kings, will be found in the *Travels* [London, 1821-1822] of Sir R. K. Porter, and those of W. J. Hamilton, vol. i p. 197. [See above, note 1 to our selection from Vincent of Beauvais.]

mountain he was so weary that he fell asleep; and when he awoke he found himself lying at the foot of the mountain. Then he prayed devoutly to God that he would suffer him to go up; and an angel came to him, and said that he should go up; and so he did.[1] And since that time no one ever went up; wherefore men should not believe such words.

vi. Gonzalez de Clavijo

The account of the embassy of Ruy Gonzales de Clavijo (d. 1412) to the court of Timour marks the very dawn of Spanish travel literature. It is "the oldest Spanish narrative of travels of any value," says Clements R. Markham at the outset of his English edition (Narrative of the Embassy of Ruy Gonzalez de Clavijo to the Court of Timour [*1859*], *p. i*). *Sent at the wish of King Henry in 1403, Clavijo purposed at the outset of his three-year journey to write a description of all the countries through which he passed. His resolve was well executed. "We may trust to his faithfulness, as much as to the vigilant and penetrating spirit he shows constantly," declares George Ticknor (1791-1871) in his classic* History of Spanish Literature, *"except when his religious faith, or his hardly less religious loyalty, interferes with its exercise" (Markham, p. vi). The following testimony of the Ark's survival, however, cannot be said to fall under Ticknor's stricture; there is hardly a trace of religious sentiment in it. The passage appears on pp. 80-82 of Markham's edition.*

The City of Calmarin,[1] Which Was the First in the World, After the Flood.

On Thursday, the 29th of May [1404], at noon, they reached a great city called Calmarin, and from it,

---

[1] [This story agrees with that of Vincent of Beauvais, whose *Speculum* was Mandeville's "great standby" (Letts, p. 29).]

[1] Etchmiazin?

distant about six leagues, they saw the great mountain
on which the ark of Noah rested, after the flood. This
city was in a plain, and on the other side flowed the great
river called Corras²; and on the other there was a very
deep and rocky valley, as broad as the flight of an
arrow; and it encircled the city, until it united with the
river. The valley and river made the city very strong, so
that it could only be attacked where the river commenced; but at this place there was a very strong castle,
with great towers, and it had two gates, one in front of
the other. This city of Calmarin was the first city that
was built in the world, after the flood, and it was built
by the lineage of Noah. The people of the city said
that, eight years ago, Tetani, Emperor of Tartary, besieged the city, and that they fought day and night for
two days, and on the third there was a parley. They
gave up the city, on condition that neither he, nor his
people should enter it, but that the citizens should pay
to him a certain annual tribute; with which the emperor
was satisfied, but he demanded that half of the people
of the city should be given up to him, to go with him to
the land of Jugania,³ where he was going to make war
on the king Sorso. When the citizens had given up
these men, the emperor attacked the city, entered it by
force, pillaged and burnt it, making breaches in the
walls, and killing many people.

The greater part of the inhabitants were Armenians;
but the land of Armenia has been taken from the
Christians by the Moors, as I will relate to you, presently. In this city there are very great edifices; and
throughout all this country, they gave the ambassadors
and their people lodging, and food, and horses; for all
the land belonged to Timour Beg.

On Friday they departed, and passed the night at a
castle, which was on the top of a rock, and belonged to
a widow lady, who paid tribute to Timour Beg⁴ for this
castle, as well as for other land which she held. In this

---

² Kur, or Cyrus.
³ Georgia.
⁴ [i.e., Tamerlane, the Tartar conqueror (1336-1405).]

castle there used to be robbers, and men who came out
to plunder travellers on the road. Timour Beg marched
against this castle, entered it by force, and killed the
lord of it, who was the husband of this lady; and he ordered that malefactors should never be allowed to as-
semble in it again: and, that they might not be able to
defend themselves, he caused the doors to be taken
away, and ordered that they should never be replaced.
He then gave it to this lady. The castle was, therefore,
without doors, and was called Egida. This castle was at
the foot of the lofty mountain of the ark of Noah; and
all these mountain ranges, after leaving the land of
Trebizond, were without woods. The lady received the
ambassadors very well, and gave them all they required.

On Saturday, the 13th of May, the road led along
the foot of the mountain of the ark of Noah. It was
very high, and the summit was covered with snow, and
it was without woods; but there was much herbage
upon it, and many streams. Near the road there were
many edifices, and foundations of houses, of stone; and
great quantities of rye was growing, as if it had been
sown by man, but it was useless, and did not come to
grain; and there was also plenty of water cresses. At
the foot of this mountain they came to the ruins of a
town long since deserted, which was a league in length;
and the people of the country said that it was the first
town that was built in the world, after the flood, and
that it was founded by Noah and his sons.

After leaving these ruins, they came to a great plain,
in which there were many streams of water, and trees,
and rose gardens, and fountains. The mountain had a
very sharp peak, which was covered with snow, and
they say that the snow never leaves this peak all the
year round, either in winter or summer, and this is on
account of its great height.

On this day the ambassadors took their siesta by a
beautiful fountain, near a stone arch; and while they
were there, the clouds moved away, and the peak of the
mountain appeared, but they suddenly returned, and
the people said that it was very seldom visible.

Next to this mountain, there was another, which also had a sharp peak, but not so high as the first, and between these two peaks there is one like a saddle, and they were all very high, and their summits were all covered with snow.

6

The 17th Century Travelers

Moving now to early modern times, we have the accounts of three 17th-century travellers: a German diplomat, a Dutch adventurer, and a French-English explorer. As background for their primary accounts we note in passing, as typical of the dependent narratives of this period, the comment of Gemelli-Careri (ca. 1651-1725), who reminded his contemporaries that the region near Erzurum "has preserved for aeons on the peak of its heighest mountain the remains of the Ark, according to the ancient traditions."* "All modern travellers agree on recognizing the soundness of his observations," says Louis Lacour of Gemelli-Careri in the article devoted to him in Hoefer's Nouvelle Biographie Générale (XIX, cols. 845-46).

* * *

i. Adam Olearius

He was "a German by nationality, a Protestant by faith, a scholar by training, and a high functionary social rank." Thus Samuel H. Baron sums up the striking person of Adam Olearius (1063-1671). Born Adam Oelschläger, he distinguished himself at the University of Leipzig and took a Latin name—Olearius—as was then the custom among scholars. After the outbreak of the Thirty Years War, Duke Frederick of Holstein enlisted his service in two embassies to the Great Duke of Muscovy and the King of Persia (1633). After his return in 1639, Olearius spent the next eight years preparing for publication the volu-

---

* Voyage du tour du monde, I (2d ed.; Paris, 1727), 559-60.

99

minous materials he had gathered. The Voyages and Travels of the Ambassadors *(1647) shows that Olearius "took advantage of every opportunity for firsthand observation" and possessed considerable "resourcefulness in gathering information. . . . No one has ever doubted the devotion to truth that Olearius declares in the preface to his book," asserts Baron, who has produced the first English translation of Olearius since 1669 and the only critical edition of the* Voyages and Travels *in any language but Russian.* "As a student of astronomy and mathematics," Baron adds, "he was imbued with the ideal of scientific objectivity." Since Baron's translation covers only part of Olearius' work (those portions relating to Russia) we have taken the following account of the Ark's survival from Book IV, p. 187 of John Davies' translation, published at London in 1662. My thanks to Professor Baron for his personal assistance to me in researching Olearius' account.*

Mount *Ararat*, upon which *Noah's* Ark rested after the deluge, and which the *Armenians* call *Messina*, the *Persians, Agri*, and the *Arabians Subeilahn*, is without comparison much higher than the *Caucasus*, and is indeed but a great black Rock, without any Verdure, and cover'd with Snow on the top, as well in Summer as Winter, by means whereof it is discover'd fifteen Leagues into the *Caspian* Sea. The *Armenians*, and the *Persians* themselves, are of opinion, that there are still upon the said Mountain some remainders of the Ark, but that Time hath so hardened them, that they seem absolutely petrify'd. At *Schamachy* in *Media* Persia, we were shewn a Crosse of a black and hard Wood, which the Inhabitants affirmed to have been made of the Wood of the Ark: and upon that accompt it was look'd upon as a most precious Relick, and, as such, was wrapp'd in Crimson Taffata. The Mountain is now inaccessible, by reason of the precipices whereby it is encompass'd of all sides.

---

* *The Travels of Olearius in Seventeenth-Century Russia* (Stanford, Calif., 1967), pp. 14-15.

ii. Jans Janszoon Struys

On June 30, 1670, Jans Janszoon Struys (d. 1694) arrived at Erivan near Ararat, a town presently on the Russian side of the border between Turkey and Russia. The following testimony to the Ark's survival resulted from his experiences there. Struys was a Dutch traveller (his name sometimes appears as Strauss) who visited a great number of countries between Europe and the Orient in the years 1647 to 1672. He was made a prisoner, sold as a slave to a Persian, and ransomed by a Georgian ambassador of the King of Poland. In 1677 he published the account of his voyages in Dutch, from which a French translation was made by Glanius in 1681 (reprinted 1684, etc.) When Eybiès claims that Struys engaged in intentional deception in describing his ascent of Ararat, he seems to betray his own rationalistic prejudice; the narrative of Struys' ascent is imbedded in a context which bears numerous marks of authenticity, and even Eybiès must admit that though Struys' travel accounts are written by "a man without education, one nonetheless finds there useful observations" (Michaud, Biographie universelle, Vol. XL, pp. 342-43). J. A. Fabricius, in his Codex Pseudepigraphicus ([1741], II, Pt. 1, 69). omits as unworthy of citation several early references to the vestiges of Noah's Ark (e.g., John Mandeville), and says, "Let Struys alone suffice." Cf. also Georgi, Allgemeines Europäisches Bücher-Lexicon, Pt. 5, p. 106. We translate from Struys' account of his third voyage, chap. 18, in Les Voyages . . . en Moscovie, en Tartarie, en Perse, aux Indes, & en plusieurs autres Pays étrangers ([1684], II, 146-62).

On the 30th [of June, 1670] we arrived at Vruvan or Erivan. This city is situated at the foot of Mt. Ararat. . . . My master intended to sell me at Erivan, but the local inhabitants expressed no desire to buy me. When he had given up hope of a sale, two Carmelite monks came to ask if I were not a surgeon. They assured me that had I any skill along that line they would give me a case for which I would be very well pàid if I succeeded. I answered that I was no surgeon and had never practiced the art.

These good men did not believe me; after they had conferred together for some time I clearly observed from their expressions that they took me for a competent surgeon but one who dared not admit it in his master's presence. So they took my master aside. . . . Said one of them: "My brother is suffering from hernia,[1] and if your slave can cure him I shall make you a present of fifty crowns." My master replied: "Let me see to it." . . . To me he said: "Are you aware that this gives you the chance to recover your freedom? If you're smart, you will take the opportunity, for you may never be afforded another so attractive or certain." . . .

The proposal troubled me deeply: I knew my master to be the most grasping and avaricious man imaginable, and he was being tempted by a sure thing—an opportunity that would knock but once. Then there was the matter of the promise of my freedom, but I feared the blows of the rod, which I would be incapable of fleeing if the operation did not succeed to his liking. But after thinking it over a bit, I resolved to do everything my master wished me to do. He praised my decision, ran to the monastery, and promised them a miracle. The monk and he came to terms on the price, and the following morning we left to find the patient, who lived as a hermit on Mount Ararat.

His hermitage was so far from the foot of the mountain that it took us seven days to reach it, and every day we covered five miles.[2] Every night we found a hut

---

[1] [Not from a broken leg, as Baring-Gould states in his *Legends of the Patriarchs and Prophets* (New York: Hurst & C., n.d.), p. 142, following J. A. Fabricius' Latin précis of the story in his *Codex pseudepigraphicus Veteris Testamenti*, II (2d ed.; Hamburg, 1741), 69-70.]

[2] [Baring-Gould *(loc. cit.)*, following Fabricius, incorrectly gives the time of ascent as five days. The seemingly exaggerated total distance of 35 miles may represent the entire journey from Erivan to

where we could sleep, and each morning the hermit who occupied it would secure a donkey and a peasant for us: the peasant to guide us and the donkey to carry our provisions and wood. Without the latter, you cannot survive on this uninhabitable mountain. The cold is so intense that a horseman can go at full gallop on the ice for three hours without danger. The only means of warming oneself is the wood one carries, for there are no bushes or trees, not even thickets or brambles, and on the entire mountain not a bit of topsoil exists.

The first clouds through which we passed were dark and thick. The others were extremely cold and full of snow, though at a little lower altitude the temperature was high and the grapes and other fruit had fully ripened. When we experienced our third cloud-layer, we thought we would die from cold: we were at the end of the line, nothing could warm us up; and if that icy interval had continued another quarter of an hour, I believe that we would have died right there. But when we could proceed no farther, we providentially came upon one of the hermitages I mentioned previously. There a great fire was built for us, but it took me more than an hour before I felt it. From that day on, the farther we climbed, the more temperate the air we breathed, and this mildness continued right to the cell of our patient. We arrived there the 7th of July.

The cell is large and well-hewn in rock, and the good hermit told me that he never felt more heat or more cold than he did just then, and neither was in evidence. He added that during the twenty-five years he had lived there he had experienced not a single gust of wind or drop of rainfall. And, said he, on the summit of the mountain, the climate is even more tranquil, for nothing ever changes there[3]; it is for this reason that

---

Ararat (some 60 km. or 36 miles). Note that at the beginning of the quoted passage Struys states that Erivan "is situated at the foot of Mt. Ararat," and that his drawing shows Ararat from the perspective of Erivan.]

[3] [This monk must have had a remarkably well-hewn cave or an even more remarkable insensitivity to climatic change! But his meterological judgments may have been considerably inferior to his exploratory skills.]

the Ark does not deteriorate and has remained for so many centuries in as pristine a state as on the first day it landed there.

While my patient was talking, I was carefully observing him. When he had finished, I made him lie down, took his pulse, and examined the arca in question. I found that he was suffering from a rupture, and that the hernial swelling resembled a large hen's egg. "How long have you had to put up with this discomfort?" I asked him. "Only a month," he replied. "Good!" said I. "The cure does not come too late; I bring you a successful remedy." I touched the ruptured spot again and told my patient with a laugh that in a week or two he would be as well as I.

The good monk was so overjoyed that he embraced me and said a hundred complimentary things, including the fact that I was quite obviously a true expert in my profession and that he was privileged to have fallen into my hands. Since his belief was important to my task, far from disillusioning him by sham modesty, I reinforced his conviction by relating numerous instances of high success in much more difficult cases. I put him in such a good frame of mind that he was half cured before I had even begun my operation! . . .

The brave hermit thanked me so profusely that I was embarrassed. He added that his sacred vows prevented him from giving me rich presents, and that he had nothing more precious than a cross attached to a little silver chain. He removed it from his neck and gave it to me; it consisted of a little fragment of reddish-brown wood,[4] and with it he gave me a piece of the rock on which the Ark came to rest. Such a high value did he attribute to these pieces of wood and rock that, in his judgment, I would be too rich if I retained them. If, on the other hand, I was willing to take them to St. Peter's Church in Rome, he assured me a recompense that

_____
[4] [cf. the descriptions of relics seen by Parrot and Wells in note 7 to the account of Faustus of Byzantium in section 2 above. Interestingly, this is the precise color of the wood fragment given to me by French explorer Fernand Navarra. See below, my account of "Ark Fever."]

would make my fortune. He had been born at Rome, he said; his name was Domingo Alessandro, and he was the son of one of the richest and most influential families of Rome. . . .

When I was ready to depart, I thought that it might not be a bad idea to obtain from him an attestation as to my experience on Mt. Ararat. He willingly gave it to me in the following terms:[5]

I have thought it unreasonable to refuse the request of Jans Janszoon [Struys] who besought me to testify in writing that he was in my cell on the holy Mt. Ararat, subsequent to his climb of some thirty-five miles.[6] This man cured me of a serious hernia, and I am therefore greatly in his debt for the conscientious treatment he gave me. In return for his benevolence, I have presented to him a cross made of a piece of wood from the true Ark of Noah. I myself entered that Ark and with my own hands cut from the wood of one of its compartments the fragment from which that cross is made.[7] I informed the same Jans Janszoons in considerable detail as to the actual construction of the Ark, and also gave him a piece of stone which I had personally chipped from the rock on which the Ark rests. All this I testify to be true—as true as I am in fact alive here in my sacred hermitage. Dated the 22nd of July, 1670, on Mt. Ararat.

Domingo Alessandro of Rome

Carrying these holy relics, whose possession fulfilled all my desires, and proud of the fine success of my first operation, I descended the mountain with my donkey

---

[5] [The attestation is recorded in Latin, and is followed by a translation into French.]

[6] [Lat., "circiter triginta quinque miliarium sursum eundo." Thirty-five miles is the product of 7 days x 5 miles/day; see above, Struys' text at our note 2.]

[7] [Lat., ". . . vera Archa Noë, ubi in persona intus fui, & illud de quo ista crux est facta, propriis meis manibus ab una camera scidi."]

and my guide. I followed the same route as before, but
I experienced far more difficulty than the first time,
particularly while the ice-laden clouds hung over a
path so rough, slippery, and steep that at each step we
ran the risk of going head over heels. Toward the foot
of the mountain, the wind, the rain, and the even more
treacherous pathway made me almost despair of getting
back at all. I did arrive—but not without vowing never
to return there in all my life. Neither the Ark nor the
rock which cradles it ('as my hermit's testimony asserts) would have an attraction sufficient to draw me
there again.

Thus I saw the famous Mt. Ararat, and my experience goes to prove that, although the climb is difficult,
the mountain is not inaccessible as many claim.

iii. Sir John Chardin

*During the 17th century many distinguished Euro-
peans were attracted to the court of Persia. Pietro della
Valle, Sir Thomas Herbert, Tavernier, and Olearius, to
name a few, returned to tell of new peoples and customs in the mysterious East. But the "greatest of them
all," says Sir Percy Sykes, was Jean Chardin (1643-
1713), a Frenchman who was knighted by English
monarch Charles II in 1681 after he had fled the persecution of Protestants following the Revocation of the
Edict of Nantes and had settled in London. In 1686 the
first volume of his* Journal du voyage . . . de Chardin
en Perse et aux Indes orientales *was published; the
three remaining volumes did not appear until 1711.
They record the detailed studies of Persia Chardin
made in his visits of 1669-1671 and 1671-1677, studies which show his "remarkable thoroughness," as
Sykes puts it. "That his knowledge of Persia, its language and its people was profound," he adds, "is
proved by the eulogies of the great Orientalist, Sir
William Jones, while the value of his work was ac-*

*knowledged by Montesquieu, Rousseau and Gibbon."** *This recognition could not have been incidental. Chardin's "modern" skepticism stands at the threshold of the Enlightenment. We have translated the following account of the Ark on Ararat from the French edition published at Amsterdam in 1711 under the title* Voyages . . . en Perse, et autres lieux de l'Orient *(II, 235-37).*

Twelve leagues[1] to the east of Erivan one sees the famous mountain where almost everyone agrees that Noah's Ark landed—though no one offers solid proof of it. When the air is clear, this mountain does not seem to be two leagues[2] away, so lofty and massive is

---

* Sir Percy Sykes (ed.), *Sir John Chardin's Travels in Persia* (London: The Argonaut Press, 1927), pp. xiv, xv. This reprinting of an early and incomplete English version of Chardin's narrative does not contain the Ararat passage.

[1] [i.e., 30 miles. More precisely, the distance from Erivan to Ararat is 36 miles.]

[2] [i.e., 5 miles. Writes Freygang, who saw the mountain in May, 1812 (*Letters from the Caucasus and Georgia, to which are added, The Account of a Journey into Persia* [London: John Murray, 1823], pp. 274, 280-81):

"I had scarcely descended from these summits when I saw before me the fertile and extensive plain of Erivan, as well as the two peaks of Ararat, which raise themselves like majestic *colossi* above the clouds. If even the remembrance of Noah and the ark were not present to one's mind, the sublime view of Ararat could not fail of producing a powerful effect upon the traveller. . . .

Although at least thirty versts off [a verst measures slightly more than a kilometer], the mountain appears through some optical deception very near the observer at Eitchmaiadzen. A wide plain extends to the foot of the hill, which up to a certain height is covered with forests, the resort of an amazing quantity of wild beasts, and of the smaller game. You rarely see the loftiest point, on account of clouds, that usually rest around it. The sky however is in general clear throughout this country; it hardly ever rains, and tempests are rare: but Ararat, attracting the clouds, seems as it were the abode of storms, and almost every day the atmosphere puts on a threatening aspect; while upon the gloomy veil of dark vapour, the rapid lightning is frequently seen darting across, or a majestic rainbow is displayed. The imagination of the religious man, as of the poet, is elevated by a scene so awful, and his feelings are the more intense, as the result of impressions not unmixed with terror."]

its appearance. However, I believe that I have seen a higher peak: if I am not mistaken, the spot in the Caucasus which I passed on my journey from the Black Sea to Akhaltsikhe is higher than the mountain we are discussing.[3] . . .

The Armenian traditions relate that the Ark is still upon the summit of this Mount Massis.[4] They add that no one has ever been able to climb to the place where it came to rest. This they firmly believe on the basis of a miracle said to have happened to a monk of Echmiadzin named Jacob, who later became Bishop of Nisibis. They relate that this monk, influenced by the commonly held opinion that this mountain was assuredly the one on which the Ark rested after the Flood, determined to climb to the summit or die in the attempt.

He got halfway up, but he could never go higher, for after climbing all day he was miraculously carried back—while asleep at night—to the same spot from which he had set out in the morning.[5] This went on for some time in this fashion, when finally God gave ear to the monk's vows and determined to satisfy his desires in part. Consequently, by an angel He sent to him a piece of the Ark, exhorting him through this messenger not to fatigue himself to no purpose in climbing the mountain, for God had forbidden mankind to have access to its summit.

That's the story, and I have two things to say concerning it. First, it is at variance with the ancient writers, such as Josephus, Berossus, and Nicolaus of Damascus, who assure us that in their time the remains of the Ark were still to be seen, and that powder made

[3] [Chardin is correct. Mt. Elbrus (5641 meters; 18,481 ft.) is the highest peak in the Caucasus. Akhaltsikhe is a Georgian city (today in the U.S.S.R.. as is Erivan); it is in the Lesser Caucasus, near the Turkish border (*Columbia Lippincott Gazetteer of the World*).]

[4] [i.e., Ararat. See note 3 to the account of William of Rubruck in section 5 above.]

[5] [It should be noted that this element of the story does not appear in the early version of Jacob's experience as set forth by Faustus of Byzantium See the introduction to the text from Vincent of Beauvais in section 3.]

from the bitumen with which it had been pitched was taken as a preservative of health. Secondly, instead of its being a miracle that no one could ever reach the top of this mountain, I should rather deem it a great miracle if anyone *did* reach its summit![6] For the mountain is without any habitation, and from the halfway point to the peak it is perpetually covered with snow which never melts, so that at all seasons it has the appearance of a gigantic mass of snow.

---

[6] [A sentiment fully shared by those of us who have succeeded in reaching the peak! See below, "Ark Fever."]

7

A 19th Century Archdeacon

Not surprisingly, the 18th-century age of "Enlightenment" provides no additional accounts of Ark sightings: the rationalists and deists of the time were not inclined to seek confirmation of biblical revelation in scientific and historical matters. The early 19th-century affirmation of Claudius James Rich in his Narrative of a Residence in Koordistan ([1836], *Vol. II, p. 124*) that his guide "Hussein Aga maintained to me that he has with his own eyes seen the remains of Noah's Ark" (entry of Feb. 25, 1821) is little better than the silence of the Enlightenment; the mountain in question was Al Judi (see the note accompanying our introduction to section 5—"Monks, Merchants, and Knights of the Later Middle Ages"), and Rich himself admits to Hussein Aga's unreliability in volume II, pp. 97-98 when he states that he "overrated the extent of his master's dominions" (entry of Dec. 19, 1820).

* * *

Archdeacon Nouri was invested episcopal head of the Nestorian church of Malabar, South India in the Chaldean Cathedral at Trichur, on his thirty-third birthday, February 7, 1896. From his age at the time one rightly infers that he was an outstanding individual. John Henry Barrows, President of the World's Parliament of Religions held at Chicago, September 11-27, 1893, in conjunction with the World's Columbian Exposition, records that, as an interpreter, Nouri was "equally ready in English, French, Turkish, Arabic, Persian, and eight other languages" and that in Arabic he was "very eloquent." "He was travelled almost everywhere," adds Barrows, "and I doubt if there is any other man now living who has made the acquaintance

110

in their homes of so large a number of distinguished people."[1] The same estimate of Nouri comes from the memoir of Frederick G. Coan, a missionary to Persia with whom Nouri spent a winter at the turn of the century. He reports that Nouri's "travels covered Australia, Africa, China, and all the countries of Europe, where he said he had met most of the crowned heads." Moreover, in the face of occasionally expressed scepticism as to Nouri's existence, we have Coan's confirmation that Nouri attended the World's Parliament of Religions where Barrows claimed to have first met him: "I had attended that parliament and had two volumes giving its records. Among those who had been photographed we found his picture."[2] Coan then recounts Nouri's discovery of the Ark in this fashion on pages 164-65 of his memoir:

Now for the story of his wonderful discovery of the ark. He said he had made three attempts to scale Mount Ararat before he succeeded. At last his toil was rewarded and he stood overwhelmed and awed as he saw the old ark there wedged in the rocks and half filled with snow and ice.[1] He got inside where careful measurements coincided exactly with the account given in the sixth chapter of Genesis. I could not but ask a rather mean question at this point, whether he saw Mrs. Noah's corset hanging up in her bedroom. The

---

[1] John Henry Barrows, *A World-Pilgrimage,* edited by Mary Eleanor Barrows (Chicago: A. C. McClurg, 1897), pp. 299-300, 310, 410. Cf. pp. 305, 312, 413 and Barrows' collection of his lectures given on the "world-pilgrimage" in *Christianity the World Religion* (Chicago: A. C. McClurg, 1897), esp. p. 341.

[2] Frederick G. Coan, *Yesterdays in Persia and Kurdistan* (Claremont, Calif.: Saunders Studio Press, 1939), p. 163. Neither in the official two-volume account of the parliament, *The World's Parliament of Religions* (ed. by John Henry Barrows [Chicago. The Parliament Publishing Co., 1893]), nor in the one volume "abstract." *The World's Congress of Religions* (ed. by J. W. Hanson [Chicago: W. B. Conkey, 1893]), does there appear to be verbal reference to Nouri. Therefore Coan probably was able to locate Nouri in one of the photographs of the parliament's platform which appear as the frontispiece and on pp. 853 and 1583 of the official volumes.

[1] [cf. the accounts in the remaining sections of Part Two.]

poor bachelor was puzzled, and after I told him it was something women wore he said he had not noticed any clothing around.

We invited him to give a lecture on his marvelous discovery in the College Chapel,[2] and missionaries, teachers and students filled the place and were most deeply interested. He sincerely believed he had seen the ark and almost convinced others he had.

He went to Belgium and tried to organize a company to take it to Chicago to the World's Fair, but they felt the risks of such a long journey were too great, in addition to the heavy expense of transporting it so far. He was much disappointed, for he knew it would be a great attraction, and that people from all over the world would go to see it. So there it lies!

---

[2] [The Presbyterian College at Lake Urumia in Persia (now Iran).]

8

An Elderly Armenian

*Living on the east coast today is an Armenian expa-
triate whom we shall call George Tamisian. As a child
he grew up in the shadow of Mt. Ararat and was taken
by his uncle to see the remains of the Ark on two occasions. When political control of Armenia passed to
the Turks, he left his native land and eventually came
to reside in the United States. A retiring gentleman,
Mr. Tamisian does not wish to be further identified. A
few years ago, however, he agreed to a revealing interview, the most relevant portions of which follow. El-
lipses in the transcription of Tamisian's responses indicate the points at which his heavy accent obscured the
words.**

INTERVIEWER: Mr. Tamisian, can you explain
what you saw on Mt. Ararat and explain Noah's Ark as
you saw it?

TAMISIAN: It's impossible anybody now to find
the pieces from Noah's Ark. I don't believe if I see with
my own eye, because when I saw Noah's Ark it was
absolutely petrified.[1] Just like pure stone, just like
stone. . . .

INTERVIEWER: You went with your uncle—
when?

TAMISIAN: Oh, I go with my uncle I was ten
years old, first.

INTERVIEWER: This was in 1902?

TAMISIAN: Yes.

INTERVIEWER: You saw it how many times?

---

* A complete tape of this interview is in the possession of the
author.

[1] [This can be reconciled with the discovery of Ark fragments by
Navarra and others if we assume that the Ark was not uniformly
petrified.]

TAMISIAN: Twice. My uncle carry me his back. We got half way with donkey. Down here they call it "smuriel"—no snow, absolutely none. And snow very little on top that hard. Ark over thousand feet long; oh, about six or seven hundred feet wide.[2]

INTERVIEWER: About how high?

TAMISIAN: High? Oh, thirty-five feet high, more. More than that.

INTERVIEWER: Then how did you get on top of it?

TAMISIAN: My uncle brought stone, piled them up, carry me shoulder, put me on top. I'll never forget, long as I live. My uncle six foot tall man. Said Georgy, look real good. I say, uncle, I see a hole in here. I'm scared. Said don't be scared. Lord done here yet. Don't worry about that. And I tried to kiss, for which I did, kiss that holy Ark. I came back, I told my father and mother. Explain to my grandaddy—my grandfather. They was 'course we believe all those things.

INTERVIEWER: Now the wood—what color was it?

TAMISIAN: Dark green.

INTERVIEWER: And was there moss growing...?

TAMISIAN: Yes, moss on top. All around.

INTERVIEWER: ...like short grass...?

TAMISIAN: Yes.

INTERVIEWER: ...was growing on it?

TAMISIAN: On, right on, on the deck.

INTERVIEWER Even with the snow?

TAMISIAN: Yes, uh-huh.

INTERVIEWER: Was there snow on the roof?

TAMISIAN: Just a little bit.

INTERVIEWER: And your uncle brushed it away?

TAMISIAN: Brushed with his hand, I'll never forget this. I say, uncle, what is that? Is that ice you're throwing down? I get up . . . Say Georgy, you about thirty feet high, huh? I say Daddy—or uncle—you

---

[2] [An understandable exaggeration coming from a ten-year-old Dimensions regularly appear greater than they actually are to small children.]

going to catch me? He say, I will. Say, don't jump. I said, no I won't. And he grab me and brought me down and we came in and I told grandfather all that I see. He say, son, you're going to be a holy man. . . .

INTERVIEWER: What was the roof like? What did it look like?

TAMISIAN: Plain, absolutely plain.

INTERVIEWER: Flat?

TAMISIAN: Uh-huh.

INTERVIEWER: And were there windows or holes?

TAMISIAN: No windows, but there holes on top just like this.

INTERVIEWER: How many? One hole?

TAMISIAN: Oh, there about fifty of—more. . . . I say, uncle what is this where air come out? He say, Oh yes that's hole. That's animals in, human in. I say, where they going? He say, oh they're out now. Nobody's in.

INTERVIEWER: Were you able to see the whole Ark from one end to another?

TAMISIAN: Oh yes.

INTERVIEWER: You walked all the way around . . . ?

TAMISIAN: Oh no, uh-uh.

INTERVIEWER: Why?

TAMISIAN: . . . I say, uncle, how in world it land on Mount Ararat? He said, water brought it to Ararat. Flood—when Flood come and cover the whole world . . .

INTERVIEWER: Was there any door in the Ark?

TAMISIAN: No, I see no door.

INTERVIEWER: You did not see a door?

TAMISIAN: Uh-uh. Maybe in, but didn't see it. I didn't see it.

INTERVIEWER: You were not able to go around . . . ?

TAMISIAN: Uh-uh.

INTERVIEWER: . . . because of the snow . . . ?

TAMISIAN: No, no. The rock so deep we couldn't go in the bottom, move around. Only one side.

INTERVIEWER: Only one side?

TAMISIAN: Uh-huh.

INTERVIEWER: There was a big rock on one side?

TAMISIAN: Oh yes, Laid down on top rock. If you looking in bottom you take one over three thousand feet deep.

INTERVIEWER: You mean it was sticking out . . .?

TAMISIAN: Yes.

INTERVIEWER: . . . and there was a cliff there . . .?

TAMISIAN: Cliff right down, yes.

INTERVIEWER: . . . and this was on the edge of the cliff?

TAMISIAN: That's right. You cannot see anything. If you looking in so dark you stay you looking in.

INTERVIEWER: Looking in where?

TAMISIAN: In the bottom—that hole.

INTERVIEWER: Oh, there's a hole?

TAMISIAN: Uh-huh.

INTERVIEWER: Very deep, and the ark is sticking over the hole?

TAMISIAN: That's right. Top mountain—no, rock, pure rock. That Noah's Ark laid down right on top of the rock. Rock was over about three thousand feet wide. Oh yes, heavy.

INTERVIEWER: I see.

TAMISIAN: High, way one place there so high it's impossible any human being climb it. From ground . . .

INTERVIEWER: About how long did you stay up there?

TAMISIAN: Oh about two hour, three hour.

INTERVIEWER: Now you saw it two times or three times?

TAMISIAN: Two, uh-huh.

INTERVIEWER: Once in 1902 and once in 1904?

TAMISIAN: That's right.

INTERVIEWER: The first time you were ten years old . . .

TAMISIAN: Uh-huh.

INTERVIEWER: . . . and the next time you were thirteen years old?

TAMISIAN: Uh-huh. I never forget this.

INTERVIEWER: So how old are you now?

TAMISIAN: Seventy-two.

INTERVIEWER: You are now seventy-two?

TAMISIAN: Uh-huh.

INTERVIEWER: It must have been a wonderful experience.

TAMISIAN: Yes, I wish I knew what I know now, 'cause what do we know? We don't looking for this kind of stuff. . . .

INTERVIEWER: Now what was Ararat like that year, the first time you went up?

TAMISIAN: Mount Ararat was straight, straight straight.

INTERVIEWER: Which side did you go up? The south?

TAMISIAN: South, toward Arabajan[?] side.

INTERVIEWER: Not Bayazid?

TAMISIAN: No.

INTERVIEWER: The Persian side?

TAMISIAN: Uh-huh.

INTERVIEWER: From Little Ararat?

TAMISIAN: That's right.

INTERVIEWER: And you went up between the two . . . .

TAMISIAN: . . . took seven day before we got all there.

INTERVIEWER: It took seven days . . . ?

TAMISIAN: Yes, sir.

INTERVIEWER: . . . from Arabajan[?] to the top of the mountain?

TAMISIAN: That's right, seven day. My uncle had food all carried on our back. We going on there. Our sheep wait bottom.

:● ●

INTERVIEWER: Can you explain any more of what the Ark looked like?

TAMISIAN: No, 'cause I was a child. . . . I couldn't see all part of it. I saw big part of it, mostly.

INTERVIEWER: Was it square or round . . . ?

TAMISIAN: Oh no, no! Long.

INTERVIEWER: But was it flat—the sides flat?

TAMISIAN: Uh-uh. Just like this.

INTERVIEWER: They tipped out?

TAMISIAN: Yes.

INTERVIEWER: They tipped out?

TAMISIAN: Uh-huh.

INTERVIEWER: And then the roof was flat?

TAMISIAN: Yes, the roof was as flat as . . .

INTERVIEWER: Could you see any part of the bottom?

TAMISIAN: Oh yes, you see bottom, sure.

INTERVIEWER: The whole bottom there . . .

TAMISIAN: Oh no, not whole. Only part of it.

INTERVIEWER: . . . was it flat?

TAMISIAN: Just as flat can be.

INTERVIEWER: And there were no windows or anything in it?

TAMISIAN: No, no window sign. I saw hole what I told you on top.

INTERVIEWER: Could you see any of the pieces of wood where it joined? Did it look like it was made of wood?

TAMISIAN: Oh yes, it was wood, there's no two ways about it.

INTERVIEWER: You could see the grain in this wood?

TAMISIAN: Oh yes, uh-huh.

INTERVIEWER: And were there nails in it?

TAMISIAN: Oh no, no nails, I've seen no nails whatsoever. You can't tell. Just like one piece.

INTERVIEWER: But you could tell it was wood?

TAMISIAN: Oh yes, it was wood. I know wood. It was not stone at all. And moldy. You put your hand on. Moldy. It's so soft, just like

INTERVIEWER: . . . moldy?

TAMISIAN: Uh-huh. Green moldy.

9

Samplings from the Cummings' Archives

For over thirty years, Mr. Eryl A. Cummings and his wife Violet, of Farmington, New Mexico, have devoted themselves to tracking down stories of Ark sightings. Mr. Cummings has, in addition, participated in expeditions to Ararat on several occasions. It is through his generosity that the materials cited below are made available to the reader. Cf. Violet M. Cummings' popularized account, Noah's Ark: Fact or Fable *(San Diego, California: Creation-Science Research Center, 1972; paperback edition, New York, New York: Pyramid Publications, 1974.)*

* * *

i. The Russian Expedition

If the average person has heard anything of modern Ark sightings, he has doubtless heard of a White Russian expedition which presumably located the Ark on the eve of the Russian Revolution. This oft-published newspaper story has been lampooned by such demythologizers of sacred history as André Parrot (not to be confused with Dr. Friedrich Parrot who made the first modern ascent of Ararat in 1829) who summarizes the expedition with caustic comment in his widely-read book, The Flood and Noah's Ark:[2]

---

[1] See below, Part Three: "Explorations of Ararat."

[2] *The Flood and Noah's Ark,* trans. by Edwin Hudson, Studies in Biblical Archaeology, No. 1 (New York: Philosophical Library, 1955), pp. 64-65. Parrot's work is particularly weakened by his naive and uncritical acceptance of Old Testament documentary criticism (J-E-P-D hypothesis).

In 1916, during the First World War, a Russian
airman named W. Roskovitsky, flying over Mount
Ararat, declared that he had observed on one of
the slopes of the mountain the remains of an ancient vessel. The Czar at once organized an expedition, which, we are told, found the remains in
question and brought back a description of them
which was conclusive as regards their identification. It is most unfortunate that no competent
person saw this report, which was lost during the
course of the Bolshevist revolution of 1917. All
we have is Roskovitsky's story, of which the least
that can be said is that if it is shorn of reminis-
censes of Genesis, scarcely anything is left. That
did not prevent several American periodicals from
proclaiming the sensational news. Serious specialist organs reserved for it the fate it deserved: silence.

*Granted, there are many exaggerated elements in such
newspaper accounts as Parrot used (he relied upon the
popular* Journal de Genève[3]*); granted also that the
parallel claim that the Russian expedition report came
into the hands of Grand Duke Cyril and General Osnobichine has proved incorrect[4]; but the researches of
the Cummings[5] have yielded (1) verifications from
relatives and acquaintances of soldiers who were actually on the expedition, and (2) corroborating information from the author of the original Russian article
(published in* Rosseya, *November, 1945) which un-
derlay the exaggerated popular accounts! It should also
be of interest to the reader that I myself spent an afternoon with the author to whom we have just referred*

---

[3] Issues of June 7 and June 14, 1949 (specific citations unfortunately not supplied by Parrot). In the June 14 issue (p. 3) the account
by Wladimir Roskovitsky is supplied in French translation by Bernard
Gagnebin.
[4] See our Part Four, the essay "Arkeology 1971," and Appendix C.
[5] All letters and affidavits which we quote below are on ,le in
the Cummings' archives.

(Colonel Alexander A. Koor) shortly before his death.

On April 4, 1940, a Mr. James Frazier, of Malotte, Washington, corroborated the story in a letter thus: "My father-in-law, John Schilleroff, told me at different times about the Ark of Noah, but he did not mention any landmarks, though he did mention the town he started from. I could not pronounce the name and have forgotten it. He was German and I do not speak German.

"Mr. John Georgesen, a Dane, formerly my neighbor here, now also deceased, told me the same story, he also having served in the Russian Army in the Ararat region. They had never met, though their accounts fully agree. They belonged to different expeditions and went at different times. The following is the story as they both told it to me.

"While in the Russian Army, they were ordered to pack for a long tramp up into the mountains of Ararat. A Russian aviator had sighted what looked to him like a huge wooden structure in a small lake. About two-thirds of the way up, probably a little farther, they stopped on a high cliff, and in a small valley below them was a dense swamp in which the object could be seen. It appeared as a huge ship or barge with one end under water and only one corner could be clearly seen from where these men stood. Some went closer, and especially the Captain. They could not get out to it because of the water, and the many poisonous snakes and insects. The Captain told them of the details."

Another letter, from an A. H. Booth, reads as follows: "John Schilleroff, a father-in-law of Mr. Jim Frazier, made a trip in company with 100 soldiers of the Russian Army and found the Ark of Noah. I heard him tell the story of his adventures there, but I cannot recall the details. Mr. Frazier, who wrote to you, is my brother-in-law. John Georgesen, formerly a neighbor of Mr. Frazier, was in another military party at the

---

* See below, Part Four: "Ark Fever."

same time. They said the Ark stands high in the mountains in a wooded valley swamp. They could see a part of the Ark, but the swamp was so infested with snakes and insects that they did not go out to it."

Still further verification comes in a letter from F. L. Chitwood, of Klamath Falls, Oregon, on July 27, 1945, in which he shared the story as told him by Mr. Booth: "I have often talked with old man Schilleroff about his experiences in climbing the mountain, but at that time I did not see the importance of getting all the information I could and making a record of it."

"I believe the Booths to be reliable people," wrote Mr. Chitwood. "I have known them for nearly forty years." He mentioned also that "these men had to contend with poisonous snakes in making the ascent."

* * *

The author of the *Rosseya* article, Colonel Alexander A. Koor (later Major General Koor), was formerly a White Russian Army officer under the Czar, who had been in command of troops in the Ararat area during the closing years of the First World War. He had also fought against the Bolsheviks, finally escaping with his wife into Manchuria, eventually reaching asylum in the United States.

Koor's military background and service in the area around Mount Ararat provided ample evidence of his qualifications as author of the *Rosseya* story, since he had personally known relatives of some of the members of the land expedition that investigated the reported discovery of the Ark.

On March 1, 1946, Col. Koor provided the following information: "Here are some data which should help our research, from the *Official Records of the Russian Caucasian Army, 1914-1917,* by General E. B. Maslovsky.*

* [In Russian. Published at Paris by "La Renaissance" in 1933; 530 pp.]

"The headquarters of the 14th Railroad Battalion was at Bayasit, just southwest of Greater Ararat, with Brigade Headquarters at Maku, southeast of Lesser Ararat, commanded by Col. Svercjkoff. The 14th Battalion came to the front in the summer of 1916, from Russia. I understand that the discovery of Noah's Ark was in the end of 1916, with the scouting parties having to wait until the summer of 1917.

"I know that Sergeant Boris V. Rujansky belonged to the 14th Battalion. I understand, and it is logical, that the first and second parties of the expedition to Mount Ararat were formed from the local force of the 14th Battalion of #-C Zamorsky Brigade, by order from the local Brigade Headquarters. Sergeant B. V. Rujansky was sent to join the party because he was a specialist. Before the war he worked in the Technological Institute of Peter the Great, and attended the Imperial Institute of Archaeology in St. Petersburg. In 1916 the 3-D Caucasian Aviation Detachment, under the command of 1st Lt. Zabolotsky, served air duty over the region at Mount Ararat, Lake Van, and Lake Urmia. This aviation detachment served the 4th Caucasian Corps, and the Army Aviation Inspector was Captain Koorbatoff. I hope 1st Lt. Zabolotsky is the man you are looking for, for he, from an airplane, sighted the Ark and started the investigation. Captain Koorbatoff was his supervisor. . . .

"I was in the Ararat region in November, 1915, during the war between Turkey and Russia. The general headquarters of the Caucasian Army sent me and other officers in command of emergency forces from Barzem and Pytergorsky for protection of the Araratsky Pass, just northwest of the peak of Greater Ararat and Zorsky Pass a few miles northwest, from the imminent Turkish attack. In June and July, the 3rd Turkish Army had broken through our forces very close to Aghri Dagh, the region of Ararat.

"It was during this military service that I learned of

the several undeciphered inscriptions and investigated archaeological sites in that region.

(Signed) Alexander A. Koor"

Col. Koor graciously shared his maps of the archaeological sites to which he had always dreamed of returning for further investigation some day, and also provided the following certified statement concerning the Russian Expedition in 1916.

"TO WHOM IT MAY CONCERN: This is to certify that I, Alexander A. Koor, former colonel and Chief-in-Command of the 19th Petropaulovsky regiment, heard the following concerning the discovery of Noah's Ark:

"(1) Lt. Paul Vasilivich Rujansky of the 156th Elisavetpolsky regiment, Caucasian Army. I knew all of Rujansky's family for years. I met them in the city of Kazan, Russia, where I attended the government Military Academy. 1st Lt. Rujansky was wounded in Ersurum when his regiment took Chaban Dede, central fort of the Ersurum fortifications. He was relieved from active duty and sent to work in the Commandant's office, in the city of Irkutsk, Siberia. After the Bolsheviks made an uprising he moved to the city of Harbin, Manchuria, where I found him in 1921.

"(2) Lt. Peter Nicolovich Leslin of the 261st Ahilchinsky regiment, also of the Caucasian Army. During the Bolshevik uprising he was arrested, but excaped from them, and in December, 1918, he joined my Petropaulovsky regiment.

"(3) About July or August, 1921, I and Lt. Leslin met 1st Lt. Rujansky in Harbin. During one of our conversations, 1st Lt. Rujansky told me about the discovery of Noah's Ark. He (1st Lt. Rujansky) didn't know about the details because he was wounded and sent to Russia, but he knew because his brother, Boris Vasilivich Rujansky, Sergeant of the Military Railroad Battalion, was a member of the investigating party which was sent to Mount Ararat to corroborate the discovery of Noah's Ark.

"(4) Lt. Leslin admitted he had also heard about the discovery of Noah's Ark, not as a rumor, but as news, from the Senior Adjutant of his Division, who had told him that Noah's Ark was found in the saddle of two peaks of Mount Ararat.

"This is all that I heard from these two officers, and I am sure both told me the truth.

(Signed) Col. Alexander A. Koor"

Thus the basic facts of the Russian aviator's discovery were fully verified; also the claims of the two former soldiers, John Schilleroff and John Georgesen, that they had participated in the two-phased Russian expedition to find the Ark were well substantiated.

ii. Hardwicke Knight

While exploring on Mount Ararat one summer day in the late 1930's, a New Zealander by the name of Hardwicke Knight stumbled upon evidence which strongly suggests that the remains of Noah's Ark are still on that mountain. The following account of his discovery is taken from material in printed and manuscript documents in the possession of Mr. Cummings, including personal correspondence which passed between Knight and himself.

Knight was still climbing the next day, and ridge was still succeeding ridge, when he crossed one more snow field. He had passed the area around Lake Kop, on the northern side of the mountain, but there were still two more ice fields to cross before he could reach the next ridge. The weary climber crossed the first, then skirted below the second. He walked over some soggy timbers at the termination of the second ice field, and climbed half way up the slope of the farther side. Was this some ancient trackway, Knight wondered idly as he passed on? Was this, perhaps, the trail to Ahora he had been hoping to find?

Suddenly he paused, then turned back. "Anxious though I was to conserve my strength," says Knight, "I was nonetheless curious, even if my curiosity had been slow to take. I satisfied myself that the soggy mass was indeed timber. It reminded me, when I felt it, of the forest trees said to be prehistoric which are submerged by the sea and appear at low tide at Walberswick on the Suffolk coast of England, or of the timbers of a Spanish galleon that are exposed in a similar way at very low tide on the Welsh coast."

"All around was the stony rubble that had rolled down the mountainside. Timbers extended in more than one direction; some were parallel and others perpendicular to them. The timbers could have been massive rectangular beams, although all I could see was the tops of them exposed level with the surface of the ground and it was not possible to tell how far they extended under the stones. What I saw looked like the frame of a very heavy wagon."

At first thought, Knight considered the possibility that he might have stumbled on the remains of a gun carriage from some mediaeval military campaign. The timbers did not look in the least like fallen logs or trees, he assures us, or he would have ignored them. "Not only were they rectangular in themselves," he explains, "but they formed a framework which was also rectangular." It was impossible to say if the timbers had been hewn, since there was no texture left upon the surface, which the discoverer described as "soggy and dark," and perhaps nine inches to a foot in width, and only a few feet of them were exposed by the melting of the ice field at its lower end. Quickly breaking off a piece of the waterlogged wood, Knight resumed his climb.

During the few moments that Knight had stopped to retrace his steps to examine the wood, he had become blanketed with the intense cold, and a severe pain in his chest had robbed him of that "composure which is necessary for a proper evaluation of an artifact," as he puts it; so, as the discovery of the wood seemed of minor significance to him at the time, and as night was coming on, he set off for the next ridge. The icy wind lashed his eyes into tears as he climbed the steep slopes, and he was obliged to sit down and wipe them when he reached the top. We will let Knight describe the scene that met his startled gaze:

> In front of me was one of the greatest and ugliest chasms in Mother Earth that I had ever seen. Immediately before me were screes that dropped thousands of feet into a black canyon, the farther side of which was equally steep and dark and remote. This great ravine appeared to be walled by steep screes and in places by precipices in both directions, cutting right across my way. Descending to the plain on my left, and cutting deeply into the very heart of the mountain on my right.

The explorer had come face to face with the Ahora Gorge, of course. By his calculations, Ahora was still ahead of him, and he would have to cross the great chasm to reach it. But no matter how he searched, he could find no way to cross to the other side without descending down the great screes thousands of perilous feet, to the black glacier that looked so forbidding below. Alone, and with so many unknown factors to consider before descending into the abyss, Knight reluctantly abandoned his plan to visit Ahora and the ruins he had hoped to explore, and set off down the side of the mountain to Igdir, to much needed food and rest.

The soggy sample of wood did not survive, and, his "evidence" gone, it was many years before Knight mentioned the timbers he had seen so close to the Great Chasm of Aghri Dagh. But the more he reflected, the more he studied and read, the more he came to see that his experience "fitted into a traditional pattern," and the more convinced he became that what he had discovered on the heights of the biblical peak might have something to do with Noah's Ark. He realized, too, that the same high shoulder of the mountain where he had found the timbers was the same area that all the old traditions had pointed out as the holy site.

"The biblical description of the Ark is explicit," says Knight. "It was an immense structure made of timbers, and what I had seen was not the whole remains of such a structure, and I have never for a moment thought so. The proportions of the timbers, however, make it seem logical to me to suppose that they are part of a very large and necessarily strong structure. Somewhere in or under the ice higher on the mountain above that place there might be a larger portion of this structure preserved. Perhaps some day," concludes Knight, "archaeologists will devise some method of searching for and finding these evidences. Such researches must surely have the blessing of God. But for my own part I am richly blessed to be one of the favored few who have been privileged to see and touch."

iii. George Jefferson Greene

In the late summer of 1952, George Jefferson Greene, an American oil pipeline and mining engineer, on a reconnoitering mission for his company around the northeastern flanks of Mount Ararat, looked down and saw a strange object protruding from the ice. The Ark! was Greene's first startled thought. He must be gazing down upon the Ark!

Reaching for his camera, Greene directed the helicopter pilot to maneuver the craft as closely as possible to the huge structure below. Closer and closer they edged, while the excited engineer recorded his discovery on film. Sidewise, head on, from closer than 100 feet away, the shutter clicked, while the sun was beginning to lower in the western sky.

When Greene returned to civilization and was able

to study the pictures he had taken, he was more than ever convinced that the great ship he had photographed on Mount Ararat was truly the Ark. When the photos were "blown up" to 8 x 10 size, the laminated sides of the structure were clearly visible. The pictures revealed other details as well: that the boat was situated on a "fault" on the mountain side; that a high cliff protected it on one side, and a sheer dropoff on the other. The glacier in which it was buried had only partly melted away, but about a third of the prow was plainly visible from the air.

Armed with a convincing portfolio of the photos he had made, he tried again and again to interest friends in forming an expedition to return with him to the mountain for a closer examination of what he had seen. At last, perhaps disheartened by the indifference of both family and friends, George Greene tucked his pictures away and left for British Guyana, where he hoped to make a fortune in a mining operation there. Here, on December 27, 1962, ten years after he had photographed the Ark, George Jefferson Greene was murdered for his gold. None of the possessions he had taken along have ever been recovered.

It is strange, as well as unfortunate, that Greene's discovery and photos were not more widely publicized at the time, or that they at least did not reach more interested eyes and ears. For it was not until after George Greene was dead and his pictures had disappeared, that Clifford L. Burdick, of Tuscon, Arizona, accidentally ran into the story.

Burdick, a geologist connected with the Natural Science Foundation of Los Angeles, California, had become interested in fossil tracks, "human or otherwise," as "indicators of geologic history and ancient life on earth."

"I spent much time in studying the giant human and dinosaur tracks near Glen Rose, Texas, found in Lower Cretaceous rocks," says Burdick. "Naturally, I was much interested when I ran across a write-up in the *Brewery Gulch Gazette* of Tombstone, Arizona, relating how a Fred Drake had found a fossil human foot in

Cretaceous rocks near Benson, Arizona. I lost little time in contacting Mr. Drake to hear the complete story. Before leaving I chanced to mention another pet scientific project I was interested in, namely, the search for the remains of Noah's Ark on Mount Ararat."

The two men had lunched together, and at the mention of Noah's Ark, recalls Burdick, "you should have seen Drake's face light up," "Why, I've seen actual photographs of the Ark," he exclaimed. "What do you mean?" demanded Burdick, who could hardly believe his ears.

"Well, this is the way it happened," explained Drake. "I was associated with an oil prospecting crew, staying in a motel in Kanab, Utah, about 1954. I became acquainted with an oil engineer by the name of George Greene, who said he had recently returned from Turkey where he had worked for an oil pipeline company. He had a helicopter at his disposal, and during his flights chanced to circle Mount Ararat near the Eastern border of Turkey.

"He was well equipped with cameras to photograph the terrain and pertinent phenomena. As he circled the north and northeast side of the mountain Greene was startled to spot a strange anomaly, an object protruding from rock debris on a mountain ledge, with the striking similitude of the prow of a great ship, parallel wooden side planking and all.

"There were six clear photographs, taken from different angles as they flew around the ship. I am sure Mr. Greene would have given me one of the photos, had I asked for one."

It was through the kindness of Fred Drake's vivid memory that we have the only authentic drawing of what the great structure on the side of Mount Ararat is like. Although admittedly "crude," it agrees remarkably with other stories describing the laminated sides of the object, the debris covering one end, the high cliff on one side, a sheer drop-off on the other.

The foregoing account from the Cummings archive is based upon personal correspondence with Mr. Fred

Drake, 406 South Arizona Avenue, Willcox, Arizona, and Mr. Clifford L. Burdick, 629 E. 9th Street, Tucson, Arizona; and personal interviews by Eryl A. Cummings with John Greene, son of the late George Greene.

10

Fernand Navarra

French amateur explorer Fernand Navarra has made three ascents of Mount Ararat; on two of these occasions he encountered strong evidence of the Ark's survival. In 1952 he saw the outlines of a vessel under the glacial ice, and in 1955, after an abortive attempt to reach the remains two years earlier, he succeeded in obtaining some of its wood with the help of his eleven-year-old son. Note well: when Jean de Riquier, one of Navarra's companions on the first ascent, expressed doubt as to the fruitfulness of Navarra's enterprise, his judgment preceded the finding of this wood.[1]

The account of Navarra's first sighting is reproduced below from the English translation of his book, L'Expédition au Mont Ararat (1953);[2] following it we translate a passage from the explorer's J'ai trouvé l'Arche de Noé ([1956], pp. 191, 195-97, 203-206, 221) in which he describes his 1955 discovery of what proved to be 5,000-year-old, hand-tooled wood. The account of Navarra's ascent to the peak of Ararat (August 14, 1952, a few days before the events recounted in the first passage below) will be given in the next section.

Impassive now, Ararat dominated us with the thirty square miles of its ice cap. Our eyes fixed on it, we tried to pierce its mystery.

The steamlets fed by the melting snows do not reach the foot of the mountain. All or almost all of them stop as soon as they begin and only the murmur of water trickling through to the enormous caverns of the invisi-

---

[1] See our essay, "Ark Fever" below.
[2] *The Forbidden Mountain*, trans. by Michael Legat (London: Macdonald, 1956), pp. 164-66.

ble crater can be heard. We felt certain that in addition
to the surface lake of Kop there was an immense interior lake, a mile to two miles in diameter, at the level of
the 13,800-foot mark which we had just reached. But
a carapace of ice at least a hundred to a hundred and
thirty feet thick covered it. This interior lake gives birth
to both the stream of Ahora and to the well of St.
James.* "The Fountain of Truth" the wise men call the
latter. Can human brains interpret the workings of God
and begin to see a logical solution of the mysteries and
the connection between the streamlets high on the
mountain and the eternal spring below, between James'
piece of wood and Noah's vessel?

It was August 17th—we had reached an altitude of
13,800 feet and the enormous ice cap stretched before
us. Two o'clock in the afternoon. The sun was at an
angle of forty-five degrees. Alone . . . on this immense
sheet of ice which dazzled our eyes. The air was bril-
liantly clear. All around us was bare and forbidding.
Our pursuit of a dream continued. . . . Below us an
eagle wheeled in the sky. Borne on the wind, it let itself
glide steadily in regular circles, imparting a silent
rhythm to the solitude.

In front of us was always the deep, transparent ice.
A few more paces and suddenly, as if there were an
eclipse of the sun, the ice became strangely dark. Yet
the sun was still there and above us the eagle still circled. We were surrounded by whiteness, stretching into
the distance, yet beneath our eyes was this astonishing
patch of blackness within the ice, its outlines sharply
defined.

Fascinated and intrigued, we began straightway to
trace out its shape, mapping out its limits foot by foot:
two progressively incurving lines were revealed, which
were clearly defined for a distance of three hundred
cubits, before meeting in the heart of the glacier. The
shape was unmistakably that of a ship's hull: on either
side the edges of the patch curved like the gunwales of

* [i.e., St. Jacob's well.]

a great boat. As for the central part, it merged into a black mass the details of which were not discernible.

Conviction burned in our eyes: no more than a few yards of ice separated us from the extraordinary discovery which the world no longer believed possible. *We had just found the Ark.*

We should have to camp here—we should *have* to ... Perhaps one day in the future it would be possible. ... We would indeed have given ten years of our lives to have had radar equipment that day!

*   *   *

On July the fifth [1955], at 7:30 A.M., we found ourselves at the foot of our "wall": the mountain of ice.

The peak of Ararat, in full view, was dazzling; but wisps of fog, sweeping across the bottom of the gorge, made the place a gloomy one. I had never encountered, and I am sure that I shall never encounter, a more desolate scene. In that place you felt yourself abandoned by God and man. This mountain of ice which, seen from the top of the moraine, had not impressed me as formidable, was now rising up against me with all its mass, sixty meters high.[1]

. . . .

We still had to cross a veritable labyrinth, with enormous crevasses on either side. It took us two hours to cover the last thirty meters. ... How would it be possible to examine this chimney of rock without being swallowed up by it?

Raphael found the solution: "Tie me good with the rope. I'll get as close as I can and try to see what's down there."

---

[1] [Readers who wish to convert metric distances throughout this passage are reminded that 1 meter=39.37 inches. Thus there are slightly over 3 ft. to each meter, and (in the instance given here) Navarra's "mountain of ice" was over 180 ft. high = 3 x 60 meters).]

After a moment of hesitation, I gave in. . . .

"There, I see it now! Yes, the boat is there, papa. I can see it as plain as day!. . . . Come see! There's a big deep crevasse and you can see down to the bottom sure as anything.". . .

I let down the climbing ladder, testing it to make sure it held. In a few minutes I was at the bottom of the crevasse—frozen to the bone by the humidity-level. Water thinly trickled down. Raphael had been able to see clearly because the chimney of rock was large enough to admit four men of my girth. It opened out into a kind of gently sloping terrace, under whose thick surface I was able, after having proceeded some thirty meters across it, to trace a dark and confused outline. It could only be the remains of the Ark which, two years earlier, I had located from the top of the ridge of the moraine—those remains which I had seen so many times since in my mind's eye and had sworn to recover!

. . . .

Soon I had removed enough snow to see the dark lines clearly. Then my joy disappeared in one fell swoop.

I had discovered, not wood but the dirt-level of the frozen moraine. From a distance such a mistake was entirely possible: the combination of dark lines really suggested the hull of a ship. But close by the illusion could no longer be sustained.

I made every effort to deny the evidence. I went forward, brushing away the snow for another fifty meters. Everywhere the same! Nothing but dirt.

I was horribly crushed. So, I had devoted eighteen years of my existence to a mirage! I had followed the tracks of the Ark historically and I had thought myself capable of recovering it geographically—after five thousand years. I had put together three expeditions, covered thousands of kilometers, risked the life of my son: all for a mirage. . . .

At this moment, Raphael's voice, sounding strange

because of the echo-effect, reached me: "Papa, have
you cut off a piece of the wood yet?"

I was too depressed to hide the truth from him. "No;
it isn't wood. It's just some dirt from the moraine."

"Have you dug down?"

In my emotional state, I hadn't thought to do so! ...

After a half hour's work, I had only dug a hole
about fifty centimeters square and twenty centimeters
deep.[2] I penetrated an ice layer, removing as much of
the dirt and ice as possible.

Then, under the crust of the broken ice, water appeared. And in the water, the end of a black wooden
beam. . . .

I was not dreaming. What I was touching with my
numb fingers in the icy water was actually a piece of
wood—and not a tree trunk, but hand-tooled wood.

There was a lump in my throat and I wanted to cry.
I longed to remain there on my knees thanking God for
having allowed me to succeed. After the most agonizing
false start, I was experiencing the greatest joy of my
life. I controlled my tears of happiness so as to be able
to yell the news to Raphael: "I've found wood!"

Not surprised at all, he called back: "Hurry up and
come back. I'm cold."

I tried to extricate the entire beam, but I couldn't
manage it even after enlarging the hole in the ice. The
beam must have been very long; perhaps it was still attached to other parts of the ship's interior structure. To
get the whole thing out, other tools than those I had
with me would have been necessary, as well as a crew
of men and many man-hours of labor.[3] So I had to
content myself with cutting, along the grain, a piece
one meter and a half long. When I got it out of the
water its weight astonished me. Its hand-tooled character struck one immediately. The compactness of it
was also remarkable, considering that it had been in

---

[2] [i.e., 1½ ft. square and 8 inches deep.]

[3] [In 1969 a SEARCH Foundation team found more pieces of wood
about seventy-five feet from this site, according to their publicity re-
leases.]

water; the water had not distended the fibers as much as one would have expected. Was this the result of bitumen?[4]

* * *

The key question, then, is the following one: What kind of construction could have been built on Ararat, at an altitude of nearly five thousand meters, some five thousand years ago?[5]

If my answer is Noah's Ark, this isn't because I prefer wishful thinking to reality. It is rather, as I said earlier, *because there can be no other explanation.*

At the present stage of our knowledge, to obtain the only possible supplementary proof of what I am claiming here would require nothing less than another expedition—an expedition with resources sufficient to bring down from Ararat all the vestiges of the Ark now in the ice. The task which I began with minimal equipment and with only my son to help me, others will

---

[4] [Navarra here alludes to Gen. 6:14: "Make thee an ark of gopher wood; rooms shalt thou make in the ark, and shalt pitch it within and without with pitch." T. C. Mitchell of the British Museum's Department of Western Asiatic Antiquities notes that "bitumen, a natural derivative of crude petroleum, is found ready to hand in Mesopotamia and Palestine, and is therefore more probably the material referred to [by *kofer,* the word translated 'pitch']" (*The New Bible Dictionary,* ed. by J. D. Douglas [1962], p. 159). Though the nature of "gopher wood" remains unidentified (see above, "Genesis and Gilgamesh" [Part One, section 3], the text following note 4), some biblical scholars hold that it was a resinous tree, on the ground of the similarity between the Hebrew *gofer* ("gopher" and *kofer* ("bitumen/pitch"). Cf. Mitchell, *ibid.,* p. 483.]

[5] [After subjecting Navarra's wood fragment to various tests, the Forestry Institute of Research and Experimentation, Madrid, Spain, estimated the age of the fragment at 5,000 years ("la edad . . . oscila alrededor de los cinco mil años"). The full report (dated April 7, 1956) is photographically reproduced in the original Spanish, with accompanying French translation, as an appendix to Navarra's *J'ai trouvé l'Arche de Noé;* also reproduced there is the wood analysis report April 15, 1956) of the Prehistory Institute of the University of Bordeaux's Faculty of Sciences, which considered the fossilized wood to derive from "an epoch of great antiquity" une époque remontant a une haute antiquité).]

hopefully be able to carry to completion with more substantial means. I would be more than happy to guide such persons and to put at their disposal my knowledge of a mountain to which I owe so many hard-won joys. With me or without me, my greatest desire is that they succeed. For the result of their labors can only provide luminous confirmation of what the skeptics call "an hypothesis," but what for me is a certitude: I have found the Ark of Noah.[6]

---

[6] [Navarra concludes with the statement which he used as the title of his book: "Jai trouvé l'Arche de Noé." On p. 219 he qualifies his claim a bit: "If the piece I found is indeed from the Ark, it belonged to its internal structure, not to its outside panelling or superstructure, which everything leads us to believe was broken apart and dispersed long ago." But it could well be that even if Navarra's wood did come from the Ark's partitions or other inner structural material, the hull might still remain intact—waiting for definitive discovery. Several of the other accounts we have cited, e.g. those of Greene and Tamisian, would seem to suggest that this is the case.]

PART THREE

Explorations of Ararat

1

The First Modern Ascent: Parrot (1829)

Dr. J. J. Friedrich W. Parrot *(1791-1841) not only distinguished himself as the first explorer in modern times to reach the summit of Mt. Ararat; he was also a respected scholar (Professor of Natural Philosophy in the University of Dorpat), an important political figure (Russian Imperial Councillor of State, Knight of the Order of St. Anna), and a warm-hearted Christian believer. He is honored by a biographical article in the* Allgemeine Deutsche Biographie. *Parrot's* Journey to Ararat *(1845) records careful scientific observations, a reverent testimony to the mountain's grandeur (p. 135), and the description of his party's Sunday devotions high among the rocks of Ararat amidst a storm of wind and snow (p. 249). When he reached the summit, Parrot erected a 3½ foot wooden Cross. Significantly, Parrot's account also reflected his conviction that geologic evidence of the Flood still existed in the Araxes area and on Ararat (pp. 117, 230-31).*

Unjustified doubt was cast on the fact of Parrot's ascent—not because he reached the summit very late in the season (October 9), but because it had long been alleged that the steep, ice-covered peak was impossible to climb at all. However, his claim was later fully established by the affidavits mentioned on pp. 187-95 of Journey to Ararat. *Says the writer of the preface to the English version of Parrot's account*s "There seems . . . to be no ground for questioning the veracity of M. Parrot, who, as a traveller as well as a philosopher, fully merited the eulogy pronounced on him by [the great German naturalist and traveller Baron F. H. Alexander] von Humboldt[1] and was 'constantly guided by

---

[1] *Asie centrale* (3 vols., 1843), II, 306.

*the love of truth'." James Bryce who himself reached
the summit of Ararat in 1876 (see below, "One-man
Conquest and a Relic"), lauds Parrot's achievement in
these words:*

Considering that his [Parrot's] expedition was
made in 1829, when hardly anything was known
about mountain climbing, that he had twice failed
before, and on one of those occasions had had a
nasty slip which might easily have cost him his
life, it is impossible not to feel warm admiration
for his spirit and constancy, and a corresponding
indignation at those persons, some of them men of
note, who branded him as an impostor and denied
that he had reached the summit at all. Too late for
his own satisfaction, for he died four or five years
[*sic:* twelve] after his exploit, his veracity and
reputation have been completely vindicated by
subsequent ascents.[2]

*The account below is taken from pp. 176ff. of the En-
glish edition of Parrot's book.*

At the first dawn we roused ourselves up, and at
about half-past six proceeded on our march. The last
tracts of rocky fragments were crossed in about half an
hour, and we once more trod on the limits of perpetual
snow nearly in the same place as before, having first
lightened ourselves by depositing near some heaps of
stones such articles as we could dispense with. But the
snowy region had undergone a great, and for us by no
means favourable change. The newly fallen snow which
had been of some use to us in our former attempt, had
since melted, from the increased heat of the weather,
and was now changed into glacier ice, so that notwith-

standing the moderate steepness of the acclivity, it
would be necessary to cut steps from below. This made
our progress a laborious affair, and demanded the full
exertion of our strength from the first starting. We were
obliged to leave one of the peasants behind at the place
where we spent the night, as he complained of illness;
two others tried in ascending the glacier,[1] stopped at
first only to rest, but afterwards went back to the same
station. The rest of us, without allowing ourselves to be
detained an instant by these accidents, pushed on unre-
mittingly to our object, rather excited than discouraged
by the difficulties in our way. We soon after came again
to the great crack which marks the upper edge of the
icy slope just ascended, and about ten o'clock we found
ourselves exactly in the place where we had arrived on
the former occasion at noon, that is to say, on the great
plain of snow, which forms the first step downward
from the icy head of Ararat. We saw from a distance of
about half a mile the cross erected on the 19th September, but it looked so uncommonly small, perhaps
owing to its black colour, that I could not help doubting whether I should be able to make it out, and to recognize it with an ordinary telescope from the plain of
the Araxes.

In the direction of the summit we had before us an
acclivity shorter but steeper than that just passed over;
and between it and the furthest pinnacle there seemed
to intervene only a gentle swelling of the ground. After
a short rest, we ascended with the aid of hewn steps the
next slope (the steepest of all), and then another ele-
vation; but now instead of seeing immediately in front

---

[1] [In his discussion of Bryce's account of Ararat, as reported in
the *Proceedings of the Royal Geographical Society* ([London], XXII
[1878], 185), Douglas Freshfield, who himself had ascended Ararat
in 1868, observed that this glacier was "the only one in the whole
of Armenia." "It was on the north side of the mountain in a narrow
chasm," he said, adding that it may be the kind known as a *glacier
remanié.* Elsewhere, however ("Early Ascents of Ararat," *Alpine
Journal,* VIII [1877], 220), he indicates that "hard slopes of névé
are probably meant."]

of us the grand object of all our exertions, a whole row
of hills had developed itself to our eyes, and completely
intercepted the view of the summit. At this our spirits
which had never fluctuated so long as we supposed that
we had a view of all the difficulties to be surmounted,
sank not a little, and our strength, exhausted by the
hard work of cutting steps in the ice, seemed hardly
adequate to the attainment of the now invisible goal.
Yet, on calculating what was already done and what
remained to be done, on considering the proximity of
the succeeding row of heights, and casting a glance at
my hearty followers, care fled, and, "boldly onwards!"
resounded in my bosom. We passed without stopping
over a couple of hills; there we felt the mountain wind;
I pressed forward round a projecting mound of snow,
and behold! before my eyes, now intoxicated with joy,
lay the extreme cone, the highest pinnacle of Ararat.
Still, a last effort was required of us to ascend a tract of
ice by means of steps, and that accomplished, about a
quarter past three on the 27th September (9th Oct.),[2]
1829, *we stood on the top of Ararat.*

What I first aimed at and enjoyed was rest; I spread
out my cloak and sat down on it. I found myself on a
gently vaulted, nearly cruciform surface, of about two
hundred paces in circuit, which at the margin sloped
off precipitously on every side, but particularly towards the south-east and north-east. Formed of eternal ice, without rock or stone to interrupt its continuity,
it was the austere, silvery head of Old Ararat. Towards
the east, this summit extended more uniformly than
elsewhere, and in this direction it was connected by
means of a flattish depression, covered in like manner
with perpetual ice, with a second and somewhat lower
summit, distant apparently from that on which I stood
above half a mile, but in reality only 397 yards, or less
than a quarter of a mile. This saddle-shaped depression

---

[2] [September 27 is the Old Style (Julian) dating; October 9, the
Gregorian. When Parrot made his ascent, Russia had not adopted the
Gregorian calendar reform.]

may be easily recognised from the plain of the Araxes with the naked eye, but from that quarter it is seen foreshortened; and as the less elevation stands foremost, while the greater one is behind, the former appears to be as high as, or even higher than the latter, which from many points cannot be seen at all. M. Fedorov ascertained by his angular measurements made in a north-easterly direction from the plain of the Araxes, that the summit in front is seven feet lower than that behind or further west; to me, looking from the latter, the difference appeared much more considerable.

The gentle depression between the two eminences presents a plain of snow moderately inclined towards the south, over which it would be easy to go from the one to the other, and which may be supposed to be the very spot on which Noah's Ark rested, if the summit itself be assumed as the scene of that event, for there is no want of the requisite space, inasmuch as the Ark, according to Genesis vi. 15. three hundred ells long and fifty wide, would not have occupied a tenth part of the surface of this depression.[3] Ker Porter, however, makes[4] on this subject a subtle comment favourable to the opinion that the resting-place of the Ark was not on the summit of the mountain, but on some lower part of it; because in Genesis viii. 5. it is said, "On the first day of the tenth month the tops of the mountains came forth;" but in vi. 16. it is stated that the window of the Ark was above; consequently, Noah could have seen

---

[3] [Seventeenth-century polymath Athanasius Kircher was well aware that "people have . . . wondered how the Ark could rest on a mountain peak without tumbling down, and they have pointed out that none of the mountains of the world has a level pasture at its summit on which the Ark could ground safely." In response, Kircher wrote in his encyclopedic *Arca Noe* that "this may be true of the Pyrenees, the Appenines, and the Alps, but the Jesuit fathers have climbed Ararat and discovered that its top is a vast plateau" (from Don Cameron Allen's précis of the book, appended to his detailed study of "renaissance rationalism in art, science, and letters," *The Legend of Noah* [Urbana: University of Illinois Press, 1963], p. 189).]

[4] *Travels in Georgia, Persia, and Armenia, &c.*, Lond. 1821, vol. i. p. 183.

only what was higher than the ship, which was therefore lower down than the tops of the mountains: on
these grounds Ker Porter is inclined to look upon the
wide valley between the Great and Little Ararat as the
place where the Ark rested. In this reasoning, however,
he takes the above quoted texts of Holy Writ in a sense
different from the literal one; for it is nowhere said that
Noah saw the mountains coming forth, but it is simply
stated that after the Ark had rested, the water subsided,
so that already on the first day of the tenth moon the
mountains began to come forth; then "after forty days
Noah opened the window which he had made in the
Ark and let fly a raven;" and, again, after three weeks,
"Noah took off the cover of the Ark and saw that the
ground was dry," respecting which he might have
formed as good a judgment or even a better from the
more elevated point than from the lower.

Should any one now inquire respecting the possibility of remains of the Ark still existing on Ararat, it may
be replied that there is nothing in that possibility incompatible with the laws of nature, if it only be assumed that immediately after the Flood the summit of
that mountain began to be covered with perpetual ice
and snow, an assumption which cannot be reasonably
objected to. And when it is considered that on great
mountains accumulated coverings of ice and snow ex-
ceeding 100 feet in thickness are by no means unusual,
it is obvious that on the top of Ararat there may be
easily a sufficient depth of ice to cover the Ark, which
was only thirty ells high.

. . . .

About half-past six in the evening, we reached our
place of bivouac, where a cheerful fire was made with
the wood that remained, a small supper cooked, and
the night as bright and warm as the preceding one,
spent agreeably. There also we found our attendants
whom we had left behind, together with our things. The
next day, about six in the morning, we set off, and

about half-past eight reached Kip-Ghioll,⁵ where the
beasts of burden were waiting for us, and about noon
on the 28th of September we joyfully entered St.
James,⁶ as the patriarch Noah, "with his sons and with
his wives and with his sons' wives," had, 4000 years
before, descended from Ararat. On the day after our
return, in our Sabbath devotions, we bore to the Lord
the offering of our thanks, perhaps, not far from the
very spot where Noah "built an altar to the Lord, and
offered thereon burnt offerings."

---

⁵ [Lake Kop.]

⁶ [The monastery which was totally destroyed, together with the
town of Arguri (Ahuri), by the terrible blow-out of June 20-23, 1840.
Wrote James Bryce in 1877 *(Transcaucasia and Ararat)* pp. 239-41):

"The last event of importance in the history of Ararat is the
great earthquake of 1840. . . .

There formerly stood a pleasant little Armenian village of
some two hundred houses, named Arghuri, or Aghurri, whose
inhabitants, . . . boasted not only of the Patriarch's vine, bearing
grapes delicious to eat, but which Heaven, in memory of the
fault they betrayed him into, had forbidden to be made into
wine; but also of an ancient willow trunk, which had sprung
from one of the planks of the Ark. Not far above the village,
on the spot where the angel of the legend had appeared to the
monk, stood the little monastery of St. Jacob, eight centuries
old. . . . Towards sunset in the evening of the 20th of June 1840
(old style), the sudden shock of an earthquake, accompanied
by a subterranean roar, and followed by a terrific blast of
wind, threw down the houses of Arghuri, and at the same
moment detached enormous masses of rock with their superja-
cent ice from the cliffs that surround the chasm. A shower of
falling rocks overwhelmed in an instant the village, the monastery, and a Kurdish encampment on the pastures above. Not a
soul survived to tell the tale. . . . Since then a few huts have
again arisen somewhat lower down the slope than the site of
Old Arghuri and without the mouth of the chasm; here dwell a
few Tatars—for the Armenians (several, happening to be away
from the village, escaped) do not seem to have returned to the
desolated spot—and pasture their cattle on the sides of the
valley which grass has again begun to clothe. But Noah's vine
and the primeval willow, and the little monastery where Parrot
lived so happily among the few old monks who had retired to
this hallowed spot from the troubles of the world, are gone for
ever; no Christian bell is heard, no Christian service said, upon
the Mountain of the Ark."]

2

A Geologist Who Wouldn't Give Up: Abich (1845)

Q. W. H. von Abich (1806-1886) was appointed Professor of Mineralogy at the University of Dorpat the year after Professor Parrot died. (See the article on him in the Allgemeine Deutsche Biographie.*) Specializing in the geology of the Caucasus, Abich soon centered an investigation on Noah's mountain. Three times weather frustrated his attempts to reach its summit. "He deserves scarcely less credit that Parrot," declares James Bryce, "for the tenacity with which he clung to his purpose under so many difficulties."[1] Finally, his fourth ascent was a (qualified) success. Bryce writes:*

When Herr Abich made his ascent in 1845 . . . he reached the eastern summit, which is only a few feet inferior in height to the western, and six minutes' walk from it, and finding the weather threatening, returned without going on to the western. The consequence was that, when, anxious to destroy the popular superstition that the stars are visible at noon from the tops of the highest mountains, he produced his companions as witnesses before the authorities at Erivan, to make a regular deposition, they turned round on him, and solemnly declared and swore that from the point which they had reached a great part of the horizon was covered by much more lofty mountains.[2]

We translate into English for the first time Abich's account of his indefatigable efforts. The original text is to

---

[1] James Bryce, *Transcaucasia and Ararat* (London: Macmillan, 1877), p. 238.
[2] *Ibid.*, pp. 236-37.

be found in the 1851 volume of the Bulletin de la
Société de Géographie.[3] *In the same issue of the Geographical Society Bulletin Abich gives a related summary of elevations and geological details, "Hauteurs
absolues du système de l'Ararat et des pays environnants" (pp. 66ff.).*

The dotted line[1] represents the route I took on more
than one occasion in my assaults on the summit of
Ararat. It is the same route that Colonel Khodzko followed in 1850.

The entire slope between the two great eruptive
areas provides a terrain which is more homogeneous,
less irregular, and easier to cross on horseback to the
point designated (3). From there, one does better, in
attaining point (5), to climb over the large trachyte[2]
promontory than to cross with very considerable difficulty the sharp and severed ridges of the enormous lava
flows (one sees them at the left; they consist of black
resinoid trachyte.) Two routes are available from this
point to the peak of the cone; they correspond to the
two sides of the giant depression which can be clearly
seen in the illustration.

I was driven back in my first attempt to reach the
summit on August 16, 1844. This occurred at 3 P.M.
on the right side of the depression, at the point numbered (8).[3] One of those sudden storms arose which

---

[3] "Notice explicative d'une vue du cône dt l'Ararat," [Paris], 4th
ser., I (1851), 515-25, 556 (we translate pp. 521-23). This article
was published simultaneously in the *Bulletin de la Société Géologique
de France,* 2d ser., VIII (1850-1851), 265-71, with accompanying
plate. Abich slightly modified the views presented here in his later
paper, "Ararat in seiner genetischen Bildung," published in the
Transactions of the German Geological Society for 1870.

[1] [On Abich's "view of Greater Ararat as seen from the peak of
Lesser Ararat in August, 1844" (Figure 2 in photo insert).]

[2] Light-colored volcanic rock consisting chiefly of potash feld-
spar.]

[3] Abich notes (p. 68) that this was also the place where the Cross
was planted by Colonel Khodzko's expedition, as described in his
narrative."]

appear so frequently on Ararat, particularly on the southern slope of that mountain system.

The same fate pursued me during the night of August 23, 1844, in my second try, when I was proceeding up the left side of the depression and had reached a height considerably above that of Lesser Ararat. The violence of the storm, which began toward midnight, combined with electrical phenomena of a highest intensity; I felt discharges all about me. The exchange between the atmospheric electricity and that of all the nearby objects was so powerful that the flashes (they looked like little phosphorescent flames) could be seen for a long time, crackling from the ends of several of our metallic instruments and darting aloft from the tips of our ice axes the moment we held them up. A heavy snow shower, which continued all night and until ten o'clock in the morning, covered the entire cone of the mountain with a blanket of snow and ice more than a foot thick. The path we had taken to cross the sharp blocks comprising the ridge of black resinoid trachytic lava (referred to above) was rendered so impassable that we had to snow slide down the steep and shifting incline which leads from the top of the aforesaid depression into its vast interior, replete with minature glaciers.

My third attempt to reach the summit of Greater Ararat occurred on September 3, 1844. I took the route by way of Lake Kop, on the northern face of the gigantic cone. This failed owing to the gradient of the ice-covered slopes, so—for my fourth try—I returned to my original plan.

On the evening of July 28, 1845, I pitched camp fairly close to point (7) on the illustration. A trachytic mass juts out here like an immense reef. It is crossed lengthwise by numerous splits and fissures, by whose help one can reach a higher level on the cone. There you again met, instead of fixed rocks, a loose terrain; this is composed of rocky debris which has undergone considerable decomposition.

Rocks very similar to those which form the central

core of Ararat abound in this area, as in the interior
of the giant depression mentioned several times above.
Evidently there is a quantity of pyrite (sulphuretted
iron)[4] in this rock, and its decomposition explains both
the breaking down of the rocks and the absence of
snow at this elevation. The sulphurous vapors that one
smells in this spot are collateral phenomena—natural
consequences of the same decomposition. The destructive effects produced by the decomposition can be observed to the full inside the valley of St. Jacob.[5]

It took me six hours to cover the full distance from
point (7) to the peak of Ararat.[6] I reached point (9)
at noon on July 29, 1845.

---

[4] [i.e., iron disulfide.]
[5] [i.e., in the Ahora gorge.]
[6] [Abich climbed the eastern rise of the summit—today named for
him; it is some thirty feet lower than the western rise which Parrot
ascended in 1829.]

3

Ascension in Style:
Khodzko (1850)

The account of Colonel Khodzko's expedition to the peak of Mt. Ararat shows how much an organized, systematic ascent in full cooperation with the local authorities can accomplish. If only this kind of operation could be reproduced 120 years later! We owe the following excerpt from that account to the article by D. Longuinoff, "Ascension de l'Ararat," published in the Bulletin de la Sociétié de Géographie for 1851.* Longuinoff was a member of the Geographical Society of St. Petersburg; after providing an introduction concerning other ascents, etc. (pp. 52-55), he translated into French the report of the Khodzko (also spelled Chodzko and Tschodsko) expedition which appeared in Russian in the journal The Caucasus, No. 80 for 1850. An abridged French version with some modifications is given in Zurcher and Margolle, Les ascensions célèbres, pp. 348-59. We translate for the first time into English from Longuinoff's text. This is how he introduces the report (pp. 54-55):

Sixty persons combined their talents in this expedition, conceived on a vast plan with its object (in line with a desire specifically expressed by Abich) to establish a long-term operation on the peak of Ararat. In this way, it would be possible to carry out the most delicate techniques of modern scientific investigation—those depending on precision instruments. First and foremost, the idea was to complete the triangulation of Transcaucasia as soon as possible. This herculean task, commenced

---

* Paris, 4th ser., I (1851), 52-65.

six years ago by Colonel Khodzko, was thus to be
brought to its successful termination by him.

A special project, approved by the commander-in-
chief of the Caucasian corps, had established in advance the entire series of trigonometric measurements
which were to be carried out in the Transcaucasian
area during the year 1850. In conformity with that
project, it was decided to make the ascent of Greater
Ararat. . . .

On the 29th of the month [July], we pitched camp
on Greater Ararat, seven versts from Sardar Baluk[1]
and close to the snow line, which had receded to an
unusual extent that year. After a last load of charcoal
and rations had arrived, Colonel Khodzko scheduled
departure for August 1.

The day was heralded by magnificent weather, and
we went right ahead with the packing of the scientific
instruments. Personal baggage was put on horseback
and we broke camp at 6 A.M. . . . At the head of the
column marched an Armenian named Simon who had
served as Abich's guide in 1845; he carried a black
Cross about a sagene in length[2] which he determined
to plant on the summit of Ararat. . . .

At 6 A.M. on the 2d of August, the detachment resumed its climb. The difficulties of the terrain multiplied, however. We surmounted the rocky ridge which
skirts the left side of the ravine and proceeded little by
little to the higher altitudes. The sky, which had been
rather clear early in the morning, became heavily
clouded; toward noon, a west wind came up, driving
swirls of icy snow and hail before it. This change in the
weather obliged Colonel Khodzko to remove everything
from the sleds except for the instruments. The Cossacks, with their chief as their example, then proceeded
to function as bearers; and they resumed their arduous

---

[1] [A Cossack station with a well, located in the middle of the wide,
semicircular valley or sloping plain between Greater and Lesser
Ararat. A verst measures slightly over a kilometer.]

[2] [1 sagene = 2.1 meters. The cross was thus about 7 feet long.]

task not with a lowering of morale, but with the intrepid, energetic, devil-may-care attitude so characteristic of the Russian soldier.

About one o'clock, we reached the northeast extremity of the rock ridge that loses itself farther on in a region of shale and stony debris which in turn is crisscrossed by layers of ice and snow. This condition extends to the foot of the last slope rising to the peak, and near it we found, upright and well into the ground, the Cross which one of Abich's men had planted there in 1845.

Here we took a short break, hoping that the weather conditions would improve. In vain! At 2:30 P.M., the wind increased in violence and, to add to the difficulties, a dense fog swallowed up the peak. The expedition therefore resolved to push ahead so as to gain the protection of the rocks of the escarpment before the storm broke. We climbed the slope halfway, but there was no chance of going farther that same day. . . . We resigned ourselves to this awkward position until the morrow.

The fury of the wind never ceased. Occasionally it would rend the thick mantle of clouds which encircled the entire mountain at that level. Then in the pale moonlight would suddenly be revealed either a corner of the Araxes valley or the contours of Lesser Ararat, whose peak was already beneath us—or we would see the gloomy precipices surrounding our inhospitable refuge which lay at an altitude considerably higher than that of Mt. Blanc.

To complete the misery, about 10 P.M. a violent electric storm arose. By the brilliance of the lightning and the force of the thunder, the expedition soon became convinced that it was at the very center of the electric discharges. At each explosion, the electricity did not zigzag across the sky in the usual manner, but instantaneously filled the place where we were with a blinding flash and green, red, and white side effects. The thunderclaps followed the lightning with no appreciable interval; their drum-like rolls were distinctly repeated over and over by echoes from the innumerable gorges of the mountain.

Toward midnight, the storm died down, but the snow continued to fall in thick flakes; those of us who did not move were covered to a depth of three or four inches. Finally, dawn broke, but it did not exactly come up to our expectations. True, the peaks were no longer enveloped by clouds, but, to compensate, the slopes of Lesser Ararat and the entire area within view below us had disappeared under an impenetrable mantle of cloud which, from our vantage point, resembled an undulating, icy sea. . . .

The company's situation had become so impossible that we resolved to continue the ascent, in the hope of finding, above the rocks, the level space or plateau-like area which we knew to be contiguous to the summit.

At 4 A.M., the expedition started off again. However, we reached the plateau only after climbing over still a third ridge of rock. The plain was on at least a fifty degree incline, and it is strewn rather heavily with pyrites, which give off an intolerable smell of sulphur.³ . . .

On reaching the middle of the plateau, the company was forced to halt some two hundred paces short of the peak: exhaustion and the wind absolutely forbade another step. Incredible effort resulted in the pitching of two tents on ground less steeply angled than the average, but even this incline was thirty to forty degrees. The detachment retained this post for three nights and two days (August 3-5), and during that time the wind, accompanied by snow, hail, and ice, kept up almost without interruption. . . .

Colonel Khodzko determined to use the morning for the exploration of the peak areas, as well as for the discovery of an advantageous location for the scientific instruments and for the high camp itself. At 8:45, he started out with the Cossacks, and a quarter of an hour later he reached the upper-level plain. . . . Three peaks

---

³ [This sulphurous odor has been commented on by several explorers who have reached the summit of Ararat. Cf. Abich's account.]

dominated. On two of them, we saw pyramidal forma-
tions, made of rocky debris and surmounted with testimonies to the Faith. These had been put up by some
soldiers who, a month before, had voluntarily climbed
Ararat under the leadership of one Tchougounkoff, and
who had reached this solitary place on July the 12th.
We rapidly climbed the closest of these summits, and
then proceeded to the second,[4] which Abich had conquered in 1845.

But great was our surprise when, on reaching the top
of that peak, we saw before us yet a third summit, incomparably higher[5] than the other two and separated
from them by a wide gully. The steep projections of
that gully, which dropped off perpendicularly to a
depth of about a sagene and a half,[6] made it hard to
cross. Nonetheless, we conquered this obstacle with the
aid of the soldiers and, at 10 o'clock in the morning (it
was the Feast of the Transfiguration[7]), Messrs.
Khodzko, Khanykoff and their compatriots stood on
the highest peak of Greater Ararat. Previously, only
Parrot and Spasski[8] had succeeded in doing this, and
they had come up by the opposite slope.

First and foremost, we set about to erect the Cross.
When our guide Simon had been otherwise occupied
and—characteristically—at the places where the climb
had been most treacherous, the Cross had been put in
the safekeeping of Cossack Dokhnoff. When he
reached the spot, that man fell on his knees, prostrated
himself three times before the sign of our Redemption,
and forthwith went to work to plant it in the
ground. Then we, his helpers, gathered around this
Christian symbol which had just been placed on the

---

[4] [The eastern summit, which is some thirty feet lower than the
western peak climbed by Parrot in 1829.]

[5] [This is an inadvertent exaggeration.]

[6] [See above, note 2.]

[7] [In the Russian, Roman Catholic, and Anglican church calendars,
Transfiguration Day is August 6. Lutherans celebrate Transfiguration
each year on the last Sunday after Epiphany.]

[8] [On Spasski, see our Appendix B.]

summit of the biblical mount, and concluded the ceremony with a fervent prayer. . . .

Before his final departure from the summit area, Colonel Khodzko had his men build a snow pyramid a sagene in height[9] where his camp had been, and on it the Cross was raised with a bronze plaque affixed. The inscription read:

IN THE YEAR 1850
FROM THE 6TH TO THE 18TH OF AUGUST
UNDER THE PROPITIOUS REIGN OF
EMPEROR NICHOLAS I
AND THE CAUCASIAN LIEUTENANCY OF
PRINCE WORONTSOFF
THE ASCENT OF GREATER ARARAT WAS
ACHIEVED BY COLONEL KHODZKO, WHO
DIRECTED THE TRIANGULATION,
N. KHANYKOFF, J. ALEXANDROFF, A. MORITZ,
J. SCHAROYAN AND SIXTY SOLDIERS.

---

[9] [i.e., seven feet high; see above, note 2.]

4

The British Empire on Ararat: Stuart (1856)

In spite of his erroneous depreciation of Parrot's and Abich's ascents,* Major Robert Stuart has left us a valuable and highly literate account of his party's conquest of Ararat. His reference to the local tradition of the Ark's survival on the mountain is especially important. We give below Stuart's report from his private journal, originally published in the Proceedings of the Royal Geographic Society *([1877], 77-92). The reader will soon discover why we have abridged it only slightly and will agree that no one need apologize for a lengthy portion of such splendid prose. Shorter but equally lucid extracts from journals and letters of various members of Stuart's party are included in Douglas W. Freshfield's article, "Early Ascents of Ararat," in the* Alpine Journal, *VIII (1877), 216-21.*

---

* Douglas W. Freshfield, also a climber of Ararat (see below, "Just Short of the Summit"), comments on Stuart's narrative ("Early Ascents of Ararat," *Alpine Journal,* VIII [1877], 213-14):

"The writer expresses strongly his disbelief in any previous ascents—except Noah's. The reason he offers for his incredulity is the positive assurance given him by an English Consul at Erzeroum, and by residents of Armenia, that all previous attempts to reach the top had failed.

The argument from authority is, however, a dangerous one for climbers in the East. The same universal consent might now be appealed to in disproof of Major Stuart's own ascent, which has long been forgotten in the country.

It would be hard to hold Major Stuart responsible for the statements of a private journal, published in his absence. But it is perhaps, to be regretted that remarks disputing the veracity of many travellers of established reputation should have been put forth by our Geographical Society without comment or explanation."]

The sun rose in all his glory at Bayazid[1] on the 11th July, 1856. There was not a cloud in the sky to intercept his rays, and, with the exception of an occasional breeze that swept lightly down from the mountains, the atmosphere was calm and still. So far as could be prognosticated in these regions of fierce and sudden changes, the weather was set in fair.

As the Expedition of which we are about to write was novel in its object, and not without importance in its results, it is but fair towards the gentlemen who were engaged in it to give to their names an early and prominent place in the narrative. These gentlemen were as follows:—The Rev. Walter Thursby, Major Fraser, Mr. James Theobald, Mr. Evans, 9th Lancers, and the writer, Major Robert Stuart. Majors Fraser and Stuart and Mr. Evans formed part of a British Staff that, during the war, had been attached to the army of Anatolia. Messrs. Thursby and Theobald were travelling in those parts for their own amusement. It would be too much to aver that the above names will live in the future traditions of the country round Ararat, for English names are distorted into curious shapes by Oriental lips; but in some form or other they will long be remembered with pious respect in the plains and villages of those parts, from their associations with the sacred heights of Aghri-dagh.

Our cortege consisted of Iss-hak Bey, Chief of the Ararat Kurds, to whose special care we had been committed by the Kaimakam of Bayazid, Hadgï Mustafa Effendi, a zaptieh, or native policeman, who, in addition to other functions, acted as interpreter between our party and the Kurds. Our dragoman, a Smyrniote, who figured in the remains of an expensive British Staff uniform and a suridji to take charge of the horses.

• •

The snow-clad cone stood out in distinct relief against the morning-sky, cold, grand, and forbidding.

---

[1] [i.e., Dogubayazit.]

By some perspective illusion, the lesser peak, though 4000 feet lower, and some miles more distant, seemed the higher of the two. This can be explained by the principles of optics; but we fear in a manner that would not interest many of our readers. One useful lesson, however, may be learned from this fact: namely, that travellers should be careful in trusting to first impressions, seeing that the senses are apt to be misled when first brought into contact with unaccustomed objects. We now struck off in a north-easterly direction across the plain. One hour from Bayazid we came to the Shekheli, a deep narrow stream as clear as crystal, that, collecting the watershed of the adjacent mountains, winds round the base of Ararat and unites with the Arras.[2] We traversed this stream by means of a handsome one-arched bridge of Genoese construction, much impaired, like all its kindred works in this country, by the hand of time and the roughness of the elements. The parapets have been swept away, the foundations show signs of weakness, and the traveller of next year will perhaps find it gone.

The plain of Bayazid, unlike those of Alishkurd, Passine, and Erzeroum is, for the most part, barren and repulsive, yielding nothing but a sparse, lank grass, insufficient for pasture. The soil is everywhere stony and the stone volcanic. After crossing the Shekheli we observed much that would interest the naturalist: small lizards of a brown colour were in some places so numerous that they started aside in scores from every footfall of our horses, while at the same time swarms of large red-winged beetles buzzed pertinaciously around us, and every now and then we crossed the shiny trail of snakes; gray partridges abound on the stony ground at the foot of the mountains, crows and swifts are seen in scanty numbers, and further on some indications of man appear in the few wretched villages which, without inhabitants in summer, form the retreat of the Ararat Kurds when the approach of winter drives them from the heights. Here the plain assumes a more genial

---

[i.e., the river Araxes.]

aspect, extensive meadows and cornfields meet the view, and beyond these was a forest of tall reeds where, according to our zaptieh, wild swine make their lairs, while bears and wolves are to be found in the neighbouring heights. Thus far we kept to the plain, skirting the base of the mountain and following the salient and reentering angles of its shoots. But at length, after doubling a surging projection composed of broken masses of basalt, we struck to the left and commenced the ascent through a broad opening enclosed between vast ridges of volcanic formation. For the first hour after quitting the plain, the ascent was, with a few rough exceptions, easy and gradual. Our path followed the windings of a noisy stream which irrigates at intervals in its course patches of fertile land, yielding at this season wheat, or barley, or hay. On one of these plateaus, which spread out to some acres, a halt was unanimously agreed upon. Offsaddling and knee-haltering our horses, we gave them the range of the pasture, where they enjoyed their brief respite from toil, rolling, grazing, and fighting by turns.

We were soon reseated in our saddles, and now our way constantly increased in difficulty, becoming at every step more rocky and acclivitous. Our trusty little horses were, however, perfectly at home at this work; with the agility and circumspection of a cat, they carried us safely and jauntily over ground that would try the nerves of any one not accustomed to the horsemanship of Armenia.

After an hour or so of this tedious work we reached what might be designated the shoulder of the mountain. Here the ground became easier, the plateaus more frequent and extensive, and sheltered spots presented themselves suitable to the abode of man. The climate too was gradually changing for the better: instead of the hot air of the plain we were now inhaling a light breezy atmosphere, tempered with an occasional dash of cold, as every now and then a gust of wind fresh from the upper snows swept down upon us. With the advance of day a mantle of rolling clouds had gathered

round the cone; near at hand, however, there was
enough for present interest. We were now about 5000
feet above the plain, and as we were slowly working
our upward way we came upon the first encampment of
the Ararat Kurds. It was situated in a sheltered hollow
where there was good water and green pasture in
abundance; the black tents of Kedar harmonised well
with the character of the surrounding scenery, while the
dwellers therein, with their swart faces, piercing eyes
and outlandish dresses, gave the finish of life to the
whole. Our unexpected arrival and strange appearance
created an immense sensation amongst these wild people. They turned out in crowds to see us, but hospitali-
ty was their first thought; wooden bowls of "Iran," or
sour milk diluted with water, were brought forward in
quick succession, and not until we were sufficiently re-
galed did they give way to their curiosity: then old men
and maidens, haggard gypsy-like women and young
children, all gathered round to survey the strangers
from Frankestan; even their dogs, which, by the way,
are famed for strength and ferocity, manifested their
excitement by a sustained chorus of angry barking.

Pushing on thence, we passed these detached encampments at frequent intervals; and at 3 P.M. we
reached the quarters of the chief himself, at an elevation of about 6000 feet above the plain.

. . . .

These Kurds, as has been already stated, change
their place of abode with the seasons. In the month of
May, when the winter is well past, and spring vegetation has made some progress, they move with their
penates, families, and all they possess, to the heights,
returning to the plain towards the end of September,
when frequent atmospheric commotions announce the
dangers of a prolonged stay at such an elevation.

Their villages in the plain, which are thus deserted
for several months in the year, are of the most primitive description, being nothing more than mud contriv-
ances; in which the inmates, sheltered from cold, pass a

long hibernation, in company with their horses, sheep, and cattle, besides vermin of different sorts in visible swarms.

Rising with the first streak of dawn, the "fingan" of hot coffee was soon got ready and circled round. Every man charged himself with a small supply of provisions and a coil of strong jack-line in addition to his trusty pole with an iron spike at one end and a hook at the other. We had also among us a race-glass, a small hatchet, and a leather bottle of rum. Thus equipped we started off in full confidence of success, being accompanied by Iss-hak Bey and the zaptieh on horseback, and two or three men on foot. There was, however, one drawback to the anticipated pleasure of the day, namely the illness of the Rev. Mr. Thursby, by which we were deprived of his company. This illness, which happily was not of a serious nature, had come on during the night, and, as he required nothing but repose, we thought we might safely entrust him to the care of our Kurdish friends.

For the first hour or so our progress was comparatively easy, the ground differing but little from that which we had traversed on the preceding day—the same green plateaus, well-watered and in some places sheltered by huge ramparts of volacnic rock. At an hour's distance from the Bey's quarters, we came upon the most elevated of the detached encampments. It numbered seven tents, and was situated upon an extensive well-watered plateau, about 6000 feet above the level of the plain. Beyond this the aspect of nature became at every step more sterile, wild, and forbidding. The radiating ridges of basalt increased in height, became more rugged and impracticable. A track, known only to the mountaineers, enabled us, however, to make tolerable progress. After two hours we were obliged to relinquish our horses; for it was now a scramble up and down precipices, and over masses of broken rock, where only men or mountain-goats could find footing. It was pleasant to see every now and then, amid all this desolation, a patch of green peep out from beneath some sheltered nook, on which was to be found in abundance forget-me-nots, double daisies, gentianella, and primulas, all growing in unromantic fraternity with wild shallots. After three hours of stiff work, we arrived at the foot of the cone, which, owing to the continued fineness of the weather, we were enabled to see to the very summit; and it was no ordinary sight. We stood in the immediate presence of the vast cone-shaped mountain, 6000 feet high, covered with eternal snow to the very base!

Arrived at the foot of the cone, our Kurdish friends declined proceeding any further, and we held a consultation as to the best mode of ascending. Independence of thought and action is the well-known characteristic of Englishmen. This spirit, we need scarcely say, manifested itself in our council.[3] The end of it was that three decided upon trying the ascent on that part of the mountain that lay just in front of us, keeping as much as possible to the snow, while the fourth, Major Fraser, chose a line for himself, bearing away to the right, in the intention of availing himself as much as possible of those parts from which the snow had disappeared. His reasons were good. He had had much experience in rough mountain work in South Africa, where snow is unknown, and he did not deem it prudent on the present occasion to essay an element that he had not proved; whereas of the others, two were experienced Alpine travellers, accustomed to glaciers and eternal snows.

For the present, leaving Major Fraser to himself, let us follow the movements of the others. The line of ascent being determined on, the grand work of the day began in real earnest. It was now six o'clock, and we had already been three hours on foot, working upwards

---

[3] [A typical self-evaluation on the part of intrepid Englishmen in the century when "the sun never set on the British Empire!" Perhaps this chauvinism accounts in part for Stuart's readiness to believe that the non-Englishmen Parrot and Abich had been unsuccessful in their attempts to scale Ararat?]

against difficulties of no ordinary character; but as yet no one dreamt of fatigue; on the contrary, it appeared as if these three hours had been but a preparative for the day's work. A bit of unleavened bread, and an occasional mouthful of snow, served to sustain the strength and to ward off hunger, without loading the stomach or touching the wind—the two great evils to be avoided on occasions of great bodily exertion. For some time we held pretty well together, making on the whole satisfactory progress. But, after the first 1000 feet put differences in our climbing powers, the snow, with which previous experience had familiarised Theobald and Evans, sorely taxed the unaccustomed limbs of Major Stuart, who accordingly turned aside to a projecting ridge of broken basalt, which extended far up towards the summit. To one standing at the foot of the cone this ridge would present the appearance of a paved road, but it consisted in reality of huge masses of basalt, thrown together by volcanic force in making way over which the utmost agility and circumspection were required to guard against the chances of broken limbs.

At this time Theobald was some hundred yards in advance. Evans and Stuart had so far held pretty well together, but the latter now giving in, the former followed, with gradually increasing interval, on the traces of Theobald. On, on they went, higher and higher; now lost to sight in a fleecy cloud, now re-appearing, but diminished to little moving specks on the upper snows. The higher they ascended the greater the difficulties they had to contend with. As the air became more rarefied the action of the lungs was quickened, and every effort told more sensibly upon the strength. At the same time the angle of the slope continued to increase, while the footing became more difficult, because the upper part of the mountain is perpetually coated with an encrustation of ice, lightly sprinkled over with snow. For, during the summer months, the heat of the sun is sufficiently powerful to melt the snow in those elevated regions whenever the absence of clouds and mists permits his rays to have their full force; but let them be intercepted but for a moment, and their effects are counteracted by the normal temperature of the atmosphere, which at all seasons is below freezing point; over the icy crust thus formed the snow, swept from the neighbouring drifts by the never-ceasing wind, collects in a thin layer as fine and as dry as powder, deep enough in some places to conceal what is beneath, but not to afford a firm foothold.

The utmost circumspection is consequently required at each step in climbing this part of the mountain; and the spiked staff will be found of invaluable service, as well in sounding the surface as in aiding the precarious efforts of the feet. Theobald and Evans, as has been already noticed, were experienced Alpine climbers, and, being strong of limb and sound of wind, they held successfully on their upward course, without check, slip, or drawback, until at 2 o'clock P.M. the former crowned the final difficulty, and found himself on the summit of Mount Ararat. He was followed at an interval of about an hour by Evans, who, though less active, had equal perseverance.

Leaving them for a while to their own musings on this solemn height, let us now return to Major Stuart, whom we left, some three or four hours back, in an exhausted state 400 feet lower down. A feverish cold, from which he had been suffering for some days previously, had much impaired his strength, and thrown him out of that condition necessary to the performance of a severe or protracted physical effort. He did not feel this at starting; the excitement of the occasion, the first flush of returning health, and the bracing effects of mountain air, had inspired him with a premature confidence in his own strength. As we have seen, he got on very fairly for a time, holding his own with the others; but the undertaking was beyond his force, and he was obliged to give in after ascending about 2000 feet of the cone. Sitting down under the shelter of one of those masses of basalt over which he had been climbing, a drowsy feeling came over him, and he was soon fast asleep. In about an hour he awoke somewhat refreshed, and, on looking around, he found himself the object of attentive consideration to a number of ibises [ibexes] grouped on a rock close by, whence they could carry on their survey in safety. Curiosity and astonishment had imparted increased lustre to their beautiful eyes as they examined with earnest gaze this strange intruder on their domains. On perceiving him move they bounded away, springing with light unerring foot from point to point over the rocks, and soon were lost to view. What had led them up so far it would be hard to say, for at the level of 13,000 feet above the sea there is no vegetation except some scanty lichen, which could not serve for food to these animals. Some small birds were also seen on the wing at this height, but of what species there was not sufficient opportunity for judging. Above this all was solitude, silence, and snow.

Major Stuart, finding himself unable to proceed higher, now addressed himself to the task of descending. To accomplish this step by step would have been too laborious; he therefore resolved to try what could be done by a glissade. The angle of the mountain-slope with the horizon was in this place at about 35°. Taking his seat then on the snow, he looked well to his balance, steadied himself with his staff, and, giving way, off he went like an arrow shot from a bow, and in the course of a few minutes he found himself once more safe and sound at the foot of the cone. Iss-hak Bey, who, from a convenient position, was keeping close watch on every movement of our party, sent forward one of his men to meet the unsuccessful climber, received him with every demonstration of respect when he joined him, gave him his pipe and bade him welcome. "The English Bey is, no doubt, very brave and very enterprising," he said, "but he has attempted what is beyond the strength of man, and what, according to the traditions of my race, is contrary to the will of Allah. You were wise not to ascend any higher, and my heart is throbbing for the two other noble Beys who are this moment hidden from view far up among the driving mists, Allah Rerem (God is good)." "Fear not, great chief," replied the Major, "they are younger and more active men than I am, and, Inshullah, they will succeed." "Bakalum" (we'll see), was the only rejoinder; and the Major, returning to the chief his pipe, lay down on a green spot, sheltered from the sun's rays by an overhanging rock, and fell into a profound sleep, more grateful than Sybarite ever knew on bed of roses. From this almost comatose state he was suddenly recalled to waking existence by the exclamations of Isshak Bey and his attendants. Theobald had just gained the summit of the mountain; at that moment there was not a cloud to intercept the view, and, notwithstanding the great height and distance, the Kurds were able with the naked eye to follow all his movements. "Mashallah!" cried the chief, "God is great, and you English are wonderful people! We have always thought, and our fathers before us thought, that God had made that holy mountain inaccessible to man; many have tried to ascend it, but no one has ever succeeded until you come, and without any preparation walk straight up from the base to the top. Allah be praised! we have heard strange things of you, but now we see them with our own eyes."[4] All this time the Kurds were straining their keen, dark eyes towards the mountain-top, and exclamations of surprise, uttered in their native tongue, followed in quick succession as they watched the movements of the two climbers. The power of vision possessed by this people is truly astonishing; almost equalling that which Europeans attain by the means of telescopes. It can only be accounted for by the constant activity imposed upon the organ by their social habits, to which perhaps may be added their simple diet and the purity of the atmosphere in which they live.

As has been already mentioned, Mr. Theobald was the first to reach the summit; it was about two o'clock when he gained the highest point, where, after somewhat less than an hour, he was joined by Mr. Evans. After making a few observations as to the shape and

---

[4] [cf. our previous note.]

extent of the top, they commenced together the work of descending, and, keeping closely to their tracks of the morning, they got back in safety to the tents at 6:30 P.M.

We must now follow the movement of Major Fraser, who, it will be remembered, chose a line of his own. Diverging from the point where the others commenced the ascent, he skirted the base of the cone until he found what appeared a more practicable slope on the south-eastern side.

The plane from this point to the summit was apparently even and unbroken, and presenting an uninterrupted surface of snow, it seemed to promise easier work for the feet and in general greater facilities of ascent: therefore, notwithstanding the want of previous experience in snow-climbing, he determined on this line. As long as the snow was soft he found the work easy enough; step by step for hours he industriously kept a direct course, and had got within 1000 feet or so of the summit when he began to experience the difficulty of footing arising from the icy incrustation already described. In attempting to strike across to what appeared an easier line, he slipped in stepping on a sheet of ice lightly covered with snow, and, losing all control over himself, downwards he went with a rapidity which promised to bring him quickly to the point from which he started in the morning. Utterly unable to arrest his downward course, all he could do was to keep himself well on his back, body rigid, and legs stuck out. Natural instinct suggested these precautions; without which he might have spun round like a trencher, been deprived of consciousness and lost. As it was he came off unhurt. After a glissade of 1000 or 1200 feet, the snow, becoming deeper and softer, collected in such quantities between his legs as gradually to retard his speed, and at length it brought him to a stop. But now what was to be done? the loss of so much time, distance, and labour in an undertaking of this kind was certainly most serious, but failure from a cause of such trifling sound as a mere slip of the foot would have been worse than mortifying, it would have been ridiculous by his easy ride over the snow; so readjusting his nerves, and bracing up his energies for a renewed effort, he made his way with some difficulty across the snow to a ridge of basalt that, commencing near the summit, extended downwards about 2000 feet. This ridge consisted of masses of basalt, and over its crest Major Fraser now sought to make his upward way. Such resolution deserved its reward; by dint of great labour and perseverance he succeeded in gaining the summit at about 3:30, having exchanged signals with Theobald and Evans, who had by this time accomplished some hundred feet of the descent. After reaching the highest point, he kept to their tracks in descending, and got back to the tents at midnight.[5] His return was hailed with great satisfaction by the rest of

---

[5] [The following is an extract from a letter of Major Fraser, written from Erzurum on July 27, 1856 (published by Douglas W. Freshfield in his article, "Early Ascents of Ararat," *Alpine Journal*, VIII [1877], 220-21):

"A fortnight ago I had a most narrow escape of losing my life. I had proceeded to Persia, partly on duty, partly for pleasure, being near Mount Ararat, determined to try and ascend the great peak. . . . When within a few hundred feet of the summit . . . I suddenly slipped, and was shot downwards with the speed of lightning upwards of 1,000 feet; but instead of being dashed to pieces on the rocks at the foot of the glacier, some 4,000 feet below, I was stopped by the sprinkling of snow lying on the surface of the ice being pushed before me, which at length formed a sufficient heap to arrest my further progress. I need not say that I became insensible from the rapidity with which I shot over the surface of the ice, as my breath was quite stopped, being at an elevation of about 17,000 feet at the moment. But I had presence of mind enough to retain possession of my ice-staff as I fell, by the aid of which, after three hours' anxious and most fatiguing labour, I at length got off the surface of the glacier without further accident. I, however, had both hands frost-bitten to the second joints of the fingers, but they recovered, though I cannot yet feel them. It does not, however, prevent my using them, as you see. . . . I felt thankful for my miraculous escape from death, though I said little to my companions. I ascended the mountain *quite alone*, and in a different direction from my companions, which much increased my danger, as had I lain there all night, the cold would have killed me. I fell asleep thrice on the summit *alone* from the intense cold, and got back to the tents of the Koords, with whom we were staying, at midnight, having been twenty hours on foot, and quite alone."]

the party, who, as night wore on, had become more and more anxious for his safety; for it is easy to conceive how great are the dangers to which one would be exposed at night on those rugged heights with no light but the delusive glare of the snow and no shelter in the event of one of those sudden storms which often burst with terrific violence in elevated mountain regions. Our apprehensions had, nevertheless, yielded to the presence of fatigue, and we were all sunk in sleep and forgetfulness, when the fierce barking of the watch-dogs recalled us to consciousness, and before we could well collect our scattered thoughts, the Major entered the tent accompanied by a guide, whom he had procured at the upper encampment. A light was instantly struck, refreshment ordered, and while these were forthcoming we listened with breathless interest to the narrative of his day's adventures.

The Bey and some of his chief men were not long in making their appearance. They had altogether relinquished the hope of seeing the Major again, looking upon him as the victim which must needs have been sacrificed for what they considered an enterprise of temerity and folly; but when they saw him back amongst them, unscathed in life or limb, then indeed they began to feel the force of what we asserted, viz., that many things forbidden to the Kurds are allowed to the English.

. . . .

We have now done with the ascent as performed by Major Fraser and Messrs. Theobald and Evans. If the subject is not worn threadbare, we would ask the reader to accompany us while we briefly relate how the same feat was accomplished by the Rev. W. Thursby and Major Stuart. It may be said that we are going a second time over the same ground. This is substantially true; but still there will be found some features of separate interest not altogether unworthy of attention.

They set out early in the afternoon of the 13th of July, having decided upon devoting two days to the work. On the first, to ascend as far as might be deemed safe before sunset; then sheltering themselves as well as they could for the night, to finish the task on the following morning. Two young Kurds accompanied them from the tents, carrying their rugs and sheepskin cloaks, together with a small supply of provisions, consisting of unleavened bread, cold mutton, a small flask of brandy, and another of tea. Very litttle experience suffices to show that in threading difficult passes or breasting steep ascents, nothing is more injudicious than haste, or more fatiguing than a false step. The muscular effort necessary to retrieve the latter takes more out of a man than a hundred paces surely and effectively made. Aware of this fact, Major Stuart and his friend proceeded slowly and cautiously, husbanding their force with the utmost care, and looking well to their footing at every step. By this means they reached the foot of the cone with strength still unimpaired. They then turned off towards the south and began the ascent on a part of the south-eastern flank, which the combined action of sun and wind denuded in summer time of snow. By 6 o'clock P.M. they had gained an elevation of about 2000 feet above the base of the cone, and here their Kurdish attendants came to a stop and refused to proceed any further, alleging in justification ancestral traditions and the fear of treading on hallowed ground. The attempt to combat such arguments would have been a simple waste of time and words. In point of fact, the young Kurds had ascended higher than had been expected of them. They were accordingly dismissed in the most gracious manner possible; but to ensure their return in the morning for the rugs and coats, it was deemed advisable to detain their guns and swords, assigning as a reason the danger of wild beasts or robbers. There was some difficulty about this, for the Kurd does not feel to be himself without his beloved weapons; but every objection was overcome by the promise of bakshish (reward) a mode of persuasion by which we verily believe the Kurd could be induced to lay down his life, much more his arms. Major Stuart and Mr. Thursby, now left to themselves, set diligently to work to prepare shelter for the night. The wind was from the west, and blew sharp and strong. About 700 yards to their left, and nearly on the same level with them, lay a field of glaciers, the only ones to be seen on the southern slopes of the mountain. Their halting-place was on a mass of limestone-boulders that varied in size from one to five feet in diameter. To their right was a bed of snow, along the inner edge of which trickled a little thread of water, which no doubt was produced by the heat of the limestone acting on the snow. Here, on the lee side of the stony bank, they scooped out a hollow by removing the boulders, and piling them up to windward, they secured to themselves complete shelter from the wind. By a handy adjustment of the boulders, a tolerably level surface was obtained, six feet long by four in width, on which they could both lie down; they chose out a couple of smooth stones for pillows, and thus, with the addition of rugs and cloaks, no bad resting-place was prepared for the night.

Sunset was at hand by the time these operations were completed, and our adventurers now sat down to contemplate without distraction this glorious spectacle. The day had been fine throughout, and at the time we speak of there was not a cloud in the sky, nor a particle of mist to be seen in the vast horizon around. The sight, travelling far over the mountains and plains of Georgia, Azerbijan andKurdistan, was fairly lost in space and found its limit only in the dim amalgamation of earth and sky. The Araxes flowed eastward a mere thread of silver on the darkening landscape, and the lofty mountains of the panorama in front seemed dwarfed by comparison in their proportions. Bright sunlight shone above, while the shades of evening were gathering on the lands beneath. These shades continued to deepen as the sun dipped lower on the horizon, until at length the darkness of night set in on the plains, while the upper regions of the mountains were still clothed in light. As long as light lingered in the western sky, the vast shadow of the mountain was to be seen

174 THE QUEST FOR NOAH'S ARK

stretching far away eastward, and clearly defining its form on the distant horizon.

The fine weather of the day did not change when darkness set in, and glorious was the sight when through the clear ether the hosts of heaven shone forth with a brilliancy and living lustre that almost dazzled the eyes. Far above the reach of lowland exhalations and in a highly-rarefied atmosphere one almost feels the presence of the heavenly bodies. Our two friends felt all the influence of this glorious sky, and of the position in which they were. Behind them was the snow-clad peak of the ancient mountain, carved, as it were, out of the dark sky. In front was the lesser mountain, regular in outline and symmetrical in form. There are many who believe that the Aghri Dagh of Armenia is identical with the Mount of Ararat of Holy Writ—others again affirm, and not without strong reasons, that on the subsidence of the Flood the Ark rested on Ghibil Indi, a mountain of Kurdistan. Without pretending to weigh the merits of these conflicting opinions we may observe that the popular belief throughout Central Asia is favourable to the former. The Kurdish tribes who dwell on the slopes and at the base of the Aghri Dagh, and whose forefathers have been there since the earliest dawn of history, the native Christians of Georgia and Armenia—all indeed who preserve the traditions of the land—are familiar with the story of the Deluge. Their account of that great event varies but slightly from that which has been transmitted to us by Moses, and they hold it as part of their faith that Noah's Ark rested on Aghri Dagh, that the hull still remains on the summit deeply buried out of sight, and investing with a sacred character the place thus chosen to be, as it were, the second cradle of the human race, they believe that to scale the mountain is not only impossible, but that any attempt of the kind would be followed with the immediate displeasure of Heaven. The failure, often disastrous, which, as they allege, had attended all such previous attempts were well calculated to strengthen this belief. They have a distinct knowledge of every visit made to the mountain

by adventurous travellers within the last fifty years, and
Iss-hak Bey furnished us with many interesting details
of the dangers which some of them had run and of the
accidents which befell them in vainly endeavouring to
gain the summit. He remembered all about Parrot's
attempt in 1829. Parrot tried on the north side, but
signally failed. Nevertheless, he published an account
of his expedition, in which he took credit for complete
success.[6] The description given by him of the top had
been adopted by the editor's of the 'Imperial Gazetteer,'
viz.: "Top gently vaulted, nearly cruciform surface,
about 200 paces in circuit, towards east this summit is
connected by a flattish depression with another summit
distant 397 yards." This description is confirmed by
Professor Abich, who, acting under instructions from
the Russian Government, made the attempt in 1845,
and according to his published narrative, reached the
summit with six companions on the 29th July.

Now, Iss-hak Bey had distinct knowledge of the
particulars of Abich's expedition as well as of Parrot's,
and pronounced it, like the rest, unsuccessful[7]—of
which, by the way, further proof will be given as we
proceed. As to the description above given, it varies almost irreconcilably with the observations of every individual of the party whose successful performances we
are now recording. The summit, as seen by them, is in
the form of a scalene triangle, the base, which is on the
eastern side, lying nearly due north and south, being
about 100 yards in length, the perpendicular about 300
yards. The base forms a ridge with an elevation of 15
yards at the southern extremity, subsiding gradually towards the north where it merges with the level of the
summit. The apex of the triangle is the highest point of
the mountain; separated from it by a dip, 70 yards
wide and 25 deep, is another point which attains very
nearly the same height. The area of the triangle is level,

---

[6] [cf. above, the introductory paragraph to Parrot's account where
his documentary evidence is cited.]

[7] [For the attestations Abich secured, in Armenian and Russian,
see his articles in the journal *Caucasus* for 1846.]

or rather slightly concave, suggesting the idea of an extinct crater. Such is the summit of Mount Ararat according to the concurrent observations of our party; we leave to others the task of accounting for the discrepancies which exist on this subject between us and other writers. Hundreds of Kurds were eyewitnesses of our ascent. These same Kurds confidently assert the failure of the travellers whose names we have quoted and of all others by whom the attempt had been previously made. To their testimony we may add that of Mr. James Brant, who, from 1835 to 1855, filled the post of British Consul at Erzeroum. The accuracy and extent of this gentleman's information as a traveller, as a man of science, and observer of passing events, give great weight to whatsoever he may say on matters connected with Armenia.

In walking on the summit of Mount Ararat one sinks about midway to the knee in the snow, which is so fine and dry, that it does not adhere to or wet the boots; but it rises like dust to the wind, blinding the eyes and penetrating the clothes and pockets. The rocks on the sides of the mountain consist chiefly of trachyte porphyry, and the effects of strong volcanic action may be seen wheresoever the natural surface is exposed. There are deep gorges, precipitous cliffs, and ridges of broken rock, from which masses occasionally detach themselves and roll to the bottom, leaving deep furrows on the snow, over which they pass. There are two extinct craters on the eastern side of the mountain, just above the saddle, which connects it with Lesser Ararat: one on a level with the bridle-path, which communicates with that part of the mountain; the other a thousand feet higher, to reach which one must climb a steep incline formed of lava and scoria. Lava, scoria, and pumice have also been found in other parts of the mountain; and from an exposed spot near the summit, there is a strong sulphureous emanation; while the parts immediately adjacent are warm to the touch. We may observe, that on this spot are to be found particles of mica, some of which are as large as a kidney-bean. Here there had evidently been volcanic action, for the surface consisted chiefly of triturated scoria and other volcanic substances. It will be remembered that in July, 1840, there was a violent eruption, which seemed to issue from a large natural chasm on the north side. This eruption destroyed the ancient monastery of St. James,[8] and buried in ruins the village of Arguri, situated more than 6000 feet above the level of the sea, and rendered venerable by the Armenian tradition, which indicates it as the place where Noah planted the vine after his descent from the mountain. Arguri signifying in the Armenian language, "the planting of the vine."

At length the first dawn of day appeared, that cold pale light that spreads over the eastern horizon when the sky is clear of clouds and the atmosphere of vapours. Rising from their bed of stone, our travellers addressed themselves at once to the work before them, in high spirits at the prospect of continued fine weather. A few mouthfuls of unleavened bread served them for breakfast, for they decided, wisely, as we think, to trust as long as possible to the strength of the ample dinner they had made overnight, by which means the lungs would be less impeded in their functions; they would have more room to expand in the act of respiration, and the system would consequently suffer less from the effects of the rarefied air. Were this plan more generally adopted by mountain climbers, we should hear less of failures from apoplectic sysmptoms, such as difficulty of breathing, vertigo, blood rushing to the head and escaping through the ears and nostrils, all of which result from a full stomach, or from a fulness of habit, either chronic or temporary, which circumscribes the action of the lungs at a time when their utmost capacity is required to obtain a sufficient supply of oxygen from the rarefied atmosphere. Most healthy men possess a reserve of strength that will carry them through a heavy day's work without food. The stomach, especially in the case of persons accustomed to regular and generous diet, may rebel against this; but after the first few mur-

---

[8] [i.e., St. Jacob's monastery.]

murings, it will settle down into a sullen acquiescence; and in such situations as we are now speaking of, the more vigorous action of the lungs will go far to supply what may be wanting.

Major Stuart and Mr. Thursby had soon full proof of the truth of these remarks. Quietly and steadily they moved upwards, making as little effort as possible, husbanding their forces, looking out the securest footing, and halting at frequent intervals. They climbed cat-like over difficult projections, or along the face of perpendicular escarpments, they hung to butting cliffs, traversed inclined sheets of ice as smooth as glass, and poised themselves on giddy pinnacles of rock. Hour after hour this laborious work continued, but, thanks to the system they had adopted, without producing fatigue, or sensibly taxing their strength.

They were marvellously aided, too, by their iron-tipped staves. The staff is to the mountain climber what the oar is to the Laplander, the helm to the ship, the break to a carriage. It helps him in all his movements, ascending and descending. If he makes a false step, it enables him to recover himself. Is the incline difficult it serves the ascent as an extra limb of ten-leg power, on the descent as a drag or lever; does he fancy a glissade down the snow, with it he steers his course, checks or modifies his speed, or brings to at pleasure. In fact its uses are so varied, and so applicable to every situation, that it must be considered an indispensable part of the mountain traveller's equipment.

On a rocky spot, about 1200 feet from the summit, and under the western lee of a high mural ridge, is a cross, which records the expedition of Professor Abich in 1845. It is made of oak, the upright being 7 feet above ground, the transverse bar 3 feet in length, and it is firmly wedged in between two large masses of rock that lie close to each other. From the action of the weather the surface of the wood has become so soft that it may be scraped off with the nail of the finger to the depth of one-eighth of an inch. On a brass plate 6 inches by 4, screwed on at the inter-section of the bars, is engraved in Russian the professor's name, and date of his ascent. Several mutton-bones, partially decomposed, lie at the foot of the cross, and a kama or short Turkish sword, which was in very fair preservation, the blade, though without a scabbard, having suffered but little from rust. Major Stuart took possession of this kama, and should any future traveller reach the summit of Mount Ararat he may, perhaps, find it on the highest point, where the Major stuck it arm-deep in the snow.

With respect to this cross, it may be asked why Abich planted it so far down from the summit, if, as he asserts, he and his party reached the highest point? It would have been easy to have found as secure a position anywhere up to 1000 feet higher.

About 9 o'clock A.M. our friends had the satisfaction of gaining the highest point of the mountain, and with hearts brimful of loyalty, and somewhat elated by the occasion, they drank their Sovereign's health, as the fittest mode of giving expression to their feelings.[9]

. . . .

Early on the morning of the 16th preparations were commenced for the return to Bayazid. A breakfast in the highest style of Kurdish cooking was got ready betimes; milk, new and clotted, mutton, roast and boiled, and fresh chupaties in abundance, all hot and smoking from the embers; then came coffee and pipes, after which the zaptieh announced that all was in readiness. The cavalcade set out, headed, as usual, by the Bey, who was mounted on his favourite mare, equipped in all the finery of gay clothes and cumbrous arms. Retracing their previous steps, they descended the mountain, crossed the plain, and arrived at Bayazid about midday, when the whole party was again honoured with a reception by the Vaali. He congratulated the English gentlemen on their achievement, adding that it would be his duty to make a special report on the subject without delay to his Government. He probably attributed the expedition to some secret motives of policy

---

[9] [Parrot, Abich, and Khodzko had considered the planting of a Cross more fitting!]

or espionage, for the Turk is slow in believing that a man in the enjoyment of his senses will expose himself to difficulties and dangers from the mere love of adventure.

Be that, however, as it may, it is now registered among the State archives at Constaninople that in August, 1856, five English gentlemen succeeded in reaching the highest point of Mount Ararat.

5

Just Short of the Summit:
Freshfield (1868)

*Douglas W. Freshfield (1845-1934), classical schol-
ar, alpinist, and editor of the Alpine Journal,*
failed to achieve the summit of Ararat. We nevertheless
include his report of the attempt because the distinguished gentleman and his party came within 800 to
1,000 feet of success. Like the American Alpine Club
expedition almost a century later, the Freshfield report
indicates the difficulties attendant on climbing Ararat.
The excerpt below is taken from Freshfield's* Travels in
the Central Caucasus and Bashan *([1869], pp. 155-
62).*

On the morning of June 7th [1868], we set off from
Aralykh on our expedition against Ararat. We were
accompanied by a Kurd chief, in the Russian service—
in whose charge the Colonel had placed us—and his
servant; four Persians, the owners of the horses, and
three Kurds, who were supposed to be mountaineers,
and capable of acting as porters.

Starting on horseback for a 'grand course' is not
quite in accordance with Alpine ideas; but when it is
remembered that Aralykh is only 2,600 feet above the
sea, and that the lower slopes of Ararat are perfectly
uniform, bare and stony, we shall be excused for
avoiding the dreary grind up them, under an Araxes-
valley sun. At first we kept a course parallel to the
river, but soon turned towards the great mountain, and
began to ascend sensibly. We next skirted the base of a
green bastion commanding the lower slopes, in the hollows and the shelves of which several groups of Kurd

---

* On Freshfield, see the 5th supplement to the *Dictionary of
National Biography.*

tents were pitched. A somewhat steep ascent led up to
the green plain which fills the space between the bases
of the two Ararats. The Little Ararat rose immediately
before us in a unbroken slope of about 4,000 feet; it is
a typical volcano, uniform on all sides, but least steep
on the Turkish, from which a Russian General is said
to have ridden up on horseback.

On our right the base and upper portion of the cone
of the Great Ararat were visible; the lower part being
masked by buttresses, and the whole mass most deceit-
fully foreshortened. On a knoll about 300 feet above
the plain we found the group of huts which have been
used as a resting-place by most of the explorers of
Ararat. These queer dwellings are underground bur-
rows, constructed like the villages on the Georgian
steppes. A door of twisted twigs, on being opened, reveals a hole in the hillside, which forms the mouth of a
long, winding, dark passage leading into two or more
chambers lighted by holes in the roof. The floor of
these horrid caverns is the natural soil, and their atmosphere is earthy and tomb-like, while the darkness that
pervades them adds to their depressing effect. The
roofs are formed of branches covered with turf, and as
there is nothing outside to distinguish them from the
solid ground, it is easy to walk over them unawares.
One of our horses, while grazing, suddenly sank into
one of these dangerous traps, and was left, with only its
forequarters emerging from the ground, in a position
from which it was extricated with great difficulty.

On the way up we halted, and discussed our arrangements with the Kurd chief. We had been told
below that we should find all we wanted at the huts;
but they now proved to be uninhabited, and it was
therefore necessary to get a further supply of bread at
one of the encampments lower down. The porters
wished also to borrow a tent. We remonstrated at the
delay this would occasion. It was quite early in the day,
for we had reached the huts at 11:15 A.M., and being
anxious to sleep as high as possible, we proposed to the
men that they should go on with us at once, carrying
our rugs, in which we were prepared to pass the night.

We had provisions enough for ourselves, and we pointed out to them, that if they were afraid of sleeping out
at such a height, or had not sufficient food to last till
morning, they would have time before nightfall to return to the huts, where they might sleep, and remount
next day to fetch down our rugs and other baggage.
The men, not unnaturally, were averse to the double
toil and trouble involved in this plan, and utterly declined to carry it out, or to join us in sleeping out without shelter and a further supply of food. We were
therefore obliged to remain at the huts, and await the
arrival of the tent and provisions.

Our position was curiously like and unlike many old
Alpine bivouacs. The surrounding pastures might have
been on the Riffelberg, and it was delightful to see
again many well-known Alpine flowers. The rhodo-
dendron indeed was sought for in vain, and were too
low for gentians; but their lack was partially compen-
sated by a new friend, a dwarf wild hyacinth, white de-
licately streaked with blue, which grew in great profu-
sion. Little Ararat, however, was sufficiently unlike a
Swiss mountain to dispel any illusion, and if that had
not sufficed, one glance down his side into the brown,
bare, burnt-up trough of the Araxes would have been
enough to recall to our minds the fact that we were in
Asia, far indeed from the old haunts.

After midday, clouds gathered, and Ararat indulged
in his usual thunderstorm. Some hours passed, but the
men did not reappear, and we were getting more and
more impatient, when about 3:30 P.M. they came into
sight, followed by a cow, carrying one of the regular
Kurd tents, too large to be useful for mountaineering,
and too heavy to be carried by our men over rough
ground. The three porters now professed themseves
ready to go without a tent, but a second thunderstorm
delayed our start till 4:30. With fuel we had load
enough for four men; but as the owners of the horses
declined to be of any service, François and Paul had to
carry one of the bags between them.

Striking up the spur behind the huts, we made our
way as directly as possible towards the mountain, tra-

versing a good deal of rough ground, and crossing several hollows, by which we lost time, and partially decieved ourselves as to the progress made. The porters halted constantly, and our pace was slow; in about an hour and a half after leaving the huts, we found ourselves in a hollow between two spurs, and nearly at the snow-level. Here the porters stopped, and declined venturing upon the snow. It was a good place for a bivouac, and, although probably 500 feet lower, we thought we were at a height of at least 9,000 feet. We knew that the moon would allow us to start at midnight, and anxious moreover to save our men the fatigue of acting as porters, we agreed to halt. The weather looked promising, so we supped on 'Liebig' cheerily over a bright fire, and then rolled ourselves up in our rugs, with little misgiving for the morrow, despite the hindrances of the day.

After a sound sleep (at least I speak for myself) we were awake and stirring at 11:30 P.M. We had a glass of hot wine all round, and started at 12:10 a.m. The first *contretemps* was the discovery that François had, despite my warning, allowed Paul to leave Tiflis without proper boots, and that it was impossible he could come on with us. He had set his heart upon ascending Ararat, and therefore very reluctantly turned back.

After climbing two snow-slopes, we gained a ridge commanding a view of the ground between us and our mountain. In front lay a deep hollow, such as in the Alps would be filled by a glacier; the ridge along which we were proceeding appeared to be connected with, or rather to form a continuation of others, by which it was possible to make the circuit of the hollow, and reach the foot of the great rocks, which we had, for convenience and old acquaintance' sake, named 'les Grands Mulets.'

In the first hour and half we had cleared a good deal of ground, and I remarked to Tucker how well we were getting on, and how 'fit' I felt. Nemesis was at hand. In another half-hour, though the ground was easy and the inclination trifling, I began to feel unwell, and experienced all the sensations of mountain-sickness, generally ascribed to the rarity of the air. In the present case, too much telega-travelling and want of training supplied a sufficient cause. Meantime the moon was shining gloriously in a cloudless sky, lighting up the huge white cone above us, and the distant ranges beyond the Araxes. Unluckily, I got worse instead of better, and was obliged to delay our progress by frequent halts. We were now beginning to climb the actual cone, and the rock-ridge, though still easy, became steeper. When fairly on the face of the 'Grands Mulets,' after three hours of feeble and intermittent progress, 'the force of nature could no further go,' and I sadly succumbed, leaving François and Tucker to go on and, as I hoped, to prosper. This was about 6 A.M. The sun was already high, and the air was pleasantly warm.

I was left on a shelf of the rock with a cup of wine and some food. For the latter I felt no inclination; as for the wine, it was soon disposed of by my dozing off and upsetting it with my arm, leaving barely a wineglassful of liquid as my provisions for the morning.

After the first doze I made an attempt to follow my companions, but soon found it useless; so I resigned myself to fate, and lay down, now in one nook of the rocks, now in another, sometimes dreaming oddly, as one does in odd places, sometimes gazing drowsily over the top of Little Ararat (12,800 feet) into Persia, or over the Kara Dagh ranges to the white line of the Eastern Caucasus. The sun got very hot, and my head ached horribly; so I scrambled round the rocks to a shaded shelf, whence I could see far into Kurdistan, a region of snowy mountains and bare valleys. A streak below me was the infant Euphrates, but I did not feel much the better for seeing it. Of the Garden of Eden no tradition seems to linger even in this land of old stories, and if these barren hills were ever clothed by the groves of the earthly Paradise, the change has been complete indeed. My state of mind at the time scarcely made me a fair judge of the view, but I will try to give the impression that produced upon me, as compared with European mountain panoramas. Most people have seen in a sculptor's studio a block of marble hewn

down to the rough outline of the group which he has it
in his mind to produce. From a distance the eye catches
a certain grandeur of effect which closer inspection de-
stroys, by revealing that the parts are in themselves but
rough and shapeless masses. So it is with these mountains of Kurdistan. On them the great sculptor, Nature,
seems to have 'tried her prentice hand' before she had
learnt how to chisel out with her graving-tools, frost
and heat, the torrent and the glacier, those exquisite
outlines of peak and valley which are a distinguishing
feature of the Alps and the Caucasus. The first impression I received was,—what a wilderness of mountains!
—in every direction nothing met the eye but snowy
masses, lying in heaps instead of ranges. The general
effect was exceedingly grand and impressive; but when
the details were examined in search of some beautiful
peak, the search was in vain. The slopes were charac-
terised by dreary monotony, and the summits were
without form or beauty. One distant mass (Bingol
Dagh?) alone deserved to escape the general condem-
nation.

Time wore on, and at length, about 1:30 P.M., a
shout above me announced Tucker's return. I augured
ill from it, for it was not a cheerful 'jödel,' but I returned a hope that he might, for my sake, be subduing
his feelings. To my surprise, the next shout came from
below, and I knew that my companion must have descended by another route. Through the light cloud that
was hanging on the mountain, I soon saw the two figures, and before long had joined them and heard their
story.

The rocks above my halting-place turned into an
arête, cut into towers, separated by deep gaps. The
climbing here was exceedingly difficult, and the passage
of some of the gaps required both care and steadiness.
Fortunately, the ridge was not very long, and in an
hour and a half from the place where I had stopped, a
snowy saddle connecting the rocks with the upper mass
of the cone was gained. Here they rested for half an
hour, at a height probably of 13,800 feet. Above them
stretched interminable snow-slopes, seamed here and

there by rocks, but, unluckily, rocks of an utterly use-less description to the climber. They were not ridges, but disconnected crags of lava, suggesting by their fantastic shapes the idea that half the animals, after leaving the Ark, had been petrified as they came down the mountain. Here was an elephant, glissading elegantly, using his trunk for an alpenstock; there a tapir, or some antediluvian-looking beast, by whose untimely fate, now for the first time discovered, naturalists have lost a species.

Before long the snow took the form of hard névé, and it was necessary to cut steps. François was by this time so exhausted that he could do no more; Tucker, however, pushed on alone, and by cutting about 1,000 steps, succeeded in reaching a point a little under 16,000 feet.* Such work, at a height equal to that of Mont Blanc, cannot be continued for ever, without long training; his breath began to fail, and his head to throb painfully, so that he was obliged to rest every twenty or thirty steps. The tremendous staircase required to reach the summit was not to be accomplished single-handed, and at 12:10 P.M.—after nearly four hours' solitary work, the top looking as far off as ever, and clouds collecting rapidly round the mountain—Tucker turned to descend. Having rejoined François, they returned quickly together down the tracks made in the ascent, avoiding the rocky arête, by slithering down the snow-slope on its left, which had been hard-frozen in the morning.

We plunged gloomily through soft snow, and over the tiresome rough lava-crags, and, despite the mists, found it easy to follow our old track to the spot where we had left the Kurds. They now shouldered with ease the burdens under which they had groaned and staggered the evening before, and led off at a quick pace for the huts, where we arrived about 6 P.M., having halted often on the way. The last part of the walk was

* We estimated it afterwards, carefully, as between 1,000 and 800 feet below the top. [In 1970, my son David came within 550 meters or 1800 ft. of the summit; see below, "Ark Fever."]

in rain, Ararat having succeeded in his daily task of collecting a shower in otherwise fine weather. We regained the huts at 6:30 P.M., having been 18½ hours out.

6

One-Man Conquest and a Relic: Bryce (1876)

James Bryce (1838-1922) was one of the most distinguished individuals ever to ascend Mt. Ararat. His brilliant career as an English statesman, jurist, and author began in 1864 when, at the age of twenty-six, he published an exceedingly important study, the Holy Roman Empire. *While Bryce was Regius Professor of Civil Law at Oxford, he published* The American Commonwealth *(1888), yet another classic work, and one which evidenced an understanding and admiration for American institutions that eventually won for him an appointment as ambassador to the United States. For his services to the Empire Bryce was created a viscount in 1913. It was neither scholarly research nor an embassy, however, which brought Bryce to the Ararat region in 1876. He was simply taking a vacation—if such a thing is possible for a man of his energy and curiosity. Bryce could no more resist climbing Mt. Ararat while in Transcaucasia than he could disregard the plight of the Armenian people with whom he associated; his humane concern for these people led him to found the Anglo-Armenian Society and to urge their cause in the House of Commons. The following is a composite account by Bryce's ascent of Ararat taken from his three publications containing narratives of the event: "The Ascent of Ararat,"* Alpine Journal, *VIII, (1877),*[1] Transcaucasia and Ararat *(1877)*[2]*; and "On Armenia and Mount Ararat,"* Proceedings of the Royal Geographical Society, *XXII (1878).*[3]

---

[1] Pp. 208-210, 211-12.
[2] Pp. 264-65, 279, 281-83.
[3] Pp. 174, 177, 183, 185-86.

Every one must be interested in a mountain which figures so largely in the early history of our race. Ararat, however, cannot be specifically identified with any particular mountain mentioned in the Bible. You remember that the phrase in the Bible is: "the Ark rested in the tenth month on the mountains of Ararat." Now Ararat is used in the Bible there, and also in one or two other places, as a name for Armenia; or, at least, for the part of Armenia in which our mountain lies, that is the northern part. Therefore the biblical passage only goes to this, that the Ark rested upon a mountain in the district which the Hebrews knew as Ararat, or Armenia. At the same time our mountain is so very much higher, more conspicuous, and more majestic than any other summit in Armenia, that one could hardly doubt that if the Biblical writer had any particular mountain present to his mind, it must have been our Mount Ararat. No one who had ever seen it could have any doubt that if the Ark rested anywhere in that part of the world, it rested upon that particular summit. It is so much higher, so much more isolated, so much more imposing than any other, that it is just the place where an ark ought to rest. And whatever the local legends may be worth, there can be no doubt that there are legends, going back for hundreds or thousands of years, which assign this particular mountain as the scene of the Flood, although the native names for the peak are Massis (Armenian) and Aghri Dagh (Turkish).

Perhaps the best thing I can do, in order to give you some idea of what the mountain is like, will be to describe, in as few words as I can, the ascent which I had the good fortune to make to the summit of Great Ararat in the month of September 1876.

Ararat is a huge conical, or rather dome-shaped mass, descending in comparatively gentle slopes and terraces to the NW. and N., but very steeply in all other directions. Towards the NE. and E., where it is pierced by a profound chasm, it presents magnificient black precipices, capped by icebeds of enormous thickness; and from this side the summit is quite inaccessible. On the opposite or SW. side, the slope is less abrupt, but this side is in Turkish territory, and is therefore in many respects less convenient for the traveller. The ascents, so far as I know, have all been made either from the NW., which was the route taken by Parrot in his third and successful attempt, or else from the SE., the line of Abich (the distinguished geologist who has done so much for our knowledge both of Armenia and the Caucasus) in 1845, and of General Chodzko in 1850; as also of the English party, whose ascent, made in 1856, has recently been fully described in the 'Geographical Society' Proceedings,' vol. xxi. No. 1[1], for although they started from Bayazid[2] on the SW. of the mountain, they do not seem to have attacked the SW. side of the cone, but to have followed, apparently by chance, the path of Abich up its SE. slope. To anyone looking at Ararat from the Aras[3] plain on the N. or E., the NW. ascent seems the easiest, for the snow slopes there, although long, are mostly gentle. Abich, indeed, tells us that he failed on this side owing to the steepness of the ice; but in 1844 mountain climbing, and especially snow work, was still in its infancy, and a party of three or four good walkers, with a rope and ice axes, ought to find this route sufficiently simple. To a solitary climber the fatigue of step-cutting would no doubt be very great, and I had reason to be glad that fortune led me to try the cone on its SE. declivity, where it is possible to make one's way to the summit with very little of that kind of labour.

My friend and I started from Aralykh, a Russian military station on the right bank of the Araxes, where we had been most hospitably entertained by the colonel in command, at 8 A.M., on the morning of Monday, September 11, 1876, with an escort of five mounted Cossacks, who were supposed to be needed as a protection against robbers. We marched at first nearly S.,

---

[1] [Bryce refers here to Stuart's party.]

[2] [i.e., Dogubayazit.]

[3] [i.e., the Araxes.]

over a very gentle slope, towards the foot of the mountain, then SW. up a slightly steeper incline; and a little before noon began to mount more rapidly, traversing the ESE. declivity in a transverse direction, and keeping behind a great lumpy buttress which reaches a height of some 7,300 feet. Passing a small Kurdish encampment, we reached, at 2 P.M., the highest Cossack military post. Here at a spot called Sardarbulach, where is one of the few springs to be found on the mountain, eight or ten men are stationed on the open alpine pasture that separates Great and Little Ararat. The height is nearly 8,000 feet above the sea, but the air is so clear that one neither perceives how far distant one still is from the base of the proper cone of Great Ararat, nor can believe that its summit is 9,000 feet above the spectator. Everyone had told us that success depended entirely on being able to sleep high, as near the snow line as possible, and we were therefore anxious to push on at once. Horses, however, could not be taken further; the Cossacks refused to carry even the trifling load of provisions and wrappings required for sleeping in the open air, and by the time that Kurds had been collected and a bargain made with them it was past four o'clock, too late to get far up before nightfall. Reluctantly, therefore, we halted at Sardarbulach, and got some sleep from nine o'clock till midnight. At 1 A.M., the crescent moon having risen high enough to give a little light, we set off with four Kurds carrying our baggage, and no less than seven Cossacks, why, it would be hard to say. Our interpreter was not strong enough to accompany us, so being unable to speak either Russian or Kurdish we had no means of communicating with any of our party, who merely knew in a general way that we wished to go to the top, and that they were to come as far with us as they could or pleased. The progress of this caravan over the rocky ground, traversed by rough volcanic ridges, which we had to cross in our north-western course towards the cone from Sardarbulach, was very slow, not only owing to the darkness, but also because the Cossacks insisted on sitting down to rest whenever the track became steeper

Mount Ararat viewed from Erivan in 1670 (reproduced from Struys' *Voyages* [1684]).

Mount Ararat, with the monastery of St. James in the fore-ground (totally destroyed with the town of Arguri [Ahuri] in the blowout of June 20-23, 1840); reproduced from Parrot, *Journey to Ararat* [1845], p. 164.

Abich's view of Greater Ararat as seen from the peak of Lesser Ararat in August, 1844 (from the *Bulletin de la Société Géologique de France*, 2nd ser. VIII [1850-1851], facing page 265).

Photograph of Navarra taken by the author on the site of the Gaz de France plant in Rouen (June 2, 1970), together with his dedicatory card to him ("To my friend John Montgomery with my best wishes. F. Navarra").

Wood fragment and map given to the author by Fernand Navarra on June 2, 1970. The fragment is taken from the large piece of 5,000-year-old tooled wood which Navarra brought back from Ararat. The hand-drawn map shows where the wood was found: above Lake Kop (3,750 meters), beyond Navarra's camp (4,100 meters), and over the glacier at a still higher level.

Ararat, with Turkish military emplacements in the foreground.

Dogubayazit

In the Kent Hotel, Dogubayazit. Standing: Dr. Montgomery, mountaineering — guide Yücel Dönmez, hotel manager Fahrettin Kolan.

Packing equipment in the Kent Hotel.

Lesser Ararat viewed from Greater Ararat in the course of our climb.

Our base camp at 3,800 meters.

David reaches his limit—550 meters from the peak—the youngest Westerner known to have attained this altitude on Ararat.

My two compaions, with Turkish ensigns, on the final approach to the peak. Abich's summit is on the left. Parrot's (actually the higher) is on the right.

The author on the peak: 1:30 P.M., Monday August 17, 1970.

The author and one of his Kurdish companions on the summit; Navarra's tattered tricolor is visible.

Dr. Montgomery removing his crampons just below the ice cap on the descent.

Benson, Arizona. Box 814   85602
March 27, 1967.

Dear Mr. Cummings,

Since I talked to you last evening, I have been called over to Benson, (35 miles from Willcox) to do some work on some mining claims and I will probably be here for several days.

Inclosed, you will see some crude drawings designating the position in which the "vessel" was filmed   and from these you might get some concept as to what I have been telling you about. I wish that it were possible that I could make a trip over there, with you all, but I think that within the next 18 months that I, too will go over there. If I remember correctly, it seems that the Scripture stated that the "ark came to rest on the mountians of Ararat" and if it did (which I thoroughly believe) it might cover a large area to exploit. If we can find it; it will be the most important discovery that the modern world has ever knewn, and it will PROVE everything but men like you and I do not requi such evidence as we are wise enough to know that it did exhist, without having to see it. It is a pity that the rest of the world dont awaken to the fact.

With the kindest of regards to you and hoping that the "great vessel" can be found, I am

Most cordially yours,

Fred E. Drake.

The Drake sketch, based upon the lost photographs of George Jefferson Greene.

Photograph showing unidentified object on the north face of Ararat. (Our colleague, Mr. Mark Albrecht, determined in consultation with several photographic experts that this object is entirely foreign to the material of the mountain.)

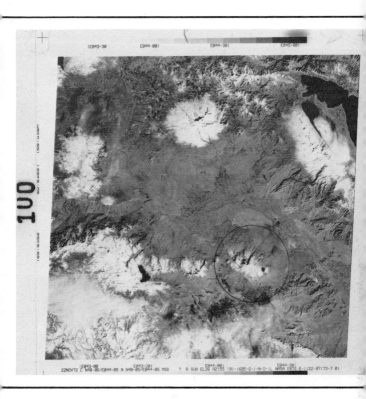

ERTS satellite photograph of Ararat Region (Greater and Lesser Ararat included).

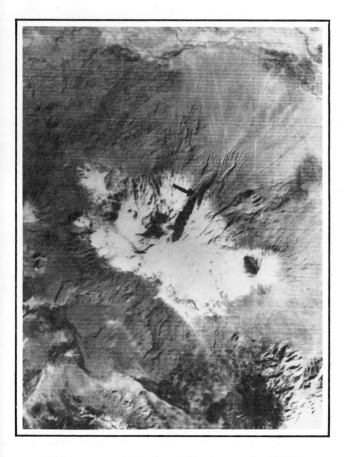

Enlargement of the Ararat Region on the ERTS satellite photograph.

SHADOW AREA

Near rectangular shape, slightly blurred, but it looks unnatural. It seems surrounded by dense shadow. (Sun time is about 10:20 A.M.) It is comparable in width to a 65' wide bridge at Pierre, So. Dakota. Length is much shorter—the bridge is about 1500' to 1600' long.

Estimated length 1,000 feet overall. Infrared film, Band 7 shows whiter area within this formation — size too small to determine.

Elongated shape—rough edges, fuzzy, likely a part of mountain terrain.

This is an approximate sketch of what appears on the film under a microscope. At this magnification, the film emulsion almost began to get grainy and break up. It is possible that the ark would have gray coloring that would be difficult to see against the ground unless it, being hollow, had snow on top of it with it melted on the ground around it. This feature is fuzzed out on the large photo, but can be seen on the smaller print. Enlargements lose detail.

Sketch of rectangular shape on Mount Ararat as displayed by ERTS Imagery. (Prepared by M. Delaney, Earth Resources Observation Satellite Center, Sioux Falls, South Dakota.)

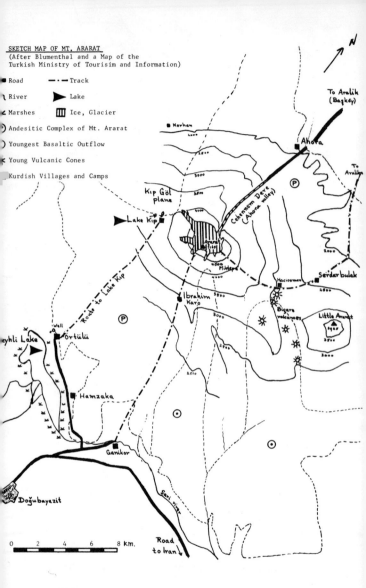

The mapping of Mount Ararat by the Archeological Research Foundation. (Taken from the combined report of the 1964 and 1966 expeditions: New York, 1967.)

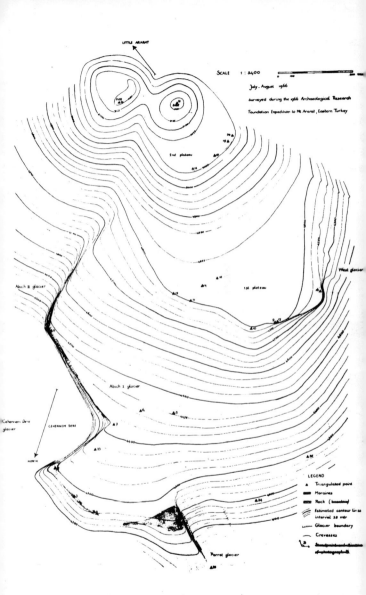

North-West glaciers of Mount Ararat

Kıp Göl plane

Our base camp was near Kıp Göl (Lake Kıp) at a height of ±3500 mtrs. Starting at Kıp Göl one can reach pt 1 *) in a 4 hours climb. First one enters a flat area, the Kıp Göl plane, which is completely covered with black moraines from the Parrot glacier. A small rivlet coming from the Parrot crosses the plane. The snout of the Parrot glacier is to the right and is completely covered with moraines, stones and grey-black dust.

Plate 1 . Base camp

Kıp Göl
base camp ↓

Kıp Göl plane ↓

Plate 2

The Kıp Göl plane seen from pt 35. Notice the huge bands of moraines at the left side of the Parrot glacier.

Pt 1. From the Kıp Göl plane one can climb streight to pt 33, and to pt 1, along grassy slopes, keeping the Parrot at our right. During the expedition we had two small tents near pt 1, some mtrs away from the ice. From pt 1 one sees the sharp edge of the 1st plateau. To the right bare rocks come up to this edge. One cannot see the summit (pt 21) from here. Close to the right one has the crevasses of the Parrot glacier. To the left there is a small wall of edge moraines leading to pt 4. On these moraines there is plenty of plant life, mostly succulent plants.

When the weather is clear, one can see the Russian mountain Alagözdağ (4095 mtrs and snow clad). Opposite one can see Tendürlik Dağ (3313 mtrs) and Aladağ (3510 mtrs) in Turkey. The Aras plane in Russia with the city of Erivan and the Aras river are clearly visible. Especially at night it is beautiful to see the many city lights in Russia.

From pt 1 to the summit (pt 21) takes three hours climbing. One has to cross several crevassed areas and has to be roped. In 1½ hour one reaches the 1st

*) With pt 1, 2, 3, etc. I mean the triangulated points 1, 2, 3,... on the map.

plateau. First one goes to pt 5 or 6 and from there one gets a slope of ± 30° to the 1st plateau (photograph C). It is best to head for a point somewhat left of pt 12, as most of the edge of the 1st plateau is badly crevassed. The slope is covered with deep snow (± 1 mtr), while the flatter areas, between pt 1 and pt 5, and on the 1st and 2nd plateau, have much less snow. Here on can meet bare ice. Especially during the afternoon the surfaces of these flat areas are melting, and water pools get formed. During the night they freeze again. Also at the summit I found a snow temperature which was close to the melting temperature. At a depth of 10 cm I measured a temperature of 0.1 °C, and at a depth of 80 cm 0.05 °C.

From the 1st plateau one can go straight to the 2nd plateau (pt 13). From there to the summit (pt 21) is only a small climb. I noticed that much snow had accumulated on the summit since my visit 2 years ago, seen by the complete covering of a military badge. From the summit one gets an uninterrupted slope down southwards to the Turkish plane. To the east one sees Little Ararat

Not far away and easy to reach is a second summit, pt 22, only 13 mtrs beneath pt 21. Standing at point 22 one gets a beautiful view on the Abich glaciers and the Ahora Valley (See photograph K). Pt 22 belongs to a small plateau, bordered by edge moraines at the South-East side. The mountain slope into the direction of Little Ararat is not covered by snow here. We noticed here a smell of sulphur. Also Blumenthal writes about this smell.

Plate 3 Little Ararat seen from point 22. Notice the edge moraines Near these moraines we found some wood probably the remains of a Turkish mountain hut.

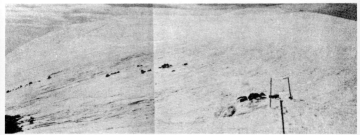

Plate 4. From the moraines visible on plate 3, and into the direction of pt 22 To the left the mountain slopes down to Mihtepe

Cehennem From pt 1 it is easy to reach pt 4, where one gets a wonderful view into the

Dere Cehennem Dere, and of the Cehennem Dere glacier

From pt 4 Little Ararat is just visible over the North-East ridge of the mountain. Also the summit is visible. The Ahora valley cuts deep into the mountain and is here hundreds of mtrs deep. We have not been into the vall nor have we been on the Cehennem Dere glacier. The sharp break off of the Abi I glacier is in the middle ± 60 mtrs high, which we measured with our ropes (See photograph B).

: 8 Point 8 was a stake we had on a rock overhanging the Cehennem Dere. From he we could see deep into the Ahoracut. The area around pt 8 was covered with mora A 30 mtrs further one can see onto the Abich II glacier which is badly crevassed he and looks like an icefall. We did not dare to plant any stakes on the glacier. That i why the contourlines of the Abich II glacier on the map are merely guessed.

Plate 5 and 6. The ice edge of the 1st plateau beneath pt 16.

To the right on plate 6 begins the West Glacier

↑ Plate 7. West glacier.

Plate 8. West glacier seen into the direction of Örtülü.

than usual. At 7 A.M. the whole party stopped at a height of about 12,000 feet, just where the first patch of snow appeared, laid down the sleeping apparatus, and made it quite clear to us that they would go no further.

At eight o'clock I buckled on my canvas gaiters, thrust some crusts of bread, a lemon, a small flask of cold tea, four hard-boiled eggs, and a few meat lozenges into my pocket, bade good-bye to my friend, and set off. Rather to our surprise, the two Cossacks and one of the Kurds came with me, whether persuaded by a pantomime of encouraging signs, or simply curious to see what would happen. The ice-axe had hugely amused the Cossacks all through. Climbing the ridge to the left, and keeping along its top for a little way, I then struck across the semicircular head of a wide glen, in the middle of which lay a snowbed, over a long steep slope of loose broken stones and sand. This slope, a sort of talus or "screes;" as they say in the Lake country, was excessively fatiguing from the want of firm foothold, and when I reached the other side, I was already so tired and breathless, having been on foot since midnight, that it seemed almost useless to persevere farther. However, on the other side, I got upon solid rock, where the walking was better, and was soon environed by a multitude of rills bubbling down over the stones from the snow-slopes above. The summit of Little Ararat, which had for the last two hours provokingly kept at the same apparent height above me, began to sink, and before ten o'clock I could look down upon its small flat top, studded with lumps of rock, but bearing no trace of a crater. Mounting steadily along the same ridge, I saw at a height of over 13,000 feet, lying on the loose blocks, a piece of wood about four feet long and five inches thick, evidently cut by some tool, and so far above the limit of trees that it could by no possibility be a natural fragment of one. Darting on it with a glee that astonished the Cossack and the Kurd, I held it up to them, made them look at it, and repeated several times the word "Noah." The Cossack grinned, but he was such a cheery, genial fellow that I think he would have grinned whatever I had said, and I cannot be sure that he took my meaning, and recognised the wood as a fragment from the true Ark. Whether it was really gopher wood, of which material the Ark was built, I will not undertake to say, but am willing to submit to the inspection of the curious the bit which I cut off with my ice-axe and brought away. Anyhow, it will be hard to prove that it is not gopher wood.' And if there be any remains of the Ark on Ararat at all—a point as to which the natives are perfectly clear—here rather than the top is the place where one might expect to find them, since in the course of ages they would get carried down by the onward movement of the snow-beds along the declivities. This wood, therefore, suits all the requirements of the case. In fact, the argument is, for the case of a relic, exceptionally strong: the Crusaders who found the Holy Lance at Antioch, the archbishop who recognized the Holy Coat at Treves, not to speak of many others, proceeded upon slighter evidence.

We found ourselves at 10 A.M. at the foot of a broken cliff which looked not exactly dangerous but a little troublesome. Here the Cossack and Kurd halted, nor could any persuasion induce them to come a step further. I am no disciple of that gospel of mountaineering without guides which Mr. Girdlestone has preached so zealously by example as well as precept. But if there is any justification for the practice, that justification exists when guides are not to be had. Moreover, as neither the Cossack nor the Kurd had ever been there before, they could not really have been of any use, except that in case of a mishap, two of us might have carried the third down or taken news to the party below.

It was therefore necessary to go on alone, and after getting entangled among some rather nasty rocks, I turned off to the left (west) and began to ascend a very long and straight slope of loose volcanic stones, lying at

---

' [Bryce is quite correct! No one is certain as to what kind of wood is meant by the "gopher wood" of Gen. 8. The English word "gopher" simply transliterates the Hebrew word *gofer;* it is not a translation or interpretation of it.]

so high an angle that progress was extremely slow. The difficulty of breathing, which had begun to be felt at 12,500 feet, was here more serious, and though it was not accompanied by headache or the other symptoms of mountain sickness, the general sensation of fatigue was so great that I did not expect to get more than a thousand feet further. To escape the censure of Mr. Leslie Stephen[5] and those other high authorities who have of late so wisely set themselves to discourage rash climbing, let me say that I had resolved to stop whenever a 'bad place' presented itself or three o'clock arrived; and both legs and lungs were so exhausted that either occurrence would have been almost welcome. The stone slope became so tiresome that at last I turned off to another rock-rib still further to the west, halting at intervals to erect piles of stones to mark the track, a piece of caution which involved a good deal of delay. Immediately to the west lay a profound and savage gully, beyond which rose another towering range of abrupt red pinnacles. Up this rock-rib, which might be called a sort of broken arête, nearly free from snow, I kept steadily for some 800 feet, till it landed me on the edge of a precipice from which the snowy summit, or rather the place where it must lie, since there was a great deal of cloud about, was visible perhaps 1,000 feet higher. Retracing my steps a little and climbing along the edge of a rather treacherous little ice slope, where one was luckily able to get some hand-hold on the rocks that enclosed it, I found myself in a sort of snow basin immediately to the SE. of the summit. It would have been possible to ascend from here up a slope of névé, but this, though quite practicable for a party, seemed too steep for a single man, who might not have found it easy to stop himself if he had once gone off. Fortunately, there was on the E. side of this great slope a declivity of friable rocks, whose angle, about 35°, would have made them easy climbing if only they had been firm enough to give good foothold.

---

[5] [The great English biographer and literary critic (1832-1904). He was an ardent mountaineer and one of the earliest presidents of the Alpine Club.]

As it was, they were troublesome, though not dangerous, and made one's progress upwards provokingly
slow. The extraordinary thing was to find them bare of
snow at a height greater than that of Mont Blanc. It
would probably have been better to have stuck to the
top of what I have called the rock-rib which I had
previously followed, instead of descending into the
basin and keeping up these rocks; but as I was sure of
being able to advance over them, and could not tell
from below that there might not have been cliffs to stop
me on the rock-rib, it seemed safer to choose these
rubbly rocks, disagreeable as they were. But future travellers may be recommended to try the rock-rib by
preference. Nearly an hour was spent on these rocks,
and as I supposed that beyond them there was probably a pretty long snow slope, success seemed again to
become doubtful, for the clouds were thickening and
there was little time left to try back in another direction
if the one first taken did not lead to the highest peak.
Rather to my surprise, the slope of snow which I
reached at the top of these rocks was very gently inclined, and after walking over it for six or seven minutes, the ground began to fall away to the north and
east; it was clear that here, at last—it was now 2:20
P.M.—was the summit.

Immeasurably extensive and grand as the view was,
it was also strangely indefinite.[6] Every mountaineer
knows that the highest views are seldom the finest; and
here was one so high that the distinctions of hill and
valley in the landscape were almost lost.

[• •]

Below and around, included in this single view, seemed
to lie the whole cradle of the human race, from Mesopotamia in the south to the great wall of the Caucasus
that covered the northern horizon, the boundary for so
many ages of the civilized world. If it was indeed here
that man first set foot again on the unpeopled earth,
one could imagine how the great dispersion went as the

---

[6] [My own ascent confirmed this judgment. See below, "Ark
Fever."]

races spread themselves from these sacred heights along the courses of the great rivers down to the Black and Caspian Seas, and over the Assyrian plain to the shores of the Southern Ocean, whence they were wafted away to other continents and isles. No more imposing centre of the world could be imagined. In the valley of the Araxes, beneath, the valley which Armenian legend has selected as the seat of Paradise, the valley that has been for three thousand years the high-road for armies, the scene of so much slaughter and misery, there lay two spots which seemed to mark the first and the latest points of authentic history. One, right below me, was the ruined Artaxata, built, as the tale goes, by Hanni-bal, and stormed by the legions of Lucullus. The other, far to the north-west, was the hollow under the hills in which lies the fortress of Kars, where our countrymen fought in 1854, and where the flames of war were so soon again to be lighted.

Yet how trivial history, and man the maker of histo-ry, seemed. This is the spot which he reveres as the supposed scene of his creation and his preservation from the destroying waters, a land where he has lived and laboured and died ever since his records begin, and during ages from which no record is left. Dynasty after dynasty has reared its palaces, faith after faith its tem-ples, upon this plain; cities have risen and fallen and risen again in the long struggle of civilization against the hordes of barbarism. But of all these works of human pomp and skill, not one can be discerned from this height. The landscape is now what it was before man crept forth on the earth; the mountains stand about the valleys as they stood when the volcanic fires that piled them up were long ago extinguished. Nature sits enthroned, serenely calm, upon this hoary pinnacle, and speaks to her children only in the storm and earth-quake that level their dwellings in the dust. As says the Persian poet:

"When you and I behind the veil are passed,
O but the long long while the world shall last,

Which of our coming and departure heeds
As the Seven Seas should heed a pebble's cast."

Yet even the mountains change and decay. Every moment some block thunders from these crags into the glens below. Day by day and night by night frost, snow, and rain are loosening the solid rock, and the ceaseless action of chemical forces is dissolving it into its primal elements, setting free the gases, and delivering over the fragments to torrents that will sweep them down into the plain. A time must come, if the world lasts long enough, when even the stately peaks of Ararat will have crumbled away and be no more. "Of old hast thou laid the foundations of the earth: and the heavens are the work of thy hands. They shall perish, but thou shalt endure: they all shall wax old as doth a garment; and as a vesture shalt thou change them, and they shall be changed: but thou art the same, and thy years fail not."

I was fortunate enough to find a shorter way down the mountain, and succeeded in regaining my friend, who had remained at the height of 11,500 feet, at half-past six in the evening—only just in time, because the sun was setting, and it was so dark that one could hardly find one's way. We descended the next day to Aralykh, and from that made our way homewards by way of Erivan and Tiflis to the coast of the Black Sea.

*[Discussion of Mr. Bryce's Paper before the
Royal Geographical Society, February 25, 1878]*

● ●

Mr. Bryce, in replying, said he was highly gratified at having his statements confirmed by such high authorities as Sir H. Rawlinson[7] and Mr. Freshfield were in their several ways. . . . With regard to the question raised by Sir H. Rawlinson as to Mount Ararat, if time had permitted he should have been delighted to discuss

---

[7] [Sir Henry Rawlinson (1810-1895), the orientalist who deciphered the Behistun inscriptions; on him, see the *Dictionary of National Biography* and G. Rawlinson's *Memoir* (1898).]

it with him at full length, beginning at Berosus, and going on to Nicolaus of Damascus, Moses of Chorene, Leo Africanus, and others, down to Dr. Theodor Noldeke,[8] who had written a valuable monograph on the subject. He could not admit that any other Ararat had superior claims to the mountain of which he had been speaking, and for which he might consider himself to hold a brief. . . . As to the pilgrimages made to the mountains in Southern Kurdistan, Berosus stated that in his time the people carried away, not only wood, but the pitch with which the Ark was smeared, and used it as a sovereign remedy for the cure of diseases. Berosus and the Assyrians had put their peak down in Southern Kurdistan; but he maintained that the author of the book of Genesis may well be held to have been better informed, and that the Ararat of the Bible, which was also the Ararat of Moses of Chroene, pointed to and was the true northern Ararat, and had nothing to do with the Assyrian one.

The President congratulated Mr. Bryce on meeting with a better fate than Dr. Parrot, since no one doubted that he had made the ascent he had described in his interesting lecture, for which he proposed the cordial thanks of the members.

---

[8] [Noldeke (1836-1930), the great German orientalist, specialized in the history of the Koran; a collection of his articles appeared in English under the title, *Oriental Sketches*.]

7

More Tantalizing Wood: Markoff (1888)

Like Bryce before him, E. de Markoff found wood high upon the unforested and uninhabited rocks of Mt. Ararat. While the circumstances under which he found it are only slightly less mystifying, the fact of the wood is just as tantalizing! Markoff (also spelled "Markow"), a member of the Russian Imperial Geographical Society, ascended the mountain in the same day his friend, E. de Kovalewsky, climbed Lesser Ararat. In a note to their account, Jules Leclercq, Member of the Central Committee of the Royal Geographical Society of Belgium, introduces the gentlemen:

The authors of this account are two young students of the Imperial University in Moscow. I had the good fortune to meet them last September when they were passing through Tiflis on their return journey from Ararat. At my strong insistence, they faithfully promised to put into my hands the story of their ascent—in the French language—for the benefit of the Royal Geographical Society of Belgium. They have kept their word. Ararat was so long considered inaccessible and has been so rarely climbed that I am delighted to make this remarkable expedition known. The reader should carefully note that August 13, Russian style,* corresponds to August 25 on our calendar.

Markoff's narrative, "Ascension du grand Ararat (13 août 1888," is part of the joint-article, "Expédition

---

* i.e., Old Style dating; see above, note 2 to our selection from Parrot's account of his ascent. Markoff reached the peak of Ararat on August 13/25, 1888.

scientifique au Caucase," published in the 1888 volume of the Bulletin de la Société Royale Belge de Géographie *(pp. 577-91). We translate for the first time into English from pp. 580-87, 590.*

At an altitude of only 12,000 feet, I had suffered a mild headache. Now it seemed that my head was caught in a vise. On reaching the spot where we were to pass the night [13,200 feet], a powerful nausea came on me; it became worse and worse and soon I was vomiting.[1] I had to forego supper. Wrapping myself in a deerskin caftan and my bourka,[2] I stretched out on my improvised bed and tried to sleep, so as to have sufficient strength for the morrow. Popoff, one of my companions, also felt a bit under the weather, but not sufficiently to prevent him from eating; the third, Ivanoff, felt fine at the outset, but after the sun went down he began to complain of terrible headaches which increased in intensity and caused him to moan all night long. . . . Though I desperately wanted to sleep, I remained wide awake the whole night.

On August 13 at 5 A.M. we were already up and packed for the climb. The sun had not yet risen, but it was light enough to see our way.

In spite of my sleepless night and my prolonged involuntary fast (I had not eaten since 4 P.M. the previous day), I felt pretty good. My hope of attaining the summit had not diminished.

Popoff, who had also tossed and turned all night, was likewise ready to tackle the mountain. As for our third companion, Ivanoff, he was not feeling very well. I suggested that he go back, but he replied that he would not desert us: he would press on as long as his strength lasted.

We left five Kurds at the place where we had slept

---

[1] [Typical symptoms of mountain sickness.]

[2] [The caftan (Russian, *kaftan,* from Turkish/Persian *qaftàn*) is an ankle-length garment with very long sleeves and a sash; it is common throughout the Near East even today, but is generally made of striped cotton or silk. The bourka is a long cloak of goat's hair; it is a garment indigenous to the region.]

and went on—nine persons in all. We took with us only the things which were absolutely necessary: provisions and bourkas. Soon we came to a conical rock on the south-east face of the mountain; that spot can be considered the snow-line. . . .

Ivanoff, feeling worse and worse all the time, eventually agreed to listen to us and go back. This was at an altitude of 13,600 feet. The rest of us went on.

From time to time, we encountered stretches of loose, gravel-covered terrain which made climbing considerably more difficult. Our feet were always slipping on this unstable surface.

Popoff climbed bravely at first, but little by little I noticed that he was lagging behind and seemed to be proceeding with difficulty. He told us that if he only had something with which to start a fire, a cup of tea would instantly restore him. On hearing this, one of our guides declared that a little higher up he had seen a pole which, he thought, could serve to make a fire. "Let's go," he said to encourage us. "We're almost where the stick is, and there you'll have your tea and can rest."

I was ready to keep going, but Popoff announced that he could not proceed farther. We therefore decided to send two of our porters to find the stick commemorating a previous ascent, and while waiting for our tea to be prepared for us we lay down on the rocks and, entirely exhausted as we were, soon began to doze.

When I woke from this half-sleep, I saw with the greatest satisfaction the bright flames on which the water was boiling for our stimulating brew. The wood of the commemorative stick was almost entirely consumed, except for two little pieces on which I noted some carving. On one of the fragments were cut, in Russian, the two letters C. B. and on the other H,.K. These are the initials of two explorers who tried some years ago to reach the summit of Ararat, but lacking the strength to do so, cut their names on a long pole which they had found on their path.[a] I still cannot de-

---

[a] [French, "une longue perche qu'ils avaient trouvée sur leur

termine with certainty who was responsible for leaving this pole there. In all probability, it was the stick Professor Abich planted on the summit in 1845; chances are, avalanches carried it to the place where we found it.[4]

After getting our second wind, we continued the ascent. The weather was magnificent: the sky clear and a light breeze blowing from the south. Directly before us the snow-covered peak glistened in the sunlight. At an altitude of 14,800 feet, I actually found a bright red living insect (a *coccinella septem punctata*) among the rock. The gradient was consistently 20° to 30°. . . .

We found ourselves at an altitude of about 16,100 feet above sea level. The thermometer registered 22.6° in the sun.[5] We wanted to rest a bit so as to do the remaining distance at a stretch, but we could not stop for very long for it was already rather late and we would have to hurry if we wanted to get back before nightfall. Moreover, a large dark cloud in the south presaged no good. Scarcely had we gone forward a few steps but we were confronted by a strong and disagreeable odor of sulphur.[6] The guides quickly and carefully put their handkerchiefs over their mouths; my head was covered by my bachelik,[7] but I finally got rid of it because of the difficulty of breathing and the fact that the sulphur smell was not bothering me too much. The wind blowing at our left spread the sulphurous odor about. Finally the sand-like expanse was conquered and at 2 P.M. we set foot on the sacred peak of Greater Ararat. . . .

chemin." What was this pole or stick doing there at an altitude well above any recorded site of human habitation—on a mountain devoid of trees? Markoff will suggest an answer, but perhaps, like Bryce's "relic" and Navarra's wood, this pole so unceremoniously used for initialing and firewood, may have had a more venerable history!]

[4] [This seems a bit unlikely. Would Abich's marker have turned up here after forty years? Thirty-two years earlier Stuart found the marker standing, but even then observed that "the surface of the wood has become so soft that it may be scraped off with the nail of the finger to the depth of one-eighth of an inch" (see above, "The British Empire on Ararat").]

[5] [This is a centigrade reading. Fahrenheit temperature was 72.5°.]

[6] [A phenomenon at the summit mentioned in several other accounts; see, for example, Abich's narrative.]

[7] [A kind of pointed hood made of goat's hair.]

We began our descent after having piled up, on the hillock to our right, a rock pyramid five feet high, which could be seen from Sardar Bulak[8] with the aid of field glasses. A few feet below the summit we affixed a metallic plate to a rock. On the plate was a commemorative inscription and a low-registering thermometer given us by the Russian Imperial Geographical Society for recording minimum temperature at the peak over a specified time.

We had hardly descended five hundred feet before the snowstorm began, immensely complicating our return from the summit. . . .

Some Advice and Directions for Explorers

It is indispensable to depart from Sardar Bulak very early in the morning, so that no later than 10 A.M. you can proceed from the point where the horses have to be left.

One must take a sufficient supply of fuel, food, warm clothing and bourkas.[9]

The place where you spend the night must not be at an altitude lower than 14,000 feet. If you start for the summit the following morning at 5 o'clock, you can be back at Sardar Bulak towards nightfall.

---

[8] [See above, note 1 to Khodzko's account.]

[9] [See above, note 2.]

8

The British Again:
Lynch (1893)

*Henry F. B. Lynch (1862-1913), senior partner of
Lynch Brothers, Eastern merchants, travelled extensively in the Levant for purposes of scientific, political,
and commercial research. Having reconnoitered the
mid-east on horseback and sailed down the Tigris to
Baghdad on a raft, Lynch was better able to expedite
British trade during his journey of 1889. At that time
he inaugurated a new river service and surveyed for a
new trade route into Persia. Lynch's second and third
journeys took him to Armenia: in September, 1893 he
climbed Mt. Ararat and in 1898 he surveyed the great
crater of Nimrud and mapped the country. (See* Who
Was Who, *1897-1915.) The lasting monument to
these expeditions consists of two thick volumes full of
very detailed and careful accounts, the editing of which
occupied Lynch a full three years before they were
published. (A Russian edition appeared at Tiflis in
1910.) It is from* Armenia: Travels and Studies *([1901],
pp. 172-78) that we have taken the selection below.*

Before six o'clock we were afoot and ready; it wanted a few minutes to the hour as we set out from our camp.[1] To the Swiss was entrusted the post of leader; behind him followed in varying order my cousin and Wesson and myself. Slowly we passed from the shore of the snow-lake to the gathering of the higher seams, harbouring our strength for the steeper gradients as we made across the beach of boulders, stepping firmly from block to block.

The broad, white sheet of the summit circle descends to the snow-lakes of the lower region in a tongue, or

---

[1] [They had made high camp at 12,194 ft.]

gulf of deep névé; you may follow on the margin of the great depression the western edge of this gleaming surface unbroken down the side of the cone. On the east the black wall of the giant causeway borders the shining slope, invading the field of perpetual winter to a height of over 14,000 feet. The width of the snow-field between these limits varies as it descends; on a level with the shoulder, or head of the causeway, it appeared to span an interval of nearly 200 yards. The depth of the bed must be considerable, and, while the surface holds the tread in places, it as often gives and lets you through. No rock-projection, or gap, or fissure breaks the slope of the white fairway; but the winds have raised the crust about the centre into a ribbon of tiny waves. Our plan was to cross the stony region about us, slanting a little east, and to mount by the rocks on the western margin of the snow-field, adhering as closely as might be possible to the side of the snow. It was in the execution of this plan—so simple in its conception —that the trained instinct of the Swiss availed. Of those who have attempted the ascent of Ararat—and their number is not large—so many have failed to reach the summit that, upon a mountain which makes few, if any, demands upon the resources of the climber's craft, their discomfiture must be attributed to other reasons: to the peculiar nature of the ground traversed, no less than to the inordinate duration of the effort; to the wearisome recurrence of the same kind of obstacles, and to the rarity of the air. Now the disposition of the rocks upon the surface of the depression is by no means the same as that which we have studied in connection with the seams which lie below. The path no longer struggles across a troubled sea of ridges, or strays within the blind recesses of a succession of gigantic waves of stone. On the other hand, the gradients are as a rule steeper; and the clearings are covered with a loose rubble, which slips from under the feet. The boulders are piled one upon another in heaps as they happened to fall, and the sequence of forms is throughout arbitrary and subject to no fixed law. In one place it is a tower of this loose masonry which blocks all further approach; in another a solid barrier of sharp crags, laced together, which it is necessary to circumvent. When the limbs have been stiffened and the patience exhausted by the long and devious escalade, the tax upon the lungs is at its highest, and the strain upon the heart most severe. Many of the difficulties which travellers have encountered upon this stage of the climb may be avoided, or met at a greater advantage, by adhering to the edge of the snow. But the fulfilment of this purpose is by no means so easy as might at first sight appear. You are always winding inwards to avoid the heaps of boulders, or emerging on the backs of gigantic blocks of lava towards the margin of the shining slope. In the choice of the most direct path, where many offered, the Swiss was never at fault; he made up the cone without a moment's hesitation, like a hound threading a close covert, and seldom if ever foiled.

At twenty minutes to seven, when the summit of Little Ararat was about on a level with the eye, we paused for awhile and turned towards the prospect, now opening to a wider range. The day was clear, and promised warmth; above us the snowy dome of Ararat shone in a cloudless sky. The landscape on either side of the beautiful pyramid lay outspread at our feet; from north-east, the hidden shores of Lake Sevan, to where the invisible seas of Van and Urmi diffused a soft veil of opaline vapour over the long succession of lonely ranges in the south-east and south. The wild borderland of Persia and Turkey here for the first time expands to view. The scene, however much it may belie the conception at a first and hasty glance, bears the familiar imprint of the characteristics peculiar to the great tableland. The mountains reveal their essential nature and disclose the familiar forms—the surface of the tableland broken into long furrows, of which the ridges tend to hummock shapes. So lofty is the stage, so aloof this mighty fabric from all surrounding forms, the world lies dim and featureless about it like the setting of a dream. In the foreground are the valleys on the south of Little Ararat, circling round to the Araxes floor;

and, on the north-east, beside the thread of the looping river, is a little lake, dropped like a turquoise on the sand where the mountain sweeps the plain.

In the space of another hour we had reached an elevation about equal to that of the head of the causeway on the opposite side of the snow, a point which I think we should be justified in fixing at over 14,000 feet.[2] We were now no longer threading along the shore of an inlet; alone the vague horizon of the summit circle was the limit of the broad, white sea. But on our left hand the snowless region of rock and rubble still accompanied our course, and a group of red crags stood up above our heads, just where the upward slope appeared to end.

Yet another two hours of continuous climbing, and, at about half-past nine, the loose boulders about us open, and we are approaching the foot of these crags. The end seems near; but the slope is deceitful, and when once we have reached the head of the formation the long white way resumes. But the blue vault about us streams with sunlight; the snow is melting in the crannies; a genial spirit lightens our toil.

And now, without any sign or warning, the mysterious spell which holds the mountain begins to throw a web about us, craftily, from below. The spirits of the air come sailing through the azure with shining gossamer wings, while the heavier vapours gather around us from dense banks serried upon the slope beneath us, a thousand feet lower down.

The rocks still climb the increasing gradient, but the snow is closing in. At eleven we halt to copy an inscription, which has been neatly written in Russian characters on the face of a boulder stone. It records that on the third day of the eighth month of 1893 the expedition led by the Russain traveller Postukhoff passed the night in this place. At the foot of the stone lie several objects: a bottle filled with fluid, an empty tin of biscuits, a tin containing specimens of rock.

---

[2] Abich (*Geologische Forschungen in den kaukasischen Landern*, Vienna, 1882, part ii, p. 455) ascribes to it an elevation of 14,600 feet.

At half-past eleven I take the angle of the snow slope, at this point 35°. About this time the Swiss thinks it prudent to link us all together with his rope. The surface of the rocks is still uncovered, but their bases are embedded in deep snow.

It is now, after six hours' arduous climbing, that the strain of the effort tells. The lungs are working at the extreme of their capacity, and the pressure upon the heart is severe. At noon I call a halt, and release young Wesson from his place in the file of four. His pluck is still strong, but his look and gait alarm me, and I persuade him to desist. We leave him to rest in a sheltered place, and there await our return. From this time on we all three suffer, even the Swiss himself. My cousin is affected with mountain sickness; as for me, I find it almost impossible to breathe and climb at the same time. We make a few steps upwards and then pause breathless, and gasp again and again. The white slope vanishing above us must end in the crown of the dome; and the boulders strewn more sparsely before us promise a fairer way. But the further we go, the goal seems little closer; and the shallow snow, resting on a crumbling rubble, makes us lose one step in every three. A strong smell of sulphur permeates the atmosphere; it proceeds from the sliding surface upon which we are treading, a detritus of pale sulphurous stones.

At 1:25 we see a plate of white metal, affixed to a cranny in the rocks. It bears an inscription in Russian character which dates from 1888. I neglect to copy out the unfamiliar letters; but there can be little doubt that they record the successful ascent of Dr. Markoff, an ascent which cost him dear.

A few minutes later, at half-past one, the slope at least eases, the ground flattens, the struggling rocks sink beneath the surface of a continuous field of snow. At last we stand upon the summit of Ararat—but the sun no longer pierces the white vapour; a fierce gale drives across the forbidden region, and whips the eye straining to distinguish the limits of snow and cloud. Vague forms hurry past on the wings of the whirlwind;

in place of the landscape of the land of promise we
search dense banks of fog.

Disappointed perhaps, but relieved of the gradient,
and elated with the success of our climb, we run in the
teeth of the wind across the platform, our feet scarcely
sinking in the storm-swept crust of the surface, the
gently undulating roof of the dome. . . . Along the edge
of a spacious snow-field which dips towards the centre,
and is longest from north-west to south-east, on the
vaulted rim of the saucer which the surface resembles,
four separate elevations may conveniently be distinguished as the highest points in the irregular oval figure
which the whole platform appears to present. The
highest among these rounded elevations bears northwest from the spot where we first touch the summit or
emerge upon the reef. That spot itself marks another of
these inequalities; the remaining two are situated respectively in this manner—the one about midway between the two already mentioned, but nearer to the
first and on the north side; the other about south of the
north-western elevation, and this seems the lowest of
all. The difference in height between the north-western
elevation and that upon the south-east is about 200
feet; and the length of the figure between these points
—we paced only a certain portion of the distance—is
about 500 yards. The width of the platform, so far as
we could gauge it, may be some 300 yards. A single
object testifies to the efforts of our forerunners and to
the insatiable enterprise of man—a stout stake embedded upon the north-western elevation in a little pyramid
of stones. It is here that we make our observations, and
make our longest halt.[3] Before us lies a valley or deep
depression, and on the further side rises the north-
western summit, a symmetrical cone of snow. This
summit connects with the bold snow buttresses beyond

---

[3] The temperature of the air a few feet below the summit out of
the gale was 20° F. The height of the north-western elevation of the
south-eastern summit of Ararat is given by my Hicks mountain
aneroid as 17,493 feet. The reading is no doubt too high by several
hundred feet. The Carey aneroid gives a still higher figure, and the
Boylean-Mariotti mercurial barometer entirely refused to work. [The
actual height of the mountain is 5165 meters or 16,946 ft.]

it, terraced upon the north-western slope. The distance down and up from where we stand to that summit may be about 400 yards; but neither the Swiss nor ourselves consider it higher, and we are prevented from still further exploring the summit region by the increasing violence of the gale and by the gathering gloom of cloud. The sides and floor of the saddle between the two summits are completely covered with snow, and we see no trace of the lateral fissure which Abich, no doubt under different circumstances, was able to observe.

We remain forty minutes upon the summit; but the dense veil never lifts from the platform, nor does the blast cease to pierce us through. No sooner does an opening in the driving vapours reveal a vista of the world below than fresh levies fly to the unguarded interval, and the wild onset resumes. Yet what if the spell had lost its power, and the mountain and the world lain bare? had the tissue of the air beamed clear as crystal, and the forms of earth and sea, embroidered beneath us, shone like the tracery of a shield?

We should have gained a balloon view over Nature. Should we catch her voice so well?—the ancient voice heard at cool of day in the garden, or the voice that spoke in accents of thunder to a world condemned to die. "It repented the Lord that he had made man, and it grieved him at his heart. The earth was filled with violence: God looked upon the earth and behold it was corrupt. In the second month, the seventeenth day of the month, the same day were all the fountains of the great deep broken up and the windows of heaven were opened. And the rain was upon the earth forty days and forty nights."

We are standing on the spot where the ark of gopher rested, where first the patriarch alighted on the face of an earth renewed. Before him lie the valleys of six hundred years of sorrow; the airiest pinnacle supports him, a boundless hope fills his eyes. The pulse of life beats strong and fresh around him; the busy swarms thrill with sweet freedom, elect of all living things. In the settling exhalations stands the bow of many colours, eternal token of God's convenant with man.

9

Problems and Palpitations: Seylaz (1910)

Louis Seylaz led his party to the top of Mt. Ararat on August 12, 1910. It was the second ascent of the 20th century. The account of the expedition published by Seylaz in Le Tour du Monde *(XVII [Aug. 26, 1911], 397-408) introduces themes which remain typical of ascents in our century: the problem of permissions and the difficulties with Kurdish porters who have become jaded and therefore more demanding. The original* Tour du Monde *article is, incidentally, a good place to find photos of a climb at the end of the Victorian period. We translate, for the first time into English, the following selection from pp. 397-98, 400-405 of the account.*

The first time I thought of Ararat seriously was in 1905. I was taking it easy at the Janssen Observatory on the peak of Mt. Blanc,[1] wondering what higher mountains I might still be able to climb. I was not playing the dilettante; I wanted to operate within the limits of the possible, so from the outset I discounted the peaks of America or of the Himalayas. Elbruz[2] and Ararat were left, therefore—but especially Ararat, for it had captured my imagination.

I had to wait some years before all the circumstances became favorable at the same time. Finally, on July 30, 1910, we embarked at Constantinople on the Austrian Lloyd line's vessel *Salzburg*. . . .

We were five in number: three Americans, a Scottish physician, and a member of the Alpine Club.[3] Eight

---

[1] [The highest mountain in the Alps.]

[2] [The highest mountain of the Caucasus.]

[3] [i.e.,Seylaz, the author of this account.]

212

days later we arrived at Tiflis, where we were joined by the Reverend L, who was making his second attempt at scaling Ararat, and by Professor Rosenthal of the Tiflis Observatory. It was through the good offices of the latter that our expedition was officially recognized as a scientific mission. This resolved the greatest difficulty we had expected to encounter, for the entire Ararat region, at the Persian-Turkish border,[4] is virtually under martial law. The police authority there is exercised by numerous military posts, from which the Cossacks patrol the countryside in every direction. . . .

On August 11, our departure [from Sardar Bulak up the mountain] had first been set for 4 A.M., but was delayed to 6 o'clock. When our [Kurdish] porters arrived, they began to argue about the weight of the packs, not wanting to carry anything above five kilograms.[5] We had to repack a number of bundles and redistribute the surplus, which gave rise to endless recriminations. Then they disputed among themselves as to who would obtain the lightest loads. The upshot was that 7:30 A.M. came before our caravan was able to set out. . . .

Except for the Kurds, no one slept much that night, some because of the cold, others on account of the hard rocks that served as our pillows. As for me, the mutton fat I had been served at Sardar Bulak did not agree with me. Thus I was able to occupy my time in admiring the stars: never, under any other sky, had I seen stars so bright or so numerous. At 2:45 A.M., the planet Venus rose above the shoulder of Lesser Ararat, resplendent with a truly remarkable brilliance. The luminosity of the heavens was marvellous to behold.

At 3 o'clock, I got out of my sleeping bag to rouse the porters, for we had agreed to set out at 4 A.M. At 4:30 only two of them were ready, packs on their backs and ice-axes in their hands. At 6 o'clock we were still waiting for the others. Finally we lost patience and started without them. . . .

---

[4] [Today, the Iranian-Turkish border.]
[5] [i.e., eleven pounds.]

Higher, even higher! Each additional meter won is a costly victory. Higher yet! Our rest stops became more frequent and every expenditure of energy agonizing. The south ridge terminates in a slope of yellowish scree which, seen from below, seems to offer an easy route for the final approach. But when we attacked it, we found it to be an abominable terrain. Actually, it is a slope of blackened ice, covered with a layer of pulverized sulphurous rocks and loose, broken stones. From that point on, we had not a single good foothold; you would search in vain for a firm support; slipping and falling became the order of the day. Sulphurous odors poisoned the little air we succeeded in gulping down. We staggered along as if drunk. Our hearts and lungs were functioning at their absolute limit; pulse rate increased to 110 and our lips turned purple. The summit was just before us, yet we despaired of reaching it. When we had gone through the agony of cutting two or three meters of ice steps, the surface slid away and we tumbled down with the debris. Would we have to give up the game and admit we were conquered?

Not on your life! I moved off this miserable stony terrain to try the ice slope on our right. Its surface was rough, and the spikes of our crampons could get a grip there. Without wasting the time necessary for step-cutting—we had to save all our energy for the final effort—we went up the slope at a run. Twenty meters, thirty°; then the slope began to level off, and suddenly it ceased entirely. A frightful gust of wind assailed us, blowing us onto the snow, where, for three minutes, we tried to get our breath.

Only then could we stand up and proclaim our victory! To the side of us was a cairn: that temple raised by alpinists to the goddess of the mountain, marking man's conquest over nature. In the cairn was a bottle containing the names of our predecessors, in particular the men of the Ivangouloff expedition which had made the ascent in 1902 to position recording thermometers in a small wooden container on the summit. Since that

---

° [1 meter = 39.37 inches = a little over a yard.]

time, no one had been on the peak. During this eight-
year interval the box had been torn from its base by
hurricane winds and now it lay half hidden in the ice,
with the instruments it was to protect.

The time was 3:15[7]; the cold was intense, and the
wind swept the peak with a violence we would never
forget, easily piercing our heavy woolen clothing. Our
fingers were so numb that we could scarcely operate
our camera. On the other hand, the realization of success chased away our fatigue: no more heart palpita-
tions, no more gaspings for breath.

The summit of Ararat is as vast as everything connected with the gigantic mountain. A battalion could go
on maneuvers there easily.[8] The peak consists of a
rolling, glacial plain.[9] The highest of the undulations is
the Abich or eastern summit.[10] About one hundred
meters away, a handsome dome of snow forms the
Parrot or western summit. It took us a good quarter of
an hour of struggling against the wind to reach the first
of these hills, though it is scarcely two hundred meters
from the cairn.

The sky was favorable all the time: not a cloud appeared on the peak or on the slopes of the mountain to
obscure our view.[11] But what does one see from the
very peak of Ararat? No less than the infinitude of
heaven and earth. . . .

The snow was in excellent condition—soft as one
could ask for. We got in line, sat down, and had ourselves a marvellous snow-slide. . . . In twelve minutes

---

[7] [A rather late hour to make the summit. Danger increases in
early afternoon owing to the melting and weakening of the ice under
the impact of the midday sun.]

[8] [cf. Khodzko's ascent with sixty soldiers in 1850.]

[9] [See above, note 3 to Parrot's account ("The First Modern Ascent").]

[10] [Our author is mistaken. The eastern summit, attained by Abich,
is some thirty feet lower than the western summit climbed by Parrot.
This difference is, of course, very slight. Colonel Khodzko was badly
off in asserting it to be 36 meters.]

[11] [Seylaz was most fortunate. This is rarely the case except in the
very early morning.]

we descended the 1100 meters it had taken us more than five hours to climb.[12] . . .

The ascension of Ararat presents no serious technical difficulty, but the rarefied air and the loose, crumbling rock make the climb extremely arduous, removing any guarantee of success. The number of unsuccessful attempt to gain the summit is considerably greater than the successes. Four years ago a member of the English Alpine Club who had climbed the majority of the great peaks in the Alps came to Ararat; he failed. During the last five hundred meters, the heart and lungs are subjected to a stiff test. On my return to Sardar Bulak, stethoscopic examination revealed that I was suffering from a mild dilatation of the right ventricle. It took several days for our systems to function normally again.

---

[12] [This was the method I also used for the descent. See below, "Ark Fever."]

10

An American Failure (1951)

*In 1951 Oliver S. Crosby and his party came within
150 feet of Ararat's summit before waning daylight
forced them to abandon their ascent. Even a well-
planned expedition such as theirs could fail! Crosby's
account, "Demavend and Ararat, 1951",* which we
have abbreviated below, shows in particular how
treacherous the mountain is.*

The rugged bulk of Ararat, towering to a height of
16,916 feet out of the plan of Dov Bayazit[1], was a
thrilling and awesome sight. On its higher reaches vast,
glistening snowfields swept steeply upward for over
three thousand feet; a hanging glacier was perched on its
south face. Massive Rock buttresses lent a note of
power and violence to the mountain, and cold, black
rivers of lava wound their way from it onto the plain
like the tentacles of some gigantic octopus. Here was a
mountain with character and variety to match its size!
The challenge of the peak filled up with quick, suffo-
cating eagerness.

We hurried on to Dov Bayazit to make the necessary
arrangements with local officials, for my leave was almost ended, and time was precious. We found the local
Sub-Prefect to be friendly but unenthusiastic about our
climb. He warned that Ararat was very dangerous, but
after much argument he finally relented and granted us
permission to proceed the following day. We were
overjoyed.

Morning found us gathered outside the Sub-Prefect's
house, studying possible routes up to the south face or

---

* *The American Alpine Journal*, IX/1 (1954), 76-87. We have
reproduced the text on pp. 81-86.
[1] i.e., Dogubayazit.

along the east ridge. The day was one of the most sparkling beauty, and we were wild to be under way, but once again it was easier said than done. Even with the help of the Sub-Prefect, it took the best part of an hour ot hire a driver and two oxen (!) to carry our provisions and climbing equipment. At long last we drove our jeep from Dov Bayazit to a point just south of the mountain where we were to meet the oxen. They were late, and we had lunch.

The two beasts arrived about one-thirty, were loaded up, and we took off across a two-mile flat of volcanic ash and thence into the foothills of Ararat. The going was easy, and we had plenty of time to gaze at the mountain's great rock shoulders, its majestic snowfields, its glacier, and the tangle of ridges fanning out from its sides. The best route seemed to lead up the south ridge facing us, although the east ridge offered the advantage of a better view of Lesser Ararat. The latter was a symmetrical red-gray cone which rose east of Ararat to an altitude of about 14,000 feet. Our inspection of the mountain was brought to a close by the gathering darkness, and it was night by the time we reached the Kurdish shepherd camp at about 11,000 feet, where we were to sleep. Our arrival caused great excitement, and we were at once surrounded by an admiring, chattering crowd which did not leave us until long after we had eaten and crawled into our sleeping bags.

The three of us were up at four the next morning, dressed, ate breakfast, loaded up for the climb, and attempted to set off. But our way was blocked by one of the armed guards of the camp, who made it clear that we were not to leave. We remonstrated; two more guards came over to support the first. It was apparent that the nomads did not want us to climb their mountain, but we were not to be put off now and raised a terrible hullabaloo. Our arguments, in broken Turkish and Persian, and the nomad consultations continued as the east grew bright and the sun rose.

We were never sure just what their objection was,

but finally, after four hours of wrangling, we were allowed to depart in an easterly direction. An escort was sent along to see that we did not turn in toward the south face of the mountain, so we were obliged to make the long detour around to the east ridge, crossing countless gullies, lava streams, and fields of jumbled black blocks as we slogged our way along. We soon outdistanced our escort, but by that time we were below the hanging glacier, and there was nothing for it but to push on around. The traverse to the east ridge took two precious hours and gained us but little altitude; it was gruelling work, and finally Pierce, who had done no climbing before, could go no further. He stopped to rest a bit and then returned slowly to the nomad camp to wait for us.

It was ten o'clock when Hermann and I finally turned our faces toward the summit of Ararat and began the real climb, starting up the east ridge from somewhere in the neighborhood of 12,000 feet. It was late, maddeningly late, but that could not be helped, and we were grateful to be on the mountain at all. The day was perfect, and the brilliant sunshine presented us with scores of breathtaking views of the south face of Ararat. We climbed steadily on the volcanic stone and moved up the ridge at a good pace.

About 1,200 feet higher we came into snow, which the hot sun had turned to slush. There was no apparent way of by-passing it, so in we plunged, slipping and sliding and wishing that we were on solid rock once more. Near the occasional outcroppings of rock the snow was swept away entirely by swift rivulets of its own water. The earth and stones of the outcroppings were oozing with water, too, and not solid enough to stand on, so we were forced to continue the uphill battle on the snow. Progress was slow and exhausting; the snow slope continued on and on, all the heat of the sun coverging on us from the great white reflector. Hermann and I pushed on, striving for altitude and working hard to keep our footing. Each step, carefully kicked in, was apt to collapse in front, in back, or on one side, breaking our pace and losing us precious time.

As we mounted in a steady zig-zag up the great snowy east side of Ararat, the air became noticeably thinner and colder, and we rejoiced to feel the snow harden under our boots. Finally, we stood well above the top of Lesser Ararat and were approaching the shoulder of Ararat proper at about 16,000 feet.

By three-thirty, despite the fact that the sun was still well up in the sky, the cold had so increased that it seemed the chill of night was on the mountain. At the same time, a piercing wind struck us and rocked us about on our feet. The change in wind and temperature took place with phenomenal quickness as we entered the shoulder snowfields leading northwest to the mountain summit. The frigid upper reaches of Ararat had a wild, rugged look. Great boulders projected from the snow all around us, teetering on the verge of a meteoric plunge down the slope. To the left the head of the cracked and broken glacier wall was just visible, the thin strip of snow across its top leading westward toward ridges and buttresses which rose almost 6,000 feet above our camp. Our route was plain enough and even gave promise of becoming less steep in time. We climbed on, watching the final peak of Ararat move nearer, grow larger and more distinct.

It came to be four o'clock and then four-thirty as we continued our progress upward through the boulder-strewn snowfield. The angle of the snow had not declined as much as we had hoped at the shoulder, but this at least allowed us to gain altitude and approach the summit more quickly. It loomed before us, tantalizingly close, and yet we seemed to move toward it at a snail's pace. The sun's outline became blurred behind a white haze of fine snow torn from the mountain and hurled across its peak by the east wind. Fortunately, this wind was at our backs, but still it reached into our muscles and lungs. The sun had no warmth to offer as it shone palely through the snow-filled air, and I began to recognize the threat which the cold held for us. Our bodies no longer generated the heat that they had as we had worked our way up the mountain, and we were chilled through if we stopped to rest more than a minute at a time.

The temperature fell further. It was five o'clock. The awareness which had been growing in our minds and which we had been trying to stifle would no longer be suppressed. We were verging on the point of no return.

There was no doubt that sufficient daylight remained to proceed to and reach the summit, which now lay directly ahead and some 150 feet above us, but this would leave us no time for the descent. We had to get ourselves off of three thousand feet of snow and ice before dark, for a bivouac on or near the summit of the mountain was out of the question, and the nearest descent route was apt to be tricky, as it lay over the west end of the glacier and down onto the snow beyond it. To traverse that untried route at night would be inviting trouble.

Reluctantly, we turned back, left the summit route, and began the passage over the top of the hanging glacier, just above the wall's face. The snow was hard and uneven there, extremely steep in places and interspersed with stretches of ice. For long distances we cut steps with the ice-axe and proceeded, a foot at a time, changing the lead frequently. There was perhaps an hour of daylight left when Hermann, who was leading at the time, suddenly broke through the snow and dropped into a crevasse. As he fell, he managed to catch himself with an elbow on either side, and I, straddling the hole, put a hand under each shoulder and helped him scramble out. We stood there for a moment, panting and wheezing with the exertion.

Handling the stiff climbing rope with stiffer fingers, we proceeded with utmost caution. The second time Hermann fell he was checked before he had got halfway into the crevasse that blocked the way. Jumping across it, we continued to the end of the glacier, across the top of a swooping buttress and came upon the upper reaches of the low snow slope. It was almost seven o'clock and the sun had set, but in the gathering gloom we sped down the smooth snow, glissading part of the way and moving on the rope and axe where the going was more unsafe. The slope was sheltered on both sides, and for the first time the air about us was quiet. Gathering reserves we scarcely knew we had, we descended well over 2,000 feet in a half hour and neared the end of the snow.

It was now quite dark, and we were somewhere in the neighborhood of 14,000 feet. The air at this altitude was fortunately not so biting as it had been on top. We were below the glacier area and the snow was not so difficult to travel on if we proceeded slowly. Indeed it was a pity when we finally saw the last of it; from then on we moved in thick blackness, guided only by various lights in the valley, some of which we took to indicate the location of the camp a good deal to the west of our position. The sky was clear, but the stars shed no useful light on the dark rocks over which we moved.

Traveling entirely by feel, we traversed buttress after buttress, couloir after couloir, moving slowly toward the west and that special ridge which should lead us to the camp. By eleven o'clock Hermann and I were exhausted, moving in a dream. We would ease ourselves down over boulders and across noisy but invisible streams until we could go no farther. Collapsing where we stood, we would hug the black rocks and lie there numbly. After about ten minutes, the cold would seep into us, tightening every muscle into uncontrollable shakes and forcing us to our feet and onward. The night was full of blind alleys, wrong turnings which brought us to precipices or difficult couloirs. We nosed our way around each obstacle like patient measuring worms, patient because there was nothing else to do.

At one o'clock we reached a cul-de-sac, for we found ourselves following down a ridge of loose rock which gradually slimmed to nothing, eaten away on both sides by converging torrents of water.

There was little chance of our making it back up the crumbling ridge, and it seemed impossible to cross the cascading waters: we were trapped in the gulley, teetering on the very brink of the westernmost stream and

enveloped in its clammy spray. Driven on by the cold
and wet, we resumed our nosing about, moving with
extreme caution. The rushing foam shone with a pale
whiteness, interspersed with black spots where there
were rocks or emptiness. By testing these dark islands
with the ice-axe, we found a precarious bridge across
the torrent. The crossing was harrowing and unbelievable, like the last minute of a nightmare in which one
slips and slithers in darkness at the brink of eternity,
but it was finally completed, and we were safely on the
far side.

The worst was now passed, for the ridge we descended became progressively less cold and less steep.
We began to obtain real benefit from our frequent rest
periods, and the departing numbness gave place to a
great sense of peace and accomplishment. Already the
memory of the agonizing night hours was fading before
the priceless experiences and sights of the day before.

A French Success: Navarra (1952)

Here is the account of the first French conquest of Mt. Ararat—made by amateur explorer Fernand Navarra a few days before he detected the outlines of a vessel under the ice at a lower altitude (see Pt. Two, sec. 10). Navarra's companion on the ascent J. A. de Riquier, reported the party's activities in his article, "Le Pays d'Ararat," which was published in Acta Geographica for 1957.[1] We give below Navarra's own account from the English translation of L'Expedition au Mont Ararat *(1953).[2]*

August 14th (5 A.M.) [1952]. We came out of our tent. In the pale morning a violent and icy wind whipped our faces. Leaden clouds, harbingers of snow, followed more and more closely over our heads. We were surprised to find the snow which had fallen during the night was bluish-green and squelched under our feet; the footprints filled with water which immediately froze. With our mountain gear and already wearing our down-lined anoraks, we were ready for the final climb. In the nearby marabout the officers were getting ready. Some of the soldiers were up, and in the shelter of the rocks the cooks, who had lit a wood fire, were making tea.

It was time to take up our packs with all the equipment for the establishment of a camp on the famous platform bordering the 16,500-foot mark. This platform was the very spot where the Ark found room enough to land. The team would spend the night of August 14th/15th in the isothermic tent, using the spe-

[1] Paris, XXI/1 (1957), 5-8.
[2] *The Forbidden Mountain*, trans. by Michael Legat (London: Macdonald, 1956), pp. 142-49.

cial equipment that had been lent to us by the Bazar de l'Hôtel de Ville in Paris. Alaedin liked our plans and agreed to join our group since he too had studied our equipment. We shared out among ourselves the cartons of films, and emergency rations and the first-aid material, which we slipped into our anoraks, and we had crampons, binoculars, cameras, ciné cameras and ropes.

The Lieutenant Atalai came out of his marabout.

"Are you taking your packs?" he asked. "I don't think you'll be able to carry them up to the summit."

We explained to him our plan of camping at the 16,500-foot contour so that we might explore the ice cap during the day of August 15th.

He understood immediately what we wanted, but, he said, he had received orders to take his troops to the summit. He owed it to himself to succeed in his attempt, while at the same time taking all necessary precautions. His detachment would set off without any load so that they could reach their goal during daylight and immediately come back down. Under the circumstances he could not be of any help to us. In a few hours, he added, we should understand the full meaning of his words when we had to drag ourselves along in the rarefied air of the summit.

So our hopes of making an exploration had to be abandoned, and only that of a victory over Ararat remained. We hoped that we might represent France that day, as on Mount Argaeus, on the summit of Noah's mountain.

We threw our useless packs into our tent and just took our ice axes. The departure was organised. Alaedin Seker put his problem to Lieutenant Atalai: he had been officially instructed to film the ascent of Ararat by the Turkish Army but could not do so unless he had some help; moreover, he could not climb at the rate adopted the previous day.

Anatol, Cumhuriyet and the officers who had witnessed these palavers and preparations now gathered together for the final effort. Lieutenant Atalai blew his whistle as the signal to start. It was half-past six. Alaedin Seker was already making heavy going under the weight of his seventeen-pound ciné camera; according to what the Lieutenant had said, no one could help him.

Hazam Calatin walked in front. He had chosen a sharp crest between two névés; its surface was made up of stones of all sizes, strewn with easily-dislodged rocks and enormous blocks of stone polished like jet. It was extremely difficult to march in these conditions and according to his physical capabilities, each of us scrambled along as best he could. These continual clamberings made us footsore right from the start, especially as the gradient, which was about one in four as far as the 13,000-foot contour, had now reached at least one in three. After the rough ground, the crest became sharper and sharper, with real razor edges to the rocks on which we cut ourselves when we fell. And as we climbed we had to keep our precarious balance, risking falls which in those conditions would have been serious. Ararat is a volcano and its rocks hardly ever vary: lavas, basalts, trachytes succeeded each other, now in sharp-angled outcrops, now in colums of blocks of varying sizes. To sum up then, we were faced with either razor-edge crests or unstable rocks, and in succession those were the difficulties which had to be overcome, difficulties which were complicated by the slope and the rarefaction of the air which was beginning to affect us.

At nine o'clock, after more than two and a half hours of this exercise—for it could not be called walking—we painfully reached the 15,400-foot mark. Everyone by then was panting and crawling. The marching column looked like ants disappearing and reappearing between the smooth black rocks. 15,782 feet —the height of Mont Blanc. The team felt on top of the world—everybody was in fine fettle. Yet there was still a regret in our minds. Kirschner, who was filming nonstop, changed his reel.

Half-past nine. The altimeter showed 15,880 feet. Everything was going well and we were feeling the benefit of our training on Mount Argeaus. Still fresh and in good spirits, we were hoping that we should avoid the mountain sickness which Demir had already suffered. We could see him toiling along two hundred yards below. He seemed to be in difficulties and we were sorry that we could not help him. We grouped together again and counted ourselves. Where was Anatol? He had disappeared somewhere among the rocks. We called him, but our muffled voices did not carry far. Cumhuriyet was there, and we congratulated him, but he only frowned—a bad sign.

Then came a moment of drama. Hazam Calatin looked at us candidly and spoke:

"I have never climbed so far before. I shall not go farther."

They were the words of an honest man. They meant that he could climb farther, that he would be able to reach the summit, but that *he did not want to*. We realised that he *could not* infringe the Law, and we resigned ourselves to letting him go. But as he made his way over the rocks, keeping his balance by waving his arms about, as though beckoning us to follow him, we thought of what lay before us. The die was cast.

We were right in the point of the angle formed by two large névés, alongside which we had to proceed until we reached a big terrace from which we should be able to see the ice cap. It was a pity that the very dense clouds at that altitude hid the valley from us. And then, in a sudden patch of clear air, there was Bayazid—Bayazid which was sweltering while we shivered.

Alaedin Sker rejoined us. He had found a friend in need, a little Turkish soldier who had kindly relieved him of carrying his camera. He told us he had been able to take a few sequences. We waited for him to get his breath back before we started again.

It was not advisable to make too long a halt on a mountain, especially at such an altitude. We realised this as soon as we resumed the ascent. Our frozen joints made it very difficult to get going again. And it was then too that the ice axes and the rope itself became insupportable in weight. Because of the very steep slope we had to lean forward, cramping our ribs, lungs and diaphragms, and this made breathing a terrible strain in the course of any strenuous movements. The rarefied air and the lower atmospheric pressure made us pant. We were gasping for breath. Every five minutes we had to stop; and we had not recovered when it was time to start again. Our heads fell forward and we drifted into sleep. Fortunately a blizzard woke us up. But despite the snow some of the men went on sleeping, while we, with the greatest difficulty, climbed higher. We checked our numbers when we reached 16,250 feet. There were barely fifteen survivors. The others had scattered and were still sleeping below, huddled among the rocks, like the victims of a raid on an invisible enemy.

At that moment we realised that *the mountain was defending itself*. No one dared to say it, but each felt that we were up against something other than natural elements. We were struggling physically and we were obsessed mentally by the same recurring thought "What will the mountain's defence be? And when will it begin?" Seeing all these sleepers falling by the wayside one after another, we were afraid when we too fell that we might not be able to rouse ourselves again. Not even so as to beat a retreat. Never had the "funkmeter" (an expression dear to Kirschner and Zubiri) given so high a reading. And supposing we had to give in before we had reached the summit?

"It's hopeless!"

Even our athlete despaired, feeling his lungs and his heart failing him for the first time in his life.

Atalai had been right. Weight was the enemy. What would we have done if we had insisted on bringing our packs? The soldiers would not have been able to carry them for us. Simply to raise one's arm became an effort; to thrust the ice axe forward so as to hook it on to a rock seemed impossible. O, cruel, disheartening Mountain of Noah, how well we realised that you would have no truck with us! This was your defence, this atrophy of our muscles, our nerves, or our very will-power. We wanted to give up and lie down to sleep. We could no longer think—we had only courage to breathe once more so as to take one step forward, driven by the necessity of reaching the goal, because we had no right to yield. The Turkish soldiers were ten yards in front of us—we could not stop, we would not sleep, we had no right to abdicate!

And Navarra waited for Kirschner and de Riquier waited for Navarra, and the team waited, fell back, reformed, fell and rose again. One fall caused another. And in our daydreams we saw again the stations of the cross in the church at Padua where our seven candles burned.

"I'm spitting my lungs up!"

"My heart is bursting!"

So long as we could talk and say anything at all, we were not beaten. We had no thoughts—you cannot think of anything at a height of more than 16,000 feet. And still we went on. We had taken more than four hours to climb from 15,400 feet to 16,400 feet. We had made our way over scree and black ice, with nothing solid for our feet to grip. Everything rolled away, everything crumbled beneath us. The slope was so steep that in a few seconds we could lose what had been gained by crawling upwards with superhuman contortions and efforts. One's whole body was flattened against that unstable mountain wall, trying to sucker itself on. We had another fifty yards to climb in our desperate, mouth-drooling state, and when we had reached the 16,500-foot mark we should have taken five hours.

At last we came to a terrace of pure ice. From that moment we were able to work together more, without clinging so desperately to the ground. And we were at last able to break a piece of the ice and suck it; our thirst was appalling, for the waterbottles had been emptied a long time before. We would have preferred hot tea, for the ice did not melt—not even in our mouths. It was absurd! For a good ten minutes we turned it round in our mouths, without receiving any sensation or moisture on our tongues. It would have been better to have something salt—yes, even something salt. We broke off more ice and tried again, for

the thirst was unbearable. It was just impossible for it
not to melt and quench that thirst a little . . . just a little . . . We were breathing heavily, dragging ourselves
forward with our throats rasping, so dry had they become with drawing in and expelling the air, for there
was no hope of breathing solely through the nose in the
approved fashion—we wanted the air to get into our
lungs any way it could, even through our pores!

"Perhaps our mouths are too frozen by the air,"
suggested Kirschner.

"I'm not sure," added Navarra, "but I think I've put
an extra coating of ice on this lump!" And he spat out
his piece of ice in disgust.

"A slice of karpüz. Just one slice of karpüz . . . karpüz . . ."

We had only one thought in mind: to get back to
Bayazid and have something to drink. We dreamed of
ayran. We saw barrel-loads of lemonade running before our eyes.

"Oh, for some lemonade . . . lemonade . . ."

Would one sell one's best friend for a glass of lemonade? Well . . . It was better not to think of such
things.

We thought we should come to the ice cap immediately after the terrace which followed the névés, but
the summit of Ararat is so constructed that after a terrace which hid the peak from us would come another,
itself concealing the next one. We were going forward in
bursts of twenty-five or thirty paces, and then stopping
for lack of breath. We were breathing very quickly.
Then we would set off for another burst. We saw a sergeant and six men above us, who had stopped twenty
yards away and sat balancing themselves precariously
on the steep slope. Kirschner joined them. Navarra was
eating sugar, and de Riquier raisins and sugar sprinkled
with alcoholic peppermint. It was better sitting. A very
keen wind kept us awake and we realised that the
mountain sickness which had almost knocked us out
and which had floored so many of our companions already, was lessening a little in intensity.

Above our heads the sky was darkened by a blanket

of heavy snow clouds. Below, at 14,750 feet, lay a sea of lighter clouds, as if seen from an aeroplane. And between these two horizons, like two shrouds, were men wandering in a lunar landscape. A fantastic, strange, inhuman world of hallucinations and near madness.

At this point a captain joined us. We looked at him in surprise, for he seemed so dazed. He was panting, and he stopped to catch his breath. When he was easier he began to pronounce a meaningless sequence of words.

"He's off his head," said Kirschner. "We better look out for ourselves."

Mountain sickness had seized the governor the day before at the camp. And yet we were only 13,500 feet up then. Prudently he had not insisted on continuing. Among the men of ancient times there were certainly some who infringed the Law. Alone, at that altitude and attacked by the same sickness, they may have slept in exhaustion and having awoken, half mad, must have climbed back down frightened to death. Not understanding the phenomenon, they may well have shouted: "There's magic there!" Hazam Calatin knew what was in store for us. Perhaps he was wise not to persist.

Lieutenant Atalai set off again with his group. In turn, we started. The soldiers seemed to split up quickly. A big ridge of ice which they had just crossed hid them from our view. We came up to it at the moment when the solitary captain, completely discouraged and "done for," stopped, unable to go farther. The big ridge changed into a wall of crevassed ice. We went forward on our hands and knees, pulling each other along. And sometimes we tumbled down too. The team was in distress, when we reached a promontory of compact ice from which we could see the ice cap stretching six or seven hundred yards towards the northwest. Beyond that the visibility was nil. Were we at the summit? No doubt it was hidden by the ice behind which the soldiers had disappeared, but after that ridge there was another, and yet another after that, and we began to wonder if we should ever come to the end of them. At least we were able to make easier progress by following the soldiers' tracks in the snow. We had the impression that we were travelling over a cupola of immense diameter as, gasping for breath, we plunged into a half-night which became darker and heavier as murky twilight descended upon us.

At that point on this barrier of ice, over which grey silhouettes were moving, we were 16,946 feet above sea level. A few more steps and we at least reached the summit of Noah's Mountain, the Holy Mountain, the Cradle of Humanity. It was half-past three when Navarra and de Riquier unfurled our tricolour and thus symbolised France's conquest—for the first time in the history of French mountaineering—of Mount Ararat.

12

The Oxford University
Exploration Club (1966)

What follows is not the account of a successful ascent of Mt. Ararat. It is a report showing the foolishness of some climbers who think Ararat can be scaled without climbing equipment, guide, or beast of burden. Moreover, the report shows the difficulties of investigating the mountain even when one is bountifully equipped with modern implements of exploration. We have taken this passage from the Bulletin of the Oxford University Exploration Club, *XV/I, (1967), pp. 1, 5-7.*

Early this year [1966] Professor and Mrs. Trease asked whether the O.U.E.C. could organise an expedition to Mount Ararat to investigate the disappearance of their son, Christopher, (Balliol), last seen near the mountain in August 1965. They offered a new van to such an expedition, should it be formed.

Mount Ararat is a recently extinct, but little investigated volcano, and it was therefore decided to combine a search for traces of Christopher Trease with a study of the geology of the mountain. . . .

Christopher Trease went to climb Mount Ararat alone, hoping to reach the summit on August 23rd 1965, his birthday. He was last seen two days before this walking down the main street of Dogubayazit on his way to climb the mountain. He was carrying a moderately heavy pack, but as far as is known, had no climbing equipment such as an ice axe or crampons. He is said to have refused an offer of an ice axe on his way out of Dogubayazit, and did not take a guide, or a donkey to carry his equipment.

Since the Expedition had no climbers, we had arranged to meet a party from Bicester who agreed to

233

take us up to the summit in the second fortnight of our stay in the area, to see if Trease had signed a book reputed to be near the summit. Hence we decided to examine the geology of the north side of the mountain for the first fortnight; during this time, Rabbie and Işçi started off on their projected tour of the mountain. They passed one night at Sedarbulak and one up at the snowline where Rabbie suffered from mountain sickness, forcing them to abandon the idea of making a complete circuit of the mountain. They made their way back to the camp at Ahora by way of Seyli Köy and Dogubayazit, arriving two or three days later. While they were on the mountain they spoke to many of the Kurdish shepherds, and found that most knew about a reward offered by Professor and Mrs. Trease, although estimates of its magnitude were generally exaggerated, and sometimes confused with the amount of money Trease was thought to be carrying. They found the Kurds invariably friendly, but unable to recognise the photographs of Trease which were shown to them, and they gave different and confusing opinions of what had happened to him.

In Dogubayazit they spoke with a guide who claimed to have offered his services to Trease but nothing new was learnt from that guide, or, indeed, from any others.

After moving camp to Ortülü, Owen and Reynolds went up the south-west side of the mountain as far as the snowline and camped there for four nights. On their way up a Kurdish shepherd approached them, asking the correct time. He was wearing a gold coloured watch with a silvery coloured expanding bracelet, on which was a pattern of incised gold V's; the make of the watch was not observed, but they thought it could possibly have belonged to Trease. A telephone call to Ankara, followed by a telegram to England later revealed that this might have been worth following up, but the encouraging reply did not reach Ankara until the return journey.

At the snowline Owen and Reynolds also suffered from mountain sickness, and this cut down the distances they were able to cover. Nevertheless, a considerable area was traversed on foot, and, with the aid of binoculars, the ice above and the rocky slopes below were scanned unsuccessfully for any signs of Trease.

The return to Ortülü was made by a more easterly route, and it was realised that anyone alone and on foot making the ascent by this way could have had some difficulty in obtaining an adequate supply of water, between leaving the plain and reaching the snow line.

Plans had been made for another trip up the snow line on the south-east side of the mountain, but these were forestalled by the puncture [of a tire on the van which detained the party for three days]; by the time this had been put right, there was no time left for any worthwhile investigations to be made.

The conventional route to the summit of Mount Ararat is through the village of Seyli Köy and thence in an almost straight line to the top; this is the route followed by an R.A.F. Expedition in early June, and later by a team from Wye College. An American Expedition (the 'American Arkological Expedition'),[1] had spent four weeks on the ice-cap, and although they had been briefed about Trease, found nothing. Neither they nor the other Expeditions found any trace of the book supposed to be near the summit,[2] and since all these expeditions had been keeping eyes open for signs of Trease, we considered it pointless to search the ground they had already covered.

From our experiences of the Kurds as suppliers of information we suggest that anything they say is to be treated with the greatest caution. Trying to sort out the truth is difficult, but when this is done, it usually turns out that either the information is well-known, or about some quite different person, as other climbers have disappeared on Mount Ararat recently.

We have divided the area into three zones for the purpose of discussing the disappearance of Trease.

From the base of the mountain at the edge of the marsh, is an area of dried grass and a semi-arid vege-

---

[1] [A somewhat garbled reference to the Archaeological Research Foundation expedition. See the section immediately following.]

[2] [No such book in fact exists.]

tation growing where it can in hollows and crevices in the black lava. This zone, extending from the base of the mountain at 6,000′ to about 10,000′ is where the Kurds graze their flocks of sheep and goats, moving higher as the dry season progresses; we would expect that if there were any remains of Trease in this area, they would have been found.

This zone passes into one of extensive boulder slopes with little vegetation; the boulders range in size from four metres across, down to less than one metre, and are often precariously balanced. It is quite possible in this zone to slip and fall, which could have serious results if help were not forthcoming. The 'zone of boulders' lies between the grazing slopes and the snow line (about 14,000′), and because there is little vegetation, the Kurds do not pass into this area.

The ice-cap with the glaciers is our third zone, and all the hazards connected with ice are present. Since, however, the Americans have made an extremely thorough search of the area, we think it unlikely that any remains of Trease will be found there.

Hence the results of the Expedition are disappointing to the extent that nothing positive has come out of our stay on the mountain; on the other hand, we feel that, together with other expeditions to the area this summer, we have covered considerable areas of the mountain.

It is possible that the remains of Trease are concealed in a crevasse or on the boulder slopes, and if so, it is unlikely that they will be found easily. The possibility of foul play, however, cannot be ruled out.

13

The Archaeological Research Foundation (1966)

An investigation of the geology, glaciology, and botany of Ararat took place in 1964-1966 under the auspices of the Archaeological Research Foundation. Seventh-Day Adventist representation was strong in this organization, and its members were generally believers in the biblical account of the Flood. The following selections are taken from the combined report of the 1964 and 1966 A.R.F. expeditions (1967), edited by Lawrence B. Hewitt, M.D.

Geological Reconnaissance of the Ararat Area
By Clifford L. Burdick, Ph.D.

Greater Ararat is perpetually covered with an ice capping down to the 14,000 foot level in summer. This ice cap is hundreds of feet thick and as it flows down the sides of the mountain, it divides into twelve fingers or glaciers, two of which are the Parrot and Abich glaciers, the latter of which tumbles down a vertical precipice thousands of feet into the Ahore[1] Gulch, with a mighty roar that can be heard for miles. Both the ice cap and the resulting glaciers move over rough terrain, which breaks them into segments, separated with crevasses. Often new falls of snow drift over these crevasses, thus hiding them from view. Climbers often fall into these crevasses.

The comparatively high snow-line is due to the light precipitation and the upward rush of dry air, from the Aras plain. This plain is a veritable bread basket for both Turkey and Russia. Although the upper and lower

---

[1] [i.e., Ahora.]

237

zones on the mountain are sterile, the middle zone, from 5,000 to 11,500 feet, is covered with good pasture, which the Kurdish sheep and goat herders make good use of.

The dangers are many. Storms and winds of 100 miles an hour and temperatures of below zero made life disagreeable for our glaciologists. At one time during the expedition our geologists were caught out on the mountain in a thunderstorm that brought with it pelting sleet and rain. After the storm an ensuing fog developed, making it difficult for them to find their way back to camp. They arrived late at night, soaking wet, cold and exhausted. Without a good sense of direction and a flashlight they might have been new victims of Ararat.

This section would not be complete without mentioning what was perhaps the most violent eruption which Ararat ever experienced. This did not occur in 1840 as some have surmised and was infinitely more terrific. Some time after Ararat attained greatest height almost the whole northeast side of the mountain blew up. A long, deep gash was opened in the mountain, known now as the Ahore Gulch. This is many miles long and thousands of feet deep and wide, and a conservative estimate would be that from one to two cubic miles of rock debris and volcanic ash were blown from the mountain. The larger surface fragments were hurled miles away, down toward the lower slopes of the northeast side, where they are yet visible.

The lighter volcanic ash was blown into the upper atmosphere and settled down as light-colored, whitish tuff on the east and northeast sides of the mountain, covering some 100 square miles of surface to a thickness of from hundreds of feet near the mountain to a few feet ten miles away. This has formed a sloping pediment of some 3-5 degrees similar to those seen in the desert southwest in Arizona. As a result, in the Ahore Gulch area is to be found the most varied rock specimens of the whole Ararat area.

This is the type of volcanic eruption that buried Pompeii and Herculaneum in 79 A.D.

The original Ararat had been deeply blanketed before that, and the only part of the original Ararat now exposed is that at the head of the Ahore Gulch where the giant explosion opened it up.

Little Ararat and other parasite cones are of more recent origin, for Little Ararat is smoother and less gullied and eroded than Greater Ararat. On the eastern slopes of Little Ararat exist the only forests in the whole area. . . .

Abich reported that in the earthquake of 1840 an avalanche of mud and water came down Ahore Gulch burying not only Ahore and St. James monastery, but covering the valley glacier to such a depth that it has insulated and preserved the ice from melting to any great extent until the present.[2] The writer noted the same situation on the Parrot glacier on the northwest side of the mountain, where the lower end of the glacier is covered deep with talus and volcanic debris. In summer where the cover is thin and toward the terminal moraine the ice melts and lets the cover rock drop into the canyon. This is also true of the Ahore glacier. In the bottom end of the Parrot glacier the melting water carries the smaller fragments downstream, but boulders weighing tons are still perched up on ice necks many feet above the glacial floor. Eventually this neck will melt and the rock will roll down hill.

The largest stream flowing down the mountain of Ararat comes down the Ahore Gulch and joins the Aras River. One wonders why there are not more streams, until it is realized that the surface of Ararat is very rough and porous and the youthful morphology of the mountain explains why fine sediment has not yet filled the interstices. For that reason the water from the melting snow sinks deep into the rock cover and may

[2] Abich, "Der Ararat in genogischer Beziehung betrachtet," *Zeitschrift b. Deutschen Geol. Gesellschaft,* XXII (1870); and Abich, "Nachrichten über eine geognostische Reise zum Ararat und insbersonder über die Verschüttung des Tales von Aguri, im Jahre 1840," *Monatsberichte über d. Verhandl. d. Gesellschaft f. Erdkunde zu Berlin,* n.s., IV (1847).

come to the surface down in the valley as springs or artesian wells.

Jacob's Well, in Ahore Gulch, where camp was made, at the 7,500 ft. elevation on the N-E side of the mountain, is fed by seepage down the mountainside in an aquifer of tuff sandwiched between lava flows. Other exposures also show beds of tuff covered with lava flows, indicating that the volcanic explosion was not the first nor the final tectonic event at Ararat.

On the north side of Ahore Gulch the strata dip about 10 degrees to the northwest, while across the canyon the black rocks dip about the same amount to the southeast, perhaps indicating that at the time of explosive eruption subterranean forces domed up the mountain as the explosion took place, forming an anticline of the remaining beds. Up through this fracture evidently flowed the later lava that built up the mountain to its full height, for the layers at the top dip parallel to those on the southeast side of Ahore Gulch. Furthermore, there is evidence that the black volcanics on the southeast side of the gulch are later than the original core of the mountain, for the bottom layers on the left going up canyon are a volcanic breccia, indicating that they were formed from broken up previous volcanic flows, while the original core seems undisturbed except for the tilting.

Instead of Ararat forming a drainage pattern radiating from the mountain, the watershed drainage flows to the Aras and Tigris and Euphrates apparently as if it did not know that Ararat existed, thus suggesting a more recent birthday for Ararat. The original drainage system may have been established from the days of Creation. Everything about Ararat suggests youth.

It has been brought out before that the bursting forth of Ararat domed the surrounding rocks such as in Ahore Gulch and the limestones surrounding Ararat, but our investigations on the shoulders of Ararat near the Ahore Gulch showed a strange tectonic phenomenon—underthrusting—that is, the upwelling magma pushed the deeper rocks aside as it made room for the rising magma, while the surface rock cover was more stationary. This was deduced from 8 bends or folds in the rock exposures.

As mentioned under the Section on Plutonic and Metamorphic Rocks (Eastern Turkey), faults in the Ararat area follow four trends, N-S, E-W, NE-SW and NW-SE. The dominant trend seems to be NE-SW and follows a fault or deep earth fracture or shear along which Ararat, Tendurek, Suphan, and Nemrut were born. When it is realized that the Ahore Gulch and its SE counterpart that cuts through the mountain is aligned along this lineament, this helps to explain the existence of the Ahore Gorge. The mountain grew from extrusions up through this old fracture, and the explosive phase naturally followed the same fracture system.

There are fractures in other directions through which flowed later lavas on the sides of the mountain; and many of these fractures are filled with red dikes, indicating oxidation of black iron to red.

The sunken ring or moat around the mountain calls for an explanation. Ararat apparently followed the same pattern as other volcanoes. As it grew it domed the surrounding rock strata to make room for the rising magma. After the volcano reached its ultimate height and maturity, it gradually reached the old age phase, and the lava began to drop back down the lava conduits into the bowels of the earth forming what is known as a caldera. As the molten magma drained back into the lower crust, it left a void or hollow, and the weight of the cover rocks caused the crust to collapse and fill the voids, thus leaving a sunken ring around the mountain, now occupied by poorly drained swampy land.

Glaciological Report

by Nicolaas A. Van Arkel, Ph.D.
Mathematical Institute, Leiden, Holland*

The Ararat complex consists of 2 individual strato-vulcanoes: Big Ararat or Büyük Agri Dag with a height of 5165 mtrs, and Little Ararat or Kücük Agri Dag with a height of 3925 mtrs.

Both vulcanoes are relatively young and must have been built up between the Young Neogene and the Quaternary. No eruptions or other vulcanic activities are known since historical times.

Little Ararat has the shape of a perfect cone, but Big Ararat has the form of a saddle. A main crater cannot be found though many small parasitic craters are situated in the flanks of the mountain, especially in the Mihtepe-and Kip Göl areas.

In Turkey the snowline is at a height of ± 4000 mtrs (Messerk. B.). Little Ararat has no snow cover during the summer, but Big Ararat has an ice sheet of ± 12 square km, at the fringes of which are small valley glaciers. The largest of these are the Cehennem Dere glacier, flowing into the direction of Ahuri, and the Parrot glacier, flowing toward Kip Göl.

The observations recorded in this report were made during the 1966 Archaeological Research Foundation glacier, flowing toward Kip Göl.

From 2 July 1966 until 3 August 1966 I was on Mt. Ararat. The actual time spent on the ice cap was from 17 July until 3 August, so 17 days. In this time 26 stakes were put into the ice and were triangulated. In addition field sketches and photographs from triangulated points were made. Only one-third of the ice cap could be covered. Lack of time, dangerous climbing and bad weather were the cause that no more area could be covered. Temperature-measurements could

---

* [With "invaluable field assistance during the time spent on the ice cap" from Swiss mountaineer Theo Koller.]

not be done as no ice-drill was available. Thickness and heaviness of the wooden stakes were also a cause that not more could be done. . . .

The first week of our stay on the ice cap was marked by bad weather conditions. We got much hail, with hailstones of ± 5 mm, and some thunderstorms. Also it could be very misty. Often the fogs came up out of the Ahora valley. Needless to say we could not work during such weather and had to stay in our tents.

The second week we had much better weather. The temperature was higher, and there was much more melting on the glaciers. However in the afternoon we got in general fogs and wind. On Tuesday 26th July we had a very bad storm during the whole day. I measured a wind velocity of up to 23 mtrs/sec. The wind came from the South, directly over the summit of the Mountain. Some stakes on the ice were blown down. Also the next day there was still much wind (± 10 mtrs/sec.). However on Thursday the weather was beautiful and we could work again.

The best time to be on Mt. Ararat is probably in August when ablation is most intensive, and the crevasses are clearly visible. In 1964 I was on Mt. Ararat in the middle of August.

PART FOUR

Ark Fever: Today's Endeavor to Find Noah's Ark

1

An Account of the Author's Successful Ascent of Ararat in August, 1970[1]

Everyone has heard of the 1849 gold rush. People who should have known better and people who did know better headed for the Cal-i-for-nay-ey to find the elusive substance of their dreams. Many failed, some succeeded, and all were stricken in varying degrees with a grievous malady called gold fever.

Now, over a century later, a not unrelated compulsion is spreading. Silvia Tipton of the Anaheim, California, *Sunday Mail,* has baptized it "Ark fever," for the stricken are willing to undergo amazing hardships in order to recover the Ark of Noah on the remote mountain of Greater Ararat in eastern Turkey. Even relatively sane and sedate professors have been bitten by this bug. I know, because I am one of them. On August 17, 1970, at 1:30 P.M., I attained the incredibly difficult 16,946 ft. peak of Ararat while engaged in this search, and my eleven-year-old son came within 550 meters of the summit, thus becoming the youngest westerner ever to reach that altitude on the mountain.

How does one fall victim to this disease? How is it treated? Can it be cured?

Before taking up these questions, it is well to note the true gravity of the affliction. While I was agonizingly endeavoring to obtain permission from a Turkish official in the frontier town of Dogubayazit to climb the mountain, his phone rang. It was the Ministry of the Interior in Ankara. Twenty Americans wanted permission to go fishing in Lake Kop on Ararat. The official

---

[1] Published in considerably abbreviated form in *Christianity Today,* July 2, 1971.

roared with laughter. There were not now, nor apparently had there ever been, fish in the minuscule lake. But sighting of a "boat in the ice" and discoveries of fragments of ancient hand-tooled wood have occurred in the immediate region of that lake. So compulsive is ark fever that it can lead to duplicity—and not necessarily to intelligent duplicity.

Ark Fever: Its Cause

Why does one give up a glorious Alsatian summertime and French haute cuisine to learn mountain climbing technique from fanatical Swiss naturists who not only sadistically put the novice through physical agonies that would make a marine corps sergeant blush, but who continually jabber in totally incomprehensible Schweizer-deutsch? Why would any sane person then alternately boil and freeze on a mountain so high that often only ten or fifteen steps can be taken without sitting down to recover one's breath in the rarified atmosphere?

The answer may come as a surprise: because of the tremendous amount of solid evidence that on the mountain the Turks call Agri Dagh—the Mountain of Agony—a substantial vestige of the Ark of Noah, if not the Ark's massive hull itself—remains to this very day, frozen in the glacial ice, but occasionally attaining the surface when the ice cap recedes under the blazing August sun.

Here we do not refer to the accounts of the Ark's survival in biblical and classical times, such as the assertion of 1st-century Jewish historian Josephus, who cites earlier, pagan writers Berossus the Chaldean, Hieronymus the Egyptian, Mnaseas, and Nicolaus of Damascus (*Jewish Antiquities* I. 89-95; nor to the Greek church father Epiphanius (4th century), who said that relics of the Ark could be seen in his day (*Panarion,* I. i. 18) nor to the Koran (11:44), where the Ark lands on "Al Judi" (i.e., the "excellent" or "approved" mountain, in the rendering suggested by modern Ahmadiyya scholar Maulvi Muhammad Ali);

nor to medieval traveller Marco Polo (13th century), who explicitly connects the landing of the Ark with Greater Ararat, and Sir John Mandeville (14th Century), whose claim that the Ark can be seen distinctly on the top of the mountain is somewhat reduced in value by his estimate of the height of Ararat as seven miles! Nor are we speaking of as relatively modern an account as that of distinguished historian and British ambassador to the United States James Bryce (author of *The Holy Roman Empire* and *The American Commonwealth),* who ascended Greater Ararat in early September, 1876, and—in his own words—"saw at a height of over 13,000 feet . . . a piece of wood about four feet long and five inches thick, evidently cut by some tool, and so far above the limit of trees that it could be no possibility be a natural fragment of one"; this "relic," said Bryce, "suits all the requirements" (*Transcaucasia and Ararat* [1876], pp. 264-66) and supports the powerful and longstanding local tradition that the Ark did in fact come to rest on Greater Ararat —a view which he accepted and defended in a spirited discussion with Sir Henry Rawlinson before the Royal Geographical Society *(Proceedings,* February 25, 1878).

Ancient traditions and 19th-century discoveries of Ark relics can certainly whet the appetite; but a full-fledged case of Ark fever, at least for a member of the hidebound academic community, requires a more substantial base. Mine was provided by Mr. and Mrs. Eryl Cummings of Farmington, New Mexico—a kindly sixty-year-old couple whose appearance suggests that their avocation is bridge or television, but who have in fact been researching modern reports of Ark sightings for more than a quarter of a century. Mr. Cummings himself has engaged in exploration on Ararat, and is one of the few Americans who stands a decent chance of continuing work in that region of touchy political relationships; and Mrs. Cummings has prepared a manuscript summarizing the recent evidence for the Ark's continued existence on Greater Ararat. Having read a brief but tantalizing notice of the Cummings' activities in the Newsletter of the American Scientific Affiliation, I contacted them in October, 1969, and arranged a meeting for early January, 1970, when Mr. Cummings was scheduled to speak in San Diego and I would be serving as Visiting Professor and Honorary Fellow of Revelle College at the University of California at San Diego. As a result of this meeting I was graciously given access to Mrs. Cummings' manuscript, and its contents sent my pulse racing; Ark fever had most certainly set in.

It would be impossible here to mention even a major proportion of the evidence. But several staggering—yet typical—illustrations can be given, particularly since in two instances I was personally able to obtain collateral substantiation.

First, the 1916 Russian expedition. Students of biblical archeology are familiar with André Parrot's little book, *Déluge et Arche de Noé* (2nd edition, 1953), in which the author includes the following sarcastic reference: "During the First World War, a Russian airman named W. Roskovitsky, flying over Mount Ararat, declared that he had observed on one of the slopes of the mountain the remains of an ancient vessel. The Czar at once organized an expedition, which, we are told, found the remains in question and brought back a description of them which was conclusive as regards their identification." The source of Parrot's reference was a 1949 issue of the *Journal de Genève,* but the same story appeared in several other publications. One of them was the Russian-language periodical *Rosseya.* Its author, the Cummingses discovered, was a White Russian colonel, Alexander A. Koor. This distinguished officer, archaeologist, and philologue had escaped from Russia after the Revolution, and had reached California by way of Manchuria. He supplied the Cummingses with a sworn statement declaring, *inter alia:* "About July or August, 1921, I and Lt. Leslin met 1st Lt. Rujansky in Harbin [Manchuria, where they had escaped from the Bolsheviks.] During one of our conversations, 1st Lt. Rujanksy told me about the discovery of Noah's Ark. He didn't know about the details because he was wounded and was sent to Russia, but he knew because his brother Boris Vasilivich Rujansky, sergeant of the Military Railroad Battalion, was a member of the investigating party which was sent to Mount Ararat to corroborate the discovery of Noah's Ark." Further investigations by the Cummingses among White Russian émigrés on the Pacific coast located relatives of two other (then deceased) soldiers who had been on the expedition, who had never met because they were in different groups, but who had narrated the same facts to their respective families; these facts were in agreement with Colonel Koor's information.

As for Colonel Koor himself, he was still alive in the spring of 1970, though he was becoming feeble with advanced age.[2] I myself spent an afternoon with him and his daughter in their modest and book-filled apartment in Menlo Park, California. I had no doubt of the Colonel's integrity and scholarly precision in conveying factual data. He, in turn, was fully confident of his sources, having known intimately the officers who gave him accounts of their sightings of the Ark on Ararat.

In 1953, an article was published by a reputable (and now deceased) journalist[3] which stated that information relating to the existence of remains of the Ark . . . is contained in documents presented to the library of the University of Geneva by Gen. Dimitri Osnobichine, an aide to the Grand Duke Cyril in Czarist days." Soon after arriving in France in April to conduct my seminary's annual European Program at the Protestant Theological Faculty of the University of Strasbourg, I flew to Geneva to check this out in the hopes that the original reports of the Russian expedition might still be preserved. I found that General Osnobichine had indeed settled in Geneva after the Revolution, that he had died there, and that he had made bequests to the University of Geneva Library. But only his printed books had apparently entered the University Library; there was no sign of personal papers or manu-

---

[2] Colonel Koor has since passed away.

[3] Henry Wales (d. 1960), "Relics of Noah's Ark," *Chicago Sunday Tribune*, March 29, 1953. The article carried a Paris by-line.

scripts. In meticulously examining the printed items, however, I came across a French pamphlet—published in 1922 in Munich, Germany!—titled, *Le Grande Duc Kirill: L' auguste gardien du trône.* This tribute to Cyril was issued by the Union of Russian Legitimist Monarchists, and from it I learned that Cyril had also escaped at the time of the Revolution. He had made his way through the Baltic countries to southern France, and a son, Vladimir, had been born to him in Finland in 1917. Research—and luck—put me in contact with a Frenchwoman of Russian extraction in Nice who provided me with the information that Vladimir was alive and well and living—not in Paris—but in Madrid! For several months I corresponded with him. He writes: "I am, and have always been, extremely interested in this and similar subjects. I shall try to get information concerning the whereabouts of Gen. Osnobichine's papers, and let you know as soon as possible."[*]

Nineteen-sixteen is over a half-century ago. If the reader tends to regard this also as ancient history, consider briefly the case of oil pipeline and mining engineer George Jefferson Greene, who in late summer of 1952 was reconnoitering for his company in a helicopter over Mount Ararat. He distinctly saw the prow of a ship in the ice. Circling within ninety feet of the object, Greene photographed it several times. On returning to the United States, he showed his excellent 8 x 10 blown-up photographs to friends and acquaintances, who declare that these pictures unquestionably showed a vessel in the ice and were not retouched or faked. Subsequently Greene went to British Guiana on another mining project—and on December 27, 1962, was murdered, apparently for gold. None of the possessions he brought to British Guiana were recovered, nor was his murder solved. But the photographs—six of them —had existed, and some thirty people had seen them. The Cummingses have the sworn testimonies of several of these persons. One of the Cummings' associates, Dr.

---

[*] For the fascinating, but ultimately negative, result of this investigation, see below, Appendix C.

Clifford L. Burdick, a geologist, obtained the most specific kind of description of the photographs from an oil man who had had contact with Greene in 1954; even "wooden side planking" could be identified on the photographed vessel. My personal conversations with Dr. Burdick while in California convinced me of his reliability and scientific acumen; it was not difficult to see why the Cummingses had found Burdick a powerful ally in an endeavor generally eliciting little more than knowing smiles of incredulity from the scientific establishment.

In August of the same year—1952—the French amateur explorer Fernand Navarra made the first of his three explorations of Greater Ararat. Though now well known in America, Navarra has gained considerable renown in his own country for his exploratory activities (space is devoted to his work, for example, in the standard French Fodor guide to Turkey). Navarra recounted his 1952 exploration in his book, *L'Expédition au Mont Ararat* (1953), which was published in English translation in London three years later. After having attained the summit of Ararat on August 14th, 1952, and having been the first Frenchman ever to have planted the tricolor there, Navarra and his companion Jean de Riquier proceeded to search for traces of the Ark. Here is his account of what they saw:

It was August 17th—we had reached an altitude of 13,800 feet and the enormous ice cap stretched before us. . . . We were surrounded by whiteness, stretching into the distance, yet beneath our eyes was this astonishing patch of blackness within the ice, its outlines sharply defined.

Fascinated and intrigued, we began straightway to trace out its shape, mapping out its limits foot by foot: two progressively incurving lines were revealed, which were clearly defined for a distance of three hundred cubits, before meeting in the heart of the glacier. The shape was unmistakably that of a ship's hull: on either side the edges of the patch curved like the gunwales of a great boat. . . .

No more than a few yards of ice separated us from the extraordinary discovery which the world no longer believed possible.

Further confirmation could not be made, for the expedition had no radar equipment with it. In July, 1953, Navarra returned to Ararat in an effort to photograph the outlines of the vessel in the ice, but he was afflicted with such severe mountain sickness that he had to return empty-handed. In a short address to the Geographical Society of France on March 12, 1955, de Riquier expressed doubt that the Ark was really there at all: "Universal mythology cites forty mountains of the Ark, but here, at Ararat, the legend still survives. Nonetheless, as for recovering a prehistoric boat on the mountain, I regard it as a vain enterprise, unless one day an extraordinary and providential eruption or glacial retrenchment should reveal it—if in fact Ararat does guard such a mystery" ("Le Pays d'Ararat," *Acta Geographica* [Paris], XXI/1 [1957], 5-8).

However, by July, Navarra was back on the mountain in company with his eleven year-old son Raphael. With great difficulty they made their way to the area where Navarra had seen the silhouette of a boat under the ice in 1952, and, on the suggestion of Raphael, he dug down and found hand-tooled wood. Lacking the tools for extensive digging, Navarra nevertheless cut off and brought back a piece 1½ meters long. Elated, he recalled both the words of Scripture, "a little child shall lead them," and the conviction of an old Armenian story-teller, "to find the Ark, one must be pure as a child." But Navarra did not let such mystical flights deter him from more prosaic, scientific checking after his return to Europe. He subjected his wood to analysis both at the University of Bordeaux (its Prehistoric Institute of the Faculty of Sciences) and at the Forestry Institute of Research and Experimentation, Madrid, Spain. The Bordeaux report (April 15, 1956) declared that the fossilized wood derived from "an epoch of great antiquity" *(une époque remontant à une haute antiquité);* and the Madrid analysis (April 7, 1956) estimated the age of the fragment at 5,000 years *("la edad . . . oscila alrededor de los cinco mil años")* Radiocarbon examinations of the wood have not dated the fragment as early as this, but contamination of the wood at a later stage in its history could well account for this fact, and the instability of the radiocarbon dating method for the sample in question is illustrated by the widely divergent results of two radiocarbon tests on the same fragment.

As for Navarra himself, the title of his second book —*J'ai trouvé L'Arche de Noé* ("I found Noah's Ark") —makes clear his view. This book, which describes Navarra's 1955 expedition in detail and includes the Bordeaux and Madrid analyses of the wood as an appendix, produced the most lively discussions in France when it appeared in 1956; it has not as yet been translated into English, and, ironically, the year of its publication also marked the appearance of the English version of Navarra's earlier—and now largely superseded —book. In concluding his second book, Navarra argued that, by process of elimination, the 5,000-year-old hand-tooled wood, at an elevation well above any known structure ever to have been erected on the mountain, is best accounted for as a portion of the Ark. He had gone this far with his son and with the most mediocre equipment; if others were to seek confirmation with better means, he "would be more than happy to guide them and to put at their disposal [his] knowledge of the mountain." "With me or without me," he wrote, "my greatest desire is that they succeed."

In 1969, Navarra returned to Ararat with a SEARCH Foundation expedition and uncovered more wood. Mr. Cummings' contacts with him in Turkey, and my afternoon with him in Rouen (June 2, 1970) confirm the integrity and constancy of his dream. In Rouen, on the site of his demolition of a vast chemical plant (he is the *président directeur général* of one of the largest industrial demolition companies in France),

he not only shared his Champagne with me, but gave
me two most valuable items of information: he assured
me that yere I to go up the mountain, my own eleven-
year-old son David could certainly survive the rigors as
had Raphael fifteen years before; and he drew me on
the spot a map of the location of his finds, with precise
elevation figures! Could any resistance survive an attack of Ark fever such as that?

Ark Fever: Its Treatment

The accounts of sightings described here (and the
many others not even mentioned because of space limitations) do not *prove* that the Ark remains on Greater
Ararat. But their coordination both in time (the sightings consistently occur in late summer, when the ice
cap recedes to the maximum) and in space (they focus
in the area of Lake Kop, on the northern face of the
mountain) are highly suggestive, to say the very least.
Some of the greatest archeological discoveries in history have occurred on the basis of following outlines of
preliminary evidence so flimsy that they make the
above accounts of Ark sightings almost conclusive by
comparison.

Surely, I reasoned, the alleged sightings warrant, at a
minimum, the most careful investigation of the mountain. Since I am in France with my family from April
to August anyway, there is no good reason why I
should not participate! If circumstances permit—if Mr.
Cummings is able to put together an expedition—my
son and I will be on it! The only way to treat Ark fever
effectively, without repressing the Jungian Ark archetype to the unhealthy recesses of the soul, is to go to
Ararat and search for the vessel *in situ!*

In March my visiting professorship terminated at the
University of California at San Diego, and we proceeded directly to France for the spring quarter of teaching
at the University of Strasbourg. During the ensuing
months I held my case of Ark fever somewhat in check
by ransacking the University of Geneva Library for the
Osnobichine documents and for information on Grand

Duke Cyril, and by my contacts with Fernand Navarra. But would I ever actually get to the mountain? Already it was July, and exploration must be carried on in August to take advantage of the maximum recession of the ice cap. Yet I had not heard from Mr. Cummings regarding the outcome of his efforts to obtain financial support for what we termed the "International Expedition, '70." (Money, incidentally, is not only the root of all evil, but also the perennial problem of explorers—from Columbus's day to our own. And, unlike Columbus, we were attempting a major operation, not at a time of booming Renaissance economy, but in a year when the stock market was depressingly low!)

Sunday morning, July 26, I was awakened by the arrival of a telegram at my Strasbourg apartment. It read: "Eryl Cummings will arrive Pan American flight 114 Monday morning July 27 Paris" and was signed by Mr. Cummings' faithful anchor man in the International Expedition, Malcolm Randall. All systems were go! My son and I took the one-hour Caravelle flight from Strasbourg to Paris that evening. At the Hôtel Perreyve, a small and typically French hotel in the Latin Quarter, just a half block from the Luxembourg Gardens—considered by many to be the most beautiful formal park in the world—we met Mr. Cummings. and his companion, red-haired Mark Albrecht of the Christian World Liberation Front (an organization presenting the Christian message to the hippies and freaked-out in the San Francisco Bay area). Here we planned our strategy. Because of the rumors of political crises in Turkey (Istanbul was temporarily under martial law), we would travel independently in two groups: Eryl and Mark would go immediately to the mountain, while my son David and I would arrive August 12, after we had obtained preliminary mountain training in Switzerland and had tidied up our office in Strasbourg. The plan was to avoid "making waves" through publicity; we would seek permissions individually, not in behalf of any monolithic and impressive organization; we would attempt to obtain limited, yet concrete, evidence of the Ark's survival in the area where past testimonies and observations had focused. Mr. Cummings's knowledge of the Turks and their psychology dictated these policies, and they were to prove their worth.

The following day we braved the overpowering heat and humidity (uncommon in Paris in the summer, but good background for Turkey!), and obtained our equipment. At the famed Galleries Lafayette we obtained our Bleuet stoves, lamps, and butane cartridges, but little else, for the needs of alpinists are too specific for a *grand magazin* however excellent. It was at La Cordée, on the rue de Rome, that we found our lightweight tents, air mattresses and sleeping bags, rucksacks, mountain boots, crampons (spike attachments for the boots, necessary for climbing on the ice cap), and the mountaineer's "third leg," alpine ice axes. After a fine lunch at nearby Printemps—one can hardly obtain a poor meal, even if one tries on a low budget, in the world's gastronomical capital!—we proceeded to a left-bank store, Au Vieux Campeur, on the rue des Écoles where students have strolled since the Middle Ages, to secure various items of high-altitude clothing. Mr. Cummings was by this time dozing on his feet from the effects of the transatlantic time change and the heat; and I was beat from a day of translation in a field prickling with technical terminology. Only David was in perfect shape, demonstrating that eleven-year-olds must not be excluded *a priori* from such ventures!

That evening David and I took the 9 o'clock flight back to Strasbourg, and the following morning Eryl and Mark flew from Paris-Orly to Istanbul. The task my son and I now faced was that of alpine training, or, more accurately, alpine training as applied to Greater Ararat, which exceeds in height the highest of the alpine peaks, Mont Blanc. We were most fortunate in having contact with Herr Theo Koller of Dübendorf, near Zurich, Switzerland, who had accompanied Mr. Cummings on a previous Ararat expedition (the 1966 Archeological Research Foundation effort, involving Harry Crawford, Lawrence Hewitt—a physician and amateur botanist—and N. A. Van Arkel, whose glaciological report on the mountain was accepted as original doctoral research by the University of Leiden). Koller was not able to accompany us personally on the practice climb, but he secured two mountaineering friends who put us through the paces after he had given us the necessary alpine theory. The weekend of August 1—the Swiss national holiday—was spent in agonizing climbing on both rock and glacier. While bonfires blazed on the hills, symbolizing Swiss independence, my son and I endeavored to become masters rather than slaves of mountain technique. On the Lockberg pass, 9 km. from Goschen near Andermatt, we were put through our paces by Herr Nyfeler and Fräulein Schreiber, whose sadistic glee in watching our ineptitude was only exceeded by the near incomprehensibility of their Swiss-German dialect!

But we survived and later realized that the rigors we had been put through were precisely the preparation needed for the far more difficult climb of Ararat.

On our return, stiff but elated, to Strasbourg, a note from Mr. Cummings was awaiting us. It indicated that he had reached Ankara safely, that an exploratory team representing another organization "evidently went prior to permit being granted and we are told were arrested," but that "Ararat is open to tourist climbers." Troubled by the rumor of arrest, but encouraged by the green light to "tourist climbers," we picked up our food supply for the mountain (addicted as we are to French cuisine and suspicious of Turkish can goods), bought several final items of equipment, such as the shocking expensive Thommen alpine altimeter that registers altitude to 6000 meters (the height of Greater Ararat is 5165 meters: 16,946 ft.), and packed our supplies and equipment. Friday the 7th we flew from Paris to Istanbul—father devouring Paul Bessière's *L'Alpinisme,* and Alpine Club of Switzerland's *Manual d'Alpinisme,* and being horrified by the discription of mountain sickness (bleeding from nose and ears, etc.) in Jacques Gautrat's *Dictionnaire de la Montagne;* his son, chuckling over two new French *Lucky Luke* cartoon books. . . .

Since Ararat is on the eastern edge of Turkey, one

must therefore traverse western Turkey to reach it, we had made arrangements to see Istanbul and the historic sites of Pergamon and Ephesus on our way. After clearing customs in the incredible confusion of the Istanbul airport (a confusion compounded by inexplicable structural alterations in progress in the concourses, reminding one strangely of New York's JFK), we flew immediately to Izmir, one hour by air to the south, where a short drive puts one in immediate contact with the ruins of Ephesus and Pergamon. We spent a day at each of these sites which invoke repeatedly the ghosts of Christian and of pagan antiquity.

Pergamon was one of the greatest centers of classical culture. Not long after its conquest by one of the generals of Alexander the Great, Pergamon became an independent kingdom (283 B.C.), and remained such until its last king bequeathed the city to his allies the Romans in 133 B. C. During its century and a half of independent existence, Pergamon boasted a library to rival that of Alexandria. Pliny the Elder, following Varro tells the charming story *(Natural History,* XIII.11) that in an effort to keep the Pergamon library smaller than the Alexandrian, by reducing the possibility of copying books for it, Ptolemy put an embargo on the exportation of papyrus from Egypt—but his rival King Eumenes of Pergamon got the better of him by inventing parchment. The story is a bit over-done (parchment was in existence at an earlier date, and Vitruvius has Ptolemy found his library in competition to the one at Pergamon!) but bibliophilistic rivalry between Eumenes II and Ptolemy Epiphanes was genuine enough (Eumenes tried to steal Ptolemy's librarian, and Ptolemy thereupon jailed the librarian), and the term "parchment" does in fact derive from "Pergamon." In E. A. Parsons' expert judgment, "Pergamon was from the 2nd century B. C. recognized as the center of production, if not the place of origin, of the finest animal skins for writing" *(The Alexandrian Library* [Amsterdam: Elsevier, 1952], p. 27; cf. F. G. Kenyon, *Books and Readers in Ancient Greece and Rome* [2nd ed.; Oxfords Clarendon Press, 1951], pp.

88-90. Parchment eventually replaced papyrus as the common writing surface, only to be itself replaced by paper at the end of our western Middle Ages in connection with the introduction of printing from movable type. As for the ultimate disposition of the 200,000 volume Pergamon library collection, we are told by Plutarch that it was given by Antony to Cleopatra. Also at Pergamon one finds the Asclepion: an ancient healing center which employed sophisticated techniques of physiotherapy and psychotherapy (including dream analysis!). On the portal death was "prohibited to enter in the name of the gods." But death did enter, and only ruins are left. Even the gods invoked have now died, for they were powerless in the face of "the last enemy." Pergamon itself is little more than a grave, and its most impressive remains are not even to be found in Asia Minor. In the late 1870s the German archeologist Karl Humann excavated the Pergamon acropolis (modeled on that at Athens) and transferred the best preserved fragments of the great Altar of Zeus to Berlin. Today this altar, magnificently re-erected, forms the center of the Pergamon Museum, on Museum Island, in East Berlin—where my son and I would see it four months later on a trip to that divided city. *Sic transit gloria mundi.*

Ephesus puts one in direct touch with the faith that was alone capable of conquering that last enemy, death, and of transforming the ancient world into Christian civilization. Here too are remains of the Hellenistic age, but even these support the judgments of its early Christian critics: more effective by far than the fecundity representations of Artemis-Diana, Bes, Serapis, and Eros in showing the toleration of immorality in Greco-Roman life is the impressive twenty-room brothel across the way from the famous library of the Roman senator Celcius (with its former status symbolizing the virtues of "culture," "intelligence," "wisdom," and "tolerance"!). But at the same time one sees the legendary and historical evidences of the new religion that regarded the body as nothing less than God's temple and exhorted believers (as Paul wrote to the Romans) to "put on the Lord Jesus Christ, and make not provision for the flesh, to fulfil the lusts thereof." The ruins of the theatre and the temple of Artemis are there—where the silversmith Demetrius, losing money as Paul's preaching against idolatry turned his fellow citizens from the purchase of his statues of Diana, whipped a crowd into frenzy with the cry, "Great is Diana of the Ephesians" (Acts 19). The traditional site of the prison where Paul was incarcerated at Ephesus and the gravesite of the Apostle John (whose later years and death at Ephesus are well attested) link the visitor with the days in which the struggling band of Christians in Ephesus constituted one of the "seven churches" of Asia singled out in John's Apocalypse. On the less significant side, we inevitably also found ourselves visiting the alleged House of the Virgin (Mary's home—of little more historical value than the comfortable house shown to us in Jerusalem two years before!) and the Grotto of the Seven Sleepers (where seven young people—and their dog—fled from the Decian persecution and awoke 300 years later!).

On our return to Istanbul, we focused our attention on the breathtaking Hagia Sophia—the Church of the Holy Wisdom—the greatest monument of Byzantine church architecture in the world. Wrote Procopius of Caesarea in the 6th century of the church's dome: it is "as if suspended by a chain from heaven." In our own time, Roman Catholic historian Christopher Dawson has rightly said of the church: "Architecture transcends its limitations and becomes impalpable and immaterial as the vault of the sky itself. . . . Never has man succeeded more perfectly in moulding matter to become the vehicle and expression of the spirit" (*The Making of Europe* [London, 1932], p. 120). With all Christian visitors we were saddened, to be sure, by the almost complete defacing of the mosaics by Moslems in the centuries since the capture of Constantinople by Ottoman Turks in 1453 (cf. Sir Banister Fletcher, *A History of Architecture on the Comparative Method* [15th ed.; London: Batsford, 1950], pp. 242-46); the

examples which remain (displaying especially the reg-
nant Christ) make only too clear what an artistic loss
has been sustained. The gigantic pasteboard plaques
with Quranic quotations, suspended from dome and
walls, seem but adolescent reminders of the conquest in
comparison. Our evaluation of the Prophet's influence
was not particularly improved by viewing his relics in
the fabulous Topkapi Palace: his skull, strands of hair,
"blessed mantle," etc.; and the harem, apartment of the
Chief Eunuch, and incalculably valuable treasury of the
conqueror of Constantinople and his successors made
us think of the radical contrast between rulers and subjects and general moral lassitude that has prevailed
where the crescent and not the cross has determined
the style of life. Surfeited by the degenerate magnifi-
cence of the Topkapi, we found nature the only suitable corrective: a boat trip to the Princes' Isles, accompanied by a swim and an ethereal fish dinner at the
Akasya restaurant on Büyükada island. Our table directly overlooked the transparent gem-blue water, and
Fodor's French guide to Turkey was fully justified in
recommending the restaurant for having "one of the
best cuisines in Turkey." And if this were not sufficient
consolation, David succeeded in finding some inexpen-
sive antique firearms for his collection, giving his father
a glorious opportunity to exercise the Ulster-Scot tal-
ent for bartering-to-the-death.

Wednesday evening the 12th we were to rendezvous with the others at Dogubayazit, the town 5 km.
south of Greater Ararat which has traditionally served
as the starting point for explorations of the mountain.
That morning, therefore, we picked up our equipment
which we had left stored at the airport, and flew a Turkish Airlines jet as far east as one can take a commercial flight in Turkey: to Erzurum by way of the capital,
Ankara. We had no time to spend in these cities, and it
was only on our return that we were able to view the
gigantic mausoleum of Atatürk (d. 1938), the founder
of the modern Turkish state, who almost literally
created Ankara as his new capital in the 1930s; and the
late 12th-century mosque Ulu Çamii at Erzurum, with

its fine colonnaded courtyard. At 12:25 P.M. we landed at Erzurum and took a cab to the station of the
"best" bus company in town. There we waited—objects of considerable curiosity in spite of the crowd—
until the departure of the bus for Dogubayazit. About 2
P.M. we stuffed ourselves into the back of the vehicle,
hoping against hope that our equipment would not fall
off the top of the bus, and settled in for a six-hour trip.
The bus was a local, to be sure, and soon we found that
we were being squeezed by veiled Moslem women who
are in the habit of occupying the rear! Undaunted, we
stayed where we were—particularly because of the
good photography possible from the rear window—and
adjusted as best we could to the powerful human odors
filling the crowded space. As the hours went by, the
terrain became more and more rough, rocky, and generally primitive.

Shortly after the sun went down behind bare, burnt-
sienna crags, the bus reached Agri—only two-thirds of
the way from Erzurum to Dogubayazit—and everyone
not going to Iran had to get out! For Dogubayazit, one
had to continue by minibus! It was by sheer providence
that we managed to get our equipment off the regular
bus and on to the minibus in the darkness. To add to
the frustration, we found that our fellow travelers consisted largely of a half-dozen Dutch beatniks (than
which no more greasy beatnik can be conceived). We
deduced that they were heading into Iran on an un-
orthodox route—probably looking for hashish, since
Dogubayazit is one of the chief points on the hashish
route from Iran to the west. This should have been bad
enough, but, like so many repressed Dutch youth, they
had incredible sex hang-ups: they were convinced that
the Turks were "after their women" and discussed this
ad nauseam during the trip. Their discussion was, however, effectively terminated by the breakdown of the
minibus in the middle of nowhere—with a flat tire. The
driver spent longer in repairing it than I could have believed possible, but the delay was made most interesting by the passing of a convoy of at least fifty Turkish
military vehicles, including armored cars with mounted

machine guns, tanks, and vans filled with troops. Such a convoy was actually not atypical: because of the fierce and longstanding hatred of the Turks toward the Russians, the Turkish government has turned its Eastern border into a vast armed camp, for the region of the mountains of Ararat constitutes the Turkish-Russian border. Thus by way of hashish and the military our bus journeyed from Erzurum to Dogubayazit introduced us experientially to the two principal reasons for the Turkish political sensitivity to Ark explorations. If one adds the Muslim antipathy to Christian investigations endeavoring to confirm the biblical site of the Ark's resting place (we have already noted that Quranic tradition locates the landing on "Al Judi," though this is not necessarily a place name at all), and the Turkish archeologists' irritation with foreign explorations which have so often denuded the country of the treasures of its past, the potential miseries associated with Ark fever begin to loom very large: and we were to find them waiting for us personally in Dogubayazit.

How relieved we were to reach the town about 10 P.M.—but how appalled to learn at our meeting place, the Kent Hotel, that Mr. Cummings and Mark Albrecht had been there but were now on their return journey to the States! What could have happened? Fahrettin Kolan, the young manager of the hotel, first gave us a sealed envelope that they had left for us. It contained a most encouraging note written a week earlier: "Our guide is Yücel Dönmez. Horsemen will see you here at the hotel Aug. 12-13 to see about taking you from Ortelu [a village north of Dogubayazit, in the foothills of Greater Ararat, from which the ascent can best be made to the area of previous Ark sightings on the northern face of the mountain] to Kop Gülü (Lake Kop). I've left Aug. 6th 4:00 A.M. for Kop. Special permission for Kop." Apparently all had gone beautifully—but why, then, the sudden departure? Another note in the same envelope read simply: "This is Sunday Aug. 9th. We are leaving for Kars to Erzurum. See Yücel our guide." And accompanying the letters was a telephone message from Eryl and Mark in Ankara re-

ceived for us at the hotel on August 11th, the day before our arrival in Dogubayazit; it said that they had
made every attempt to reach us, and that they were
leaving Ankara for home on the 12th. Immediately I
tried to contact them at their Ankara hotel, but they
had already departed!

The only thing to do, then was to get the story from
those who were there. I questioned Fahrettin Kolan,
who said something about soldiers going up the mountain for Eryl and Mark. Kolan said, moreover, that
botanist Lawrence Hewitt, who had been with Mr.
Cummings on the 1966 Archeological Research Foundation expedition, was himself in the hotel! I phoned
his room, and while waiting for him to join us in the
lobby, saw a short, muscular, mustached man enter at-
tired for the mountain. Kolan said that this was Yücel
Dönmez, Mr. Cummings' guide! Mr. Hewitt arrived,
and while David and I wolfed a not unappetizing *shish
kabab,* we got the full story (entirely confirmed months
later in the States by Mr. Cummings himself).

Another exploratory group had indeed started up the
mountain without full permission and had been called
back by the authorities. At this point Eryl and Mark
arrived in Dogubayazit and quietly proceeded, on the
basis of Mr. Cummings' reputation there, to obtain
local permission to climb to Lake Kop. With Yücel as
guide they reached the location of the previous sightings. Hardly had they begun their investigations, however, when a squad of Turkish soldiers appeared at
their base camp and requested them to return. There
was no question of arrest; only of polite insistence.
Why? The authorities, as a result of the problem with
the other group, felt that equity now demanded that all
Americans be kept off the mountain for the rest of the
summer.

As for us—what now? It would seem that we could
not now so much as set foot on the mountain. Dr. Hewitt, darkly suggesting political machinations, doubted
that we could accomplish anything. Yücel, however,
wanted a try at the local authorities on our behalf. It
now became clear why Mr. Cummings had left before

we arrived: this gave us an independent and free hand to try to get on the mountain as if we had no connections with him. Had we met in Dogubayazit, our evident mutual relationship could have worked to the detriment of any further climbing that summer.

The next two days oscillated between bureaucratic agony and the sublimation of our frustration by exploring the town and its evirons. The local official—a kind of territorial governor in this Eastern province under the martial law of the gendarmerie, serving as police—had gone to Ankara, and it was unclear when he would return; without him, no permissions whatever for Ararat. Thursday morning, therefore, we trudged the unpaved, dust-blown main street of Dogubayazit, a town that can best be conceived of if one imagines Dodge City before the arrival of Matt Dillon (or, more historically, Wyatt Earp). Horse-drawn wagons give the illusion of the Old West, and the citizens commonly carry sidearms or rifles. Later, the town doctor would tell us that much of his time was spent patching up gun and knife wounds inflicted by the people on each other. The Turks in these frontier areas would of course prefer to inflict wounds on their old enemies the Russians (and it is the Russians over the border who are afraid of the fierce Turks here, not the reverse as one would expect!); but under present conditions, when diplomacy reduces the opportunity to shoot or stab Russians, the people must settle for lesser internecine joys. On the outskirts of the town are military camps surrounded by barbed wire; tanks can be seen in practice manuevers, and from time to time the muffled sound of cannon fire comes from target ranges set up on the lower foothills of Ararat.

Greater Ararat herself, however, entirely steals the scene. The frontier town, the machinery of modern war —all drops to insignificance in the face of the towering mountain. It entirely dominates the view to the north of Dogubayazit—rising suddenly out of the broad plain, its peak covered with perpetual ice and (except very early in the morning) its summit lost in clouds and mist. To the immediate east of the great mountain stands conical Lesser Ararat, like a servant in humble and constant attendance on his master. Inevitably one's time perspective is altered by this sight: from the 20th century of the military camps and the 19th century Old West suggested by the town, one's thoughts are driven back millennia to that day when "God made a wind to pass over the earth, and the waters assuaged" and "the Ark rested upon the mountains of Ararat." It is not easy to keep one's attention on the problems of the present when viewing the very cradle where human civilization was reborn.

But the problems of the present could not be ignored. If we miraculously obtained permission to get on the mountain, we would need to be conditioned for it. Acclimatization is an essential of successful mountaineering, particularly where great heights are involved. We had to get used to operating at a very high altitude. It has been shown, for example, by the use of a decompression chamber, that a person subjected to the equivalent of Ararat's height will lose consciousness in 15 to 20 minutes when no acclimatization has occurred (j. Gautrat, *Dictionnaire de la Montagne* [Paris: Éditions du Seuil, 1970], p. 10). Fortunately, Dogubayazit itself serves as a preliminary acclimatization for the mountain, since the Bayazid plateau is between 4,000 and 5,000 feet above sea level. To help the process along, we determined to climb to a historic monument near Dogubayazit which simply could not be missed. This is the Palace and Mosque of Ishak Pasha, begun in the 17th century and completed in 1785 by the governor of Bayazid. It is constructed on a rocky crag above the town and appears to have come directly out of the Arabian Nights. The buildings are considered to be one of the finest examples of Ottoman-Turkish civil architecture, with some Seljuk influences. We found the climb to the palace hard going; we were obviously not used to the rarefied atmosphere, and breathing was difficult. But this was just what we needed, and the view from the minaret of the mosque was truly rewarding: Ararat in the distance, a miniature Dogubayazit not far away, and evidences of still uninvestigated archeological sites in the rocky terrain close to the palace. As the sun set, workmen were just finishing their day's labor in the palace (limited restorative work is now required at the ancient monument), so we were invited to ride back to town in the back of their open truck. The driver went as if pursued by the mountain spirits themselves, and we were nearly blown away; but we could not very well complain about a trip down so much less demanding than the trip up!

The next afternoon (Friday) we obtained our audience with the local authority, who had finally returned from Ankara. Communication was not easy, owing to the official's (1) nonexistent English, (2) exceedingly weak German, and (3) general taciturnity. Efforts were made to operate in German (this is usually the best linguistic solution for westerners in Turkey, since vast numbers of Turkish laborers have gone to and returned from West Germany in recent years, thereby establishing German as a kind of pragmatic second language), but the local authority's German proved too feeble. Fortunately, the town physician—a dynamic and personable young man—could be summoned from the hospital nearby, of which he serves as director, and his assistance as interpreter and amiable go-between brought matters to resolution with maximum speed (i.e., in about the time necessary for boiling and drinking the magnificent *tchay*—Turkish tea— which accompanies all discussion, whether trivial or profound). Official: "It is absolutely out of the question to climb Ararat. A directive states that no Americans will be permitted on the mountain for the rest of the summer, owning to the violation of our rules by the American group seeking the Ark." Montgomery: "But we have nothing to do with that group. Moreover, we are residents of France [shows official *Carte de Séjour*]. What harm would it do for us to go to Lake Kop with Mr. Yücel Dönmez as guide? You know him well and can trust him." While the local authority contemplates this and is fingering the *Carte de Séjour,* the telephone rings; it is the call from Ankara which we mentioned at the outset of this account: twenty Americans

are trying to obtain permission to "fish in Lake Kop."
The official's reaction is the appropriate mixture of
humor and irony. "You see? I am very sorry, no one
goes to Lake Kop; the political situation is very frag-
ile." Montgomery: "But surely if you regard us as
French . . .?" Official: "Kop is not possible. But perhaps we could make an exception for the south face.
Let us determine if you have ever had contact with the
following persons. [A list of about a dozen persons
connected with the other exploratory group was then
read off. Dr. Hewitt's name was also mentioned].
Montgomery: "The only one I have met personally is
Dr. Hewitt, and I had my first contact with him in the
Kent Hotel right here in Dogubayazit night before
last." Official: "You are not connected with Dr. Hewitt?" Montgomery: "I have no relationship whatever
with the group you mention, and Dr. Hewitt is, as far
as I know, engaged in independent botanical work
here." Official: "In this case, I give you special permission to climb the south face, but Ankara positively for-
bids my allowing you to go to Kop. And if you have
any contact—even by chance—with Dr. Hewitt while
he is collecting specimens in the foothills, you will immediately have to get off the mountain altogether. We
are not taking any chances on collusion. The Russians
believe CIA agents are trying to use the mountain to
their own advantage. This we shall not permit." Montgomery: "We shall abide by the rules and hope for a
more relaxed situation next year."

So, by an exceedingly narrow margin, we obtained
permission to ascend Ararat. True, we could not reach
the Kop area—the area of previous Ark sightings—but
half the mountain *was* open to us. The permission we
had received was given to no other American group, so
that the 1970 exploratory season recorded half of our
people (Mr. Cummings' party) as the only Americans
to climb officially on the north face of Ararat, and ourselves as the only ones to engage in similar activity on
the south face! Later, when we returned to the States,
we would find that even in the short time Eryl and
Mark spent in the Lake Kop region they obtained some

very interesting and important photographs. Our "International Expedition, '70" could be regarded—through the hand of providence—as a remarkably successful effort at surveying the total situation. Such a preliminary operation would be of inestimable value, and an absolutely necessary prerequisite, for all further investigations in depth when and if the political temperature cooled in Turkish-Russian relations.

Moreover, a possibility had now opened that I had not seriously considered before: the possibility of climbing to the very top of Ararat! Originally, the thought had been to restrict ourselves to the immediate area of Kop (about 3750 meters); now, though Kop was off-limits, there was no reason (except physical incapacity) not to climb the south face to the summit. The Ark was surely not on the south face, but Ark fever could be treated temporarily by a ssuccessful climb to the very peak of the mountain where Noah recommenced human civilization. From that summit it would at least be possible to see the promised land of the northern face, in preparation for further work there. *Deo volente.*

Yücel, however, was not so sure. Did I realize just how difficult a feat it was? The mountain is 5,165 meters—16,946 feet—high, over a thousand feet higher than the highest mountain in western Europe (Mont Blanc, on the French-Italian border, whose height is 15,781 feet). I know this, and other even more sobering facts, such as the treacherous character of the glacial ice sheet above the 4000 meter snow line (in the midday heat of the sun, the ice melts irregularly, allowing the unwary climber to disappear without a trace in the permanent ice cap). I was also acquainted with the history of the relatively few ascensions of Ararat: from the first in 1829 by Prof. Dr. Frederick Parrot of the University of Dorpat to that of Navarra in 1952—and the tragic stories of those such as Christopher Trease of Balliol College, Oxford, who was never seen again after the commencement of his climb to the summit on August 21, 1965. At the same time, I knew that a brawny physique was less a guarantee of success in mountain climbing than what John Wayne has immortalized in the expression "true grit": Hermann Buhl, the phenomenal climber who attained the 8,125 meter summit of Nanga Parbat entirely by himself (1953), was so slender and unathletic in appearance that he was frequently ridiculed by other climbers—until they found themselves incapable of matching his performance. Moreover, I had the fine example of James Bryce, specialist in medieval and modern history, a scholar's scholar, who attained the peak of Ararat by himself in 1876! Could I do it? There was only one way to find out, and those so afraid of failure that they do not venture are removed at the outset from any possibility of success!

At 3:15 A.M. on Saturday we struggled out of bed in our semi-primitive rooms at the Kent Hotel. There was no water, of course: Dogubayazit has water only from about 2 P.M. to 11 P.M., when the midday heat melts the ice on Ararat and the mountain streams flow down to the town. By 4 A.M. we were jolting along, in a truck of indeterminate antiquity with no speedometer at all, to the rendezvous point where we would be met by the Kurds (the ancestral nomadic inhabitants of the mountain) hired by Yücel to supply mules and horses for the first leg of our ascent. As the truck jounced along, the sun slowly and majestically climbed above the horizon and etched with gold the cloud cover of Ararat, finally dispelling the mist and leaving the mountain to dominate and overshadow everything in sight. From that moment on, it was clear that Ararat herself had become the chief character in our drama: today, as in Father Noah's time, she served as berthing place for the loftiest dreams and the most profound hopes of those in contact with her.

Less than a half an hour after the truck had reached its destination—one of the last reasonably level meadows before the ground begins to rise sharply in the Ararat foothills—we saw Kurds approaching with our animals. Three mules were required for the camping equipment, rucksacks, and food. Once the beasts had been loaded and we had mounted our horses, our little

caravan proceeded to wend its way up, always up.
Yücel and the Kurds managing the mules went on foot.
The only difficulty lay in persuading one of the Kurds
who had taken an overly-concerned interest in David,
owing, in part, to his slender appearance, that David
was fully capable of controlling his own horse, and did
not need to be led like a woman!

By 8 A.M. we were ready for our first real stop. We
had already attained 2,500 meters, and wisps of cloud
could be seen below us. Two hundred more meters and
we found ourselves in a Kurdish camp—the home
camp of several of our mule drivers. According to
time-worn custom (it has doubtless changed little since
Parrot in the 19th century—or Struys in the 17th—was
on the mountain), we were invited to partake of food
and drink with the men of the tribe. Sitting cross-
legged in the central tent, on rugs the Kurds themselves
weave from goat hair, we did our best to eat the meat
and flat loaves of bread offered to us out of common
dishes—while vainly brushing away the flies that
seemed to be everywhere at once. Since the meat was
thoroughly cooked on the spot, it posed no health haz-
ard, and the taste could be pretty well disguised by lib-
eral drafts of strong tea; but we were careful not to dip
our bread into the large dishes of creamy yogurt—re-
membering Swiss mountaineer Theo Koller's vivid description of three weeks of deathly illness resulting
from imbibing the yogurt of the Kurds!

As the terrain became rougher and our path steeper,
we encountered unavoidable animal problems. At
about 3,250 meters, one mule was killed by a snake
(poisonous snakes are not uncommon on Ararat) and
the baggage had therefore to be redistributed among
the remaining beasts, who were already profusely
sweating from the strain. My horse, who lacked nothing
in spirit but who had passed his prime, was unable to
carry me the last two hundred or so meters to the site
of our base camp, so I had to join Yücel on foot. Finally, the mules could be driven no further over the sharp,
loose rocks, and we had to lug the equipment the last
few meters ourselves. At 4:30 P.M. and at an altitude

of 3,800 meters, with the haze rolling in below us and the night fast coming on, we set up the base camp on a rocky level between the slope we had just covered and a much steeper slope of rocky debris ascending dizzily above us.

The gusts of cold wind stiffened our fingers as we set up the tents by driving the stakes into the stony soil and bracing the tent ropes with rocks. The base camp area was so small that it was (if I may be permitted an ancient vaudevillianism) like playing a trombone in a telephone booth to keep our feet out of our equipment and food while preparing dinner and getting ready to retire for the night. The food was sufficient consolation, however. Seeing no reason to suffer beyond the necessary, I had brought from la belle France such delicacies as *crevettes,* Alsatian *pâté de foie gras,* and a large bottle of Kronenbourg (famous in Strasbourg since 1664). Our survival was thus assured—at least gastronomically.

We of course slept in our clothes; in fact, we slept in all the clothes we had (the down jackets were especially effective). Snug in our sleeping bags, however, David and I experienced the negative effects of the oxygen-deprived atmosphere for the first time: both of us independently suffered the same odd, nightmarish dreams. Had Carl Gustav Jung but lived long enough to analyze their archetypical significance! But most troubling was the claustrophobic common impression that the tent was closing in on us. Added to this was our constant noseblowing during the night, for the altitude aggravated any natural sinus condition. It was actually a great relief to find in the morning that only sinus had been involved: I had thought in the night that I was perhaps suffering the nosebleeds characteristic of mountain sickness!

August 16, 7:30 A.M.: what a strange place to be on the 12th (or any other!) Sunday after Trinity. No green coloration was present anywhere; apparently the mountain was liturgically low church . . . With monstrous bags under our puffy eyes we ate breakfast in the gray, inhospitable dawn, and set to work repacking our things in preparation for the afternoon ascent. It was necessary to remove from our rucksacks everything not absolutely essential to the one-night bivouac on the way to the summit; at the same time, we must not leave anything behind which was needed at the altitude where we were going. Throughout the morning and afternoon the weather remained the same: it was heavily overcast; a sea of mist below seemed to separate us entirely from the world we normally knew, and corresponding mist have sometimes left the feeling that we were disembodied spirits in limbo (though the *limbus infantium* and the *limbus patrum* seemed equally inappropriate to our baptized, new covenant selves!). Occasionally the higher mists would clear, showing the majestic peak towering above us.

During the moments of idleness before beginning the late afternoon climb, we contemplated how easy it would be—theoretically—to reach Kop from where we were. Our altitude was almost precisely that of Kop: but two hours or more or less level hiking would be needed to circle the mountain to it. *Hupage Satana:* "Get thee hence, Satan!" We had to put such temptation behind or run the risk of destroying all possibility of further work on the northern face another year.

At 4 P.M. we commenced the next stage of the climb: not to the peak for that was still (even at this altitude) too far away, but to a bivouac point from which, after another night's sleep, we would make the final climb. The ascent was fatiguing in the extreme, not only because of the sharply increased gradient of the slope and the constant slipping and sliding of the loose rocks, but expecially because of the reduced oxygen content of the air. Shortly before reaching the shelf of rock constituting the bivouac area, David was unable to proceed farther on his own; at this point Yücel—one of the finest athletes I have ever seen—carried him on his back for perhaps 200 meters of most difficult terrain. The last hour of climbing to the bivouac was done in almost total darkness. At one point, however, even extreme fatigue seemed to evaporate as in the pale moonlight we saw looming *below* us to the right, the

conical peak of Lesser Ararat (3925 meters: 12,903
feet). We were now higher than Fujiyama!

9:30 P.M.: we dragged our numbed selves into the
bivouac area, which was little more than a semi-level
spot protected from the powerful winds by a rocky
outcropping. It was essential to eat as rapidly as possible so as to allow maximum time for sleeping, since
the final ascent to the peak on the morrow had to take
place before the midday sun made the ice cap impossi-
bly treacherous. Thus we had to look forward to a very
early rising time even though our exhaustion was almost complete. To make matters worse, the extreme
altitude slowed the boiling of water so that almost an
hour slipped away while we prepared our supper of
soup and hot chocolate. I served as cook and found the
cold wind so penetrating that I could hardly hold the
ladle steady to pour the hot beverages. After drinking
as much hot liquid as we could, we literally fell into our
sleeping bags.

The temperature must have dropped below zero in
the night. Even with down sleeping bags, down jackets,
and all the clothing such high altitude climbing demands, we nearly froze. When we forced ourselves
awake at 6:30 A.M. (we had hoped to be able to get
up an hour earlier, but that was simply impossible),
frost had covered our sleeping bags. Breakfast consisted of coffee and more hot soup, and again the delay involved in getting the water to boil—even with our excellent Bleuet butane stove—was excruciating.

We began the final ascent at 7:30 A.M. On leaving
the bivouac area the incline became significantly
steeper and the loose rock more unpredictable, and
after about an hour of climbing David reached his
physical limit. Had there been any possibility of going
on, he would have taken it, but the combined effort of
terrain, altitude, and fatigue left no choice. His dis-
couragement at not reaching the summit was mitigated
by the knowledge of what he *had* accomplished: he attained 4615 meters—practically the altitude of the ice
cap in August, and a scant 550 meters from the peak
itself. Navarra's twelve-year-old son had climbed only

to 3100 meters in the Lake Kop area on the north face. Indeed, David had climbed higher than the summit of Mt. Whitney in the Sierra Nevadas, and had become, as far as we knew, the youngest westerner to have reached such a height on Ararat. This was more than a little consolation as David painfully began his descent to the base camp with another member of the party.

This left Yücel, his Kurdish companion, and myself to battle a two-front war against the elements and the clock. The sun was rising higher and higher in the sky, and its intense heat at this altitude would, in a few hours, turn the ice above us into a Venus fly trap, capable of digesting its victim without warning. By noon the storm clouds would commence their movement across the summit and the high winds would whip the loose snow to gale-like proportions. It was imperative that we reach the peak without delay.

But that was exactly the problem. The available oxygen seems to diminish in geometric proportion as one approaches the final goal. It becomes a major task just to place one foot in front of the other. Our rate of ascent was visibly showing even before we sat down on the edge of the ice cap to strap our crampons to our mountain boots. Naturally, we had left all overnight supplies at the bivouac area to be picked up on our way down, now we eliminated every ounce of nonessential clothing.

The last 200 meters were perfectly monstrous. Even the sight of several Turkish military ensigns stuck in the ice 100 meters from the top—stark reminders of the current political importance of the mountain—gave no comfort. When the murderous sun shone directly upon us through the rarefied air, only fifteen minutes were needed to acquire second-degree sunburn; and the very instant the racing winds carried a snow cloud across the sun, the temperature plummeted and we shivered from gripping cold.

As noon approached we could see the two summits of Greater Ararat just before us—the eastern, a few feet lower than the true (western) peak. With gusts of snow obscuring our vision it was easy to understand how geologist Hermann Abich, in the fourth recorded ascent of Ararat 1845), climbed the eastern, not the western peak, and thus in fact did not attain the true summit of the mountain. Again and again I wondered how I could possibly force my leaden foot to function. At best I could take but 50 steps without resting, and sometimes the number dropped to 10! On either side of our path holes were visible: weak spots on the ice where the sun's heat had produced irregular melting. These openings revealed bottomless shafts into the ice; an unwary climber could easily disappear forever with a single false step.

The sight of the peak so close to us was the factor that assured success. It was unthinkable, regardless of fatigue, lack of oxygen, or anything else, to come this far and give up short of the summit! So we agonizingly placed one foot ahead of the other, on as firm ice as we could find, and at 1:30 P.M., Monday, August 17, 1970, we stood on the very peak of Noah's mountain!

It was incredible, unbelievable. Through the swirling mist we knew that Iran and Russia lay below us, and in the snow at our feet we found the canister and tattered tricolor of Navarra's French expedition of 1952. On August 14, 1952, when Navarra was experiencing the surge of emotion I now felt, what would I have said had a prophet told me that I would stand on the summit of Ararat eighteen years later? Doubtless I would have regarded such a prediction as sheer madness. How little we know of divine operations! Thornton Wilder has well noted that our human folly especially displays itself in thinking that our "powers of observation are clearer than the devices of a god."

We remained on the summit less than a half an hour. Weather conditions were steadily worsening, and we had to descend while our tracks were still visible. The continual weakening of the ice and the drifting of the snow made our "powers of observation" less than ideal for following an old path, to say nothing about establishing a new one. So after taking a number of photographs—none of which we consider of potential value to the CIA!—and recovering as much strength as possible in the deoxygenated air, we commenced the long descent.

The trip down took far less time than the trip up. As soon as possible we removed our crampons, thus permitting shoe-skiing (a fine technique as long as one is quick enough to use his ice axe as a brake when his feet go out from under him, as they invariably do). In spite of several heart-in-the-throat falls with the prospect of arriving on the rocks below the snow line even quicker than desired, we found ourselves back at the bivouac area almost before we knew it. There we had tea, recovered our wind, and continued shoe-skiing down the tongues of snow and snow patches that extended part of the way down to the base camp. By 6 P.M. we were at the camp, relating to David and the others the details of the climb. In the hour before dark we ate ravenously and celebrated the success with a Moët which I had brought for the occasion.

The next morning (Tuesday the 18th), we rose at 7 A.M., broke camp, soon made rendezvous with the horses and mules, and by mid-morning were adroitly avoiding the yogurt at the Kurdish encampment. I could not resist a magnificent hand-made rug, crocheted by the wife of the Kurd who accompanied Yücel and me to the summit, so I had the ambivalent satisfaction of making a direct contribution to Kurdish economic development! About 1 P.M. David bade fond farewell to his steed (rider's cramp lessened by difficulty in parting with my horse), and a little over an hour later we were in Dogubayazit. General recovery accompanied by sunburn treatment occupied the afternoon, and at 6 P.M. we departed by a specially arranged minibus for Erzurum. On the way, an Iranian making the bus trip with us graciously insisted on buying our dinner— a most delicious product of Turkish open-hearth cooking which typically benefited, as does French cuisine, from a knowledge of sauces. By 2 A.M. we were fast asleep in a fine little hotel recommended by Yücel. Rising late the next morning (Wednesday), we were still able comfortably to make our 12:55 P.M. flight to Istanbul by way of Ankara. That evening we had again reached the center of civilization, Paris, and after a week in Edinburgh (the military Tattoo) and Belfast (Montgomery relatives in County Antrim), we returned to the States. Ark fever was soon repressed—for another year at least—by the immediate task of injecting a knowledge of Hellenistic Greek into the crania of entering Trinity graduate students, and the preparation of apologetics lectures for the fall term.

But when David and I look at each other, we recognize the symptoms of a common malady: a nervous itch to get back to that mountain. For on the northern face, in an area so delimited by the convergence of past sightings that Mr. Cummings has been almost on top of it, is a mysterious object that may well prove to be the greatest archeological find of the centuries. We have come too close ever to forget it.

Ark Fever: Its Prognosis

Short of joining an archeological equivalent of Alcoholics Anonymus ("Ark Analysts Anonymous"?), what are our chances of a successful cure? Since only the recovery of the vessel itself would serve the purpose what are the possibilities of its actually coming about?

I believe that they are excellent. Recent letters from our contacts in Turkey have been most encouraging with regard to securing permissions for the north face of Ararat. Apparently our endeavors to avoid high-pressure tactics and public relations methods are succeeding where the hard-sell approaches of others accomplished nothing but to set back Ark exploration. Of course, no one can predict the future temperature of the politically volatile Turkish border situation, and even less can be certain of the divine timetable in matters of this kind. But doors seem to be opening and we must be prepared to step boldly across the threshold.

And the evidence for the existence of the vessel continues to mount. Several months after our return to the States, a private meeting took place in a west Chicago home. Mr. Cummings, David and I met with a gentleman whose disenchantment with other efforts to find the Ark brought him to us. He played for us a taped interview, a copy of which is now in my possession, wherein an elderly but perfectly lucid Armenian, now living in the U.S., recounted his personal visits to the Ark in the company of his uncle when in 1902 he was a boy of ten living near Greater Ararat. The specificity of the information provided on the tape heightens greatly its prima facie value, and offers still another link in the chain of testimony extending from Berossus to the immediate present.

"What of it?" may well be the question in the minds of some readers. "Even if the Ark turned up, do you seriously expect it would convert men, or even change their view of the Bible?" Such questions have to be faced. Certainly the discovery of the Ark could not be regarded as a final apologetic for the reliability of the Bible, nor as a panacea for Christian missions! In spite of the remarkable and persistent confirmation of biblical history by archeological finds of the last seventy-five years (cf. Werner Keller's survey, *The Bible as History*), one can always find some yet unsolved problem if he wishes. The critics who once maintained that Moses could not have writtten the Pentateuch since writing was not even in existence at that time, and who were subsequently confronted with archeological proof of four different writing systems available to Moses in the Egypt of his day, then shifted to other Old Testament "absurdities." Pascal correctly observed (*Pensées,* No. 430) that "enough light exists for those whose only desire is to see, and enough darkness for those with a contrary disposition." Perhaps he was thinking of Jesus' narrative of the rich man in hell who wanted to have the beggar Lazarus return from paradise to warn his brothers of their impending fate and bring them to repentance, but was told: "If they hear not Moses and the prophets, neither will they be persuaded, though one rose from the dead."

But it would be no less a mistake to devalue the significance of a political recovery of the Ark. The most radical biblical criticsm since the onset of modern ra-

tionalism in the 18th century has been directed against
the Book of Genesis, and particularly against its allegedly mythical early chapters. Surely a precise confirmation of the historicity of the details of Genesis,
chapters 6-8, could not help but devalue the coinage of
such interpretations, if not discredit an approach to the
biblical materials which seldom gives them even the
benefit of doubt Aristotle demanded for Homer's *Iliad*
and *Odyssey!*

The presence of Flood accounts in the traditions of
peoples throughout the globe and the place of Noahic
events in the Hebrew, Moslem and Christian religions
would create almost universal interest in a major discovery relating to the Deluge. The missionary value of
the find would be staggering, if only on the level of
providing a common ground for the general presentation of the biblical message. Beginning with Turkey itself, where efforts to set forth the claims of Christianity
meet with considerable official and unofficial discour-
agement (cf. B. Acord, "A Plea for Turkey," *International Christian Broadcasters Bulletin,* October, 1970),
opportunities for active discussion of the scriptural
message would certainly accompany the news of the
find in all parts of the world.

Moreover, the story of the Ark is not "just another
Bible story." It is fraught with such profound symbolic
import by way of the imagery of mountain, flood, and
deliverance by divine grace that those who are touched
by it can experience genuine pre-evangelism. Mircea
Eliade, perhaps the greatest living phenomenologist of
religion, has stressed the place of the "Cosmic Mountain" in universal religious symbolism. In his work,
Images et Symboles (Paris: Gallimard, 1952), he notes
that such peaks as Mount Meru of Indian tradition, the
Norse Himingbjor, etc. were regarded as the center of
all things, the point where creation began, and the one
place not submerged at the Deluge. Temple construction often directly represented Cosmic Mountain symbolism; Elaide illustrates by way of the ancient Near
Eastern *ziggurats* and "the colossal construction of the
temple of Barabudur, which is shaped like an artificial

mountain. To ascend it is equivalent to an ecstatic journey to the Center of the World; upon reaching the breakthrough into another state; he transcends profane space and enters into a 'pure region.' " The association of worship with mountain symbolism readily follows from the fact that a mountain seems to be the very point of contact between earth and heaven; and, characteristically, the Cosmic Mountain is frequently associated with the Cosmic Tree, connecting heaven and earth and offering the possibility of a sacrificial ladder between these realms. A. H. Krappe (*La Genèse des Mythes* [Paris, 1952]) shows that the "mountain has frequently been taken as the location of the Land of the Dead: the derivation of the Celtic and Irish fairy-hills." Spanish poet and philosopher of art Juan Eduardo Cirlot comments, in his *Diccionario de Simbolos Tradicionales:* "This myth has obvious connections with the myth of Entanglement—of the castle inextricably entangled in a wood—and also with the story of Sleeping Beauty. . . . In Western tradition, the mountain-symbol appears in the legend of the Grail, as Montsalvat (the 'mountain of salvation')." Thus the imagery of the mountain involves not only creation but more especially redemption, even as the related tale of Sleeping Beauty speaks of the death-like sleep of a fallen race which can only be conquered by a kiss of love from a Prince who prophetically enters the world of death from the outside. Both depth psychology (Carl Gustav Jung) and the comparative study of religious symbolism unite in regarding the mountain as a prime archetype of the most fundamental creative and redemptive human needs; and Ararat is doubtless the best known sacral peak in all the world. Here, to broaden J. R. R. Tolkien's perceptive phrase concerning New Testament events, "Legend and History have met and fused."

In the Bible, mountains carry powerful symbolic weight (one thinks immediately of Sinai, Tabor, Gerizim, the Mount of Transfiguration, and Golgotha itself). And the act of Noah's deliverance—by God's grace alone through water and wood—led the early church inevitably to see the entire event as a typological forerunner of salvation as offered in the New Covenant. The Ark itself was conceived as a symbol of the church (only those who seek the grace there offered can survive the flood of a sinful world); church architecture itself was indelibly stamped with this imagery (e.g., the "nave"—from the Latin *navis,* "ship"). In early Christian inconography—in the catacombs, for example—the Ark was used to symbolize the place of burial or casket, from which God would raise the believer at the Last Day even as He delivered Noah from the deadly waters of the Flood. Moreover, as Cardinal Daniélou stresses, "the Flood became an image of baptism. . . . Even as Noah had faced the sea of death in which sinful humanity had been annihilated, and had come out of it, so has the newly baptized descended into the baptismal font to confront the dragon of the sea in a supreme combat and to emerge victorious" (*Sacramentum Futri. Études sur les origines de la typologie biblique* [Paris, 1950], p. 65; see also Daniélou's *Les Symboles Chrétiens Primitifs* [Paris, 1961]). As early as the first half of the 2nd century, the great apologist Justin Martyr gave classic expression to the symbolism of Noahic deliverance (*Dialogue with Trypho,* cxxxviii, 1-2):

> The righteous Noah with the other people of the Flood, namely his wife, their three sons and their sons' wives, added up to the number eight and afforded the symbol of that day, eighth in number but first in power, on which Christ rose from the dead. Now Christ, "the first born of every creature," has become in a new sense the head of another race, of those whom he has brought to a new birth, by water, faith and the wood which holds the mysteries of the Cross, just as Noah was saved in the wood of the Ark, floating on the waters with his family.

Here the Ark is the Cross, and rightly so, for it is the Cross that establishes the church, conquers death, and gives meaning to the baptismal acts that serve as secondary referents of Noah's symbolism.

Daniélou has correctly observed that Noah's Ark functions as "the instrument of eschatological deliverance." The stress on eschatology—the last things, the events of the end time—is the prime element in the New Testament treatment of the Deluge. Two New Testament passages are determinative: II Peter 2-3, and Matthew 24:37-39 (parallel with Luke 17:26-27). In Peter, the assurance of Christ's Second Coming is set over against the scoffing of unbelievers, and the destruction by water in Noah's day is paralleled with the destruction by fire which will accompany the Lord's final advent (3:5-7); the rescue of Noah is presented as evidence that "the Lord knoweth how to deliver the godly" and "to reserve the unjust unto the day of judgment to be punished" (2:5-9). These Petrine chapters are the inspiration of the moving spiritual, "Well, well, well" so effectively rendered by the Australian "Seekers"):

> God told Noah, "Build me that ark;
> Build it out of hickory bark."
> Rain started falling, water start to climb
> God said: "A fire not a flood next time." . . .
>
> The Lord said: "Fire coming, judgment day;
> All mankind gonna fetch away;
> Brothers and sisters, don't you know
> You gonna reap just what you sow?"

In Matthew 24 and Luke 17 Noah is likewise mentioned in connection with the end time, the Second Coming of our Lord, and the final judgment. Declares Jesus: "As the days of Noah were, so shall also the coming of the Son of man be. For as in the days that were before the flood they were eating and drinking, marrying and giving in marriage, until the day that Noah entered into the ark, and knew not until the flood came, and took them all away; so shall also the coming

of the Son of man be." The context of both the Matthew and the Luke passages is especially concerned with
the signs and conditions preceding the Second Advent.
After listing a number of such conditions, Jesus states
explicitly that the day and hour of the Coming are
known to no man (Mt. 24:36); this is immediately
followed by the Noahic reference just quoted. The impossibility of specifically dating the end time in no way
reduces the force of Jesus' comparison between Noah's
day and the last times: the Greek text expresses "just
as" by *hōsper*[5] (not just the simple word "as", but that
word with the enclitic suffix having "intensive and extensive force"—Bauer-Arndt-Gingrich; Blass-Debrun-
ner; A. T. Robertson), reinforced by *houtōs*. This
most powerful comparative construction is actually repeated *twice* in the three-verse Matthew passage. The
strength of the construction is seen even more clearly
when one realized that it appears in Jesus' emphatic
assertion of the one sign that shall be given to his
wicked and perverse generation, the sign of the prophet
Jonah: "*Just as* Jonah was three days and three nights
in leviathan's belly, so shall the Son of man be three
days and three nights in the heart of the earth" (Mt.
12:38-40; Lk. 11:29-30[6]). In citing the Noahic parallel, Jesus seems to be saying: "Though you cannot
calculate the day of my Coming—and though none of
the previous signs I have given you are specific enough
to allow such prediction—keep especially in mind the
precise correspondence between the last days and the
days of Noah."

But what exactly is the point of comparison? The
text itself expressly states (and II Peter expands on the
same theme) that the days of Noah were characterized
by rank secularism, so that judgment came on the
world unawares, and only very few were saved. This
much is demanded by the passages themselves. Yet
perhaps there is something more.

It is a prime mark of God's dealings with men in

---

[5] Luke uses *kathōs*, which is likewise emphatic.
[6] Again employing *kathōs*.

Scripture that he gives them—creatures of earth that they are—visible signs and evidence of His spiritual truth and power. Again and again in biblical history, miracles offer concrete proof of the true God and bring unbelievers and doubters to their senses. Elsewhere I have stressed the apologetic importance of events such as Elijah's victory over the prophets of Baal, Jesus' healing of the paralytic, and, above all, His resurrection from the dead as visible proofs of revelational claims ("Inspiration and Infallibility," in *The Suicide of Christian Theology* [Bethany, 1970]). Similarly, the "sacramental" devices of the Bible, such as circumcision or the sea (cf. I Cor. 10:1-4) in the Old Testament, and water, bread and wine in the New serve as concrete, earthly means of conveying invisible, spiritual benefit. This general approach is summed up by Jesus' question in dialogue with Nicodemus (John 3:12): "If I have told you earthly things, and ye believe not, how shall ye believe, if I tell you of heavenly things?"

Will there be "earthly things" provided as specific signs and warnings of the end of the age? Jesus' answer is yes, for Matthew 24 and its parallels tell us of natural calamities, wars, etc. that will precede His return. Could an even more explicit sign be in preparation for a world that has largely forgotten the days of Noah and cares little for anything but "eating and drinking, marrying and giving in marriage"? Is it possible that God has reserved the very vessel that, like the wooden Cross, saved those who entrusted themselves to it, so as to bring it forth as a most concrete indicator of the return of the days of Noah? Such a sign would no more force the conversion of those who prefer their values to God's values than the manifest miracles of Christ convinced the men of His time who would not subject their lives to Him. But to deny Him they had to resort to such absurdities as "he casts out devils by the prince of devils"; and the weight of evidence for God's truth has pushed unbelievers to comparable irrationality in every age. Might the God of all grace—who, as in the case of doubting Thomas, so often goes the second mile in offering His truth to the undeserving—not present one final confirmation of His Word to those who "hearing can still hear" before He brings down the curtain on human history?

The Bible does not require an affirmative answer to this question, but such an answer would be entirely consistent with the divine operations as recorded in Holy Writ. Perhaps, in this light, Ark fever becomes not so much the product of an overheated brain as the consequence of dangerously close contact with a burning bush and tongues of fire.

2

*Arkeology 1971**

A recent *New Yorker* cartoon shows a bearded, robed prophetish figure ascending a mountain. Halfway up he encounters a one-word signpost: "Think." The final drawing shows him reversing course and descending! Should this be the posture of those addicted to what I have called "Ark fever"? Is there enough evidence for the thinking person to believe that Noah's

From *The New Yorker*, Nov. 27, 1971.

* First published in *Christianity Today*, Jan. 7, 1972, pp. 50-51 in somewhat abbreviated form.

ship or a substantial vestige of it remains on Greater Ararat in Turkey? Has the last year provided any additional data? Is "arkeological" work continuing?

Literary detection has yielded some negative, together with a considerable quantity of positive, evidence. On the negative side, I have been able to establish that the March 29, 1953 *Chicago Sunday Tribune* article on the 1916 Russian expedition to Ararat contained serious misinformation—misinformation that has conditioned more than one subsequent writing on the Ark's survival. The author, Paris correspondent Henry Wales, who died in 1960, claimed that "information relating to the existence of remains of the Ark . . . is contained in documents presented to the library of the University of Geneva by Gen. Dmitri Osnobichine, an aide to the Grand Duke Cyril in Czarist days." A year's research has run down this claim and exploded it. After thoroughly checking the books given by Osnobichine to the University of Geneva Library and finding nothing, I was successful in tracing Grand Duke Cyril's surviving son Vladimir (he lives in Madrid), who sent me the following personal note: "I have never come across the report in question among my father's archives. I most certainly should have noticed any such document because I am, and have always been, extremely interested in this and similar subjects." Vladimir promised to make every effort to locate Osnobichine's living relatives, and several months later I received a registered letter at my Strasbourg address from Mme Alexandre Iordanow-Osnobichine of Rome. The General was her husband's uncle, and she stated that "no report, no document or notes" concerning the Russian expedition of 1916 could be found "amongst the personal or family papers that came to my husband after the General's death in 1956"; moreover, General Osnobichine had been in the Caucasus only from 1892 to 1894 and had never been aide-de-camp to Grand Duke Cyril.*

Now it should be strongly emphasized that these

---

* All of the correspondence here referred to has been collected in Appendix C.

facts do not put the Russian expedition sighting of 1916 in question (we have sworn testimonies from the families of now-deceased soldiers who were on the expedition; and I myself conversed with White Russian colonel Alexander Koor shortly before his death some time ago concerning his contacts with officers who had reliable data on the expedition and its sighting of what was unquestionably a ship on Ararat.). But the Osnobichine-Cyril connection must now be relegated to the realm of myth—or journalistic invention, which is much the same thing!

Positively, a year's work with the literary sources has powerfully reinforced my conviction that the continued existence of the Ark on Ararat is one of the strongest traditions relating to biblical history—a tradition far stronger than those which have been successfully employed by modern Palestinian archeologists as keys to their great discoveries attesting the accuracy of biblical accounts. Here is but a sampling of important post-Josephus references to the Ark's survival on Ararat: Theophilus of Antioch (2nd C. A. D.); Haithon of Gorhigos (14th C.) and his contemporaries Odoric of Pordenone and merchant traveller Pegolotti; 17th C. Dutch traveller J. J. Struys, who, in giving medical assistance to a hermit, climbed for a week on Ararat and obtained a sworn statement from this 25-year inhabitant of the mountain as to the Ark's survival and was given a piece that the hermit had taken from it; the 17th C. German merchant traveller Oelschlager (Olearius) who notes that "time hath so hardened the remainders of the Ark, that they seem absolutely petrify'd"; and 19th C. ecumenical prelate Archdeacon Nouri, who, after three unsuccessful attempts, scaled Ararat to find "the ark wedged in the rocks and half filled with snow and ice." Such literary traditions, taken in conjunction with 20th C. sightings by the Russian expedition, mining engineer George Greene, and French amateur explorer Navarra, give the best of reasons for continuing up Ararat after meeting the pensive warning sign!

And this is precisely what my son David and I again

did in 1971. Beginning immediately after our return from Turkey in September of 1970, we sought to overcome the perennial obstacle of securing government permissions for the next year. When we were nicely in motion and the possibilities looked bright, the government changed (March, 1971)! Since ministry personnel in Ankara were replaced, we had to start over. By June high offices in Turkey had assured us that we could proceed, but in the complex relations among governmental departments and between the administration of the volatile eastern region of the country in the Ankara central government, the general situation remained in doubt. During the first week of July a tactical meeting took place over the magnificent cuisine at the historic Maison Kamerzell in Strasbourg: our chief compatriot, Mr. Eryl Cummings of Farmington, N.M., would go immediately to Turkey to deal with the permissions problem in depth and would meet us on the mountain when we arrived the week of August 9.

As it turned out, because of continuing tensions within the Turkish bureaucracy between those who favored our cause and those who did not, Mr. Cummings allowed discretion to serve as the better part of valor and personally forewent exploration; he wisely saw that to press the permissions too far might have created much graver problems for the future. David and I, however, were able to operate in terms of the limited permissions secured and were thus the only Americans on the restricted north face of Ararat in the summer of 1971 (even as I had been the only American to reach the summit from the south face in 1970).

Leaving my wife and girls to the glories of the Büyük Efes hotel in Izmir, I took David to eastern Turkey by way of the antique gun shops of Istanbul (he is a collector). We flew to Erzurum, and then drove the northern road to Igdir. We then had to hire a tractor to take us over a virtually impassable route through swollen streams to the mud-hut village of Ahora, where we slept on the floor of the mayor's one-room home (with mayor and family!). Securing horses for ourselves and donkeys for the supplies, we proceeded to the 3,600-

meter level of Lake Kop—the focal center of past sightings. Treacherous climbing with crampons and ice axes brought us to 4,150 meters, a bit above the location of Navarra's discoveries. Though we were not able to add a personal sighting to past accounts, we staked out the area in preparation for detailed work by our full crew another year. Meanwhile, Mr. Cummings, below in the foothills, had been engaged in securing a series of overlapping telescopic photographs of the entire area at the relevant altitude. This will help greatly in analyzing one particularly tantalizing color slide that seems to show a huge object wedged in a crevasse—an object perhaps "absolutely petrify'd"!

Further work now waits on another August and the grace of the Turkish authorities. Reinhold Niebuhr once said that the Church is like the Ark: you couldn't stand the stench within if it weren't for the storm without. Our investigation is also like that: we couldn't stand the strain of Ararat if the winds of unbelief in the authority of God's Holy Word didn't impel us to do all that is possible to confirm its entire trustworthiness.

3

How Not to Find the Ark [1]

In 1970 and 1971, Ark searchers faced a grim prospect owing to the political situation in eastern Turkey. Demonstrations by leftist students in Istanbul made waves that splashed against the Ankara government, and the government, in turn, pounded on key areas of potential dissent.

Mt. Ararat, the geographical and symbolic center of the native Kurdish population of ancient Armenia, constituted such a hot spot, for the Kurds in Russian Erivan, just across the Turkish border from Ararat, could well claim that Turkish Kurds deserved "liberation"—Russian-style—from Turkish "oppression." So in 1970 the only Westerners permitted on Ararat were those who were willing to stick to an "orthodox" trail on the mountain's southern face; Americans (because of negative Russian-American relations) were discouraged from doing even that, and only by special permission was I allowed on August 17 to conquer the summit. In 1971, the situation remained basically unchanged, but my son David and I were able to do some preliminary work on the crucial north face (the side of the mountain that overlooks the Russian border and where all Ark sightings have concentrated).

The middle of this summer (1972), however, brought a dramatic change in the permissions atmosphere. The south face—the route from Dogubayazit—was suddenly declared off-limits and the north face opened up!

Our own plans had been laid months before this shift in the political climate. On Thursday, May 25, David

---

[1] Reprinted, with slight omissions, from *Christianity Today*, Dec. 22, 1972, p. 42.

and I drove from Strasbourg, France, to Frankfurt, Germany, for a vital planning session. Three days later, in London, we met in private with a member of the Turkish presidential family. We were assured of clearances to work in the key area on the mountain, and we were informed that a certain American organization still soliciting funds for Ararat work would never be allowed back on the mountain, because of that organization's activities in the Near East in 1970.

With assurance of government clearance at the top level, we carried out operations in August on the north face, eliminated the east side of the Ahora gorge as a possible resting place for the vessel, and obtained complete photographic coverage of the west side of the gorge in preparation for future systematic coverage of the area between the gorge and the site of Navarra's 1955 find, above Lake Kop, of 5,000-year-old hand-tooled wood. Our expedition activities came off like clockwork, aided by a translator and two gendarmes supplied by the Turkish government.

The only clouds across the exploratory horizon came from the presence of five well-meaning arkeologists who appeared as if by magic when the north-face restrictions were—as they put it—"providentially relaxed."[2] The possibility that their activities may herald a tidal wave of similar efforts leads me to some words of admonition, based upon their work and upon that of the American organization referred to earlier.

My advice is given negatively, in deference to the supposed death-wish of Ark searchers who really do not want to carry out a thorough search for fear it will prove them wrong—as in the case of the traveler in *Bishop Blougram's Apology* who "saw the Ark a-top of Ararat;/But did not climb there since 'twas getting late,/and robber bands infest the mountain's foot." In order not to find the Ark, robber bands are by no

---

[2] John D. Morris, *Adventure on Ararat* (San Diego, Ca.: Institute for Creation Research, 1973).

means necessary; the following techniques will certainly suffice!

1. Insult the Turkish government. One of the members of the highly publicized American organization that tried unsuccessfully to operate on Ararat in 1970 was so disturbed by the refusal of Ankara to provide his group with appropriate permissions that he castigated the Turkish government in comments to Greek journalists. As a result, this organization is permanently *persona non grata* in Turkey.

2. Obtain only local permissions to climb; don't bother with red tape or the central government in Ankara. This procedure was followed by the five-man team that turned up this summer. Without clearance from Ankara, the group had no gendarme protection. The Kurds on the mountain enjoy a certain amount of bullying and pilfering in the absence of gendarmes, so the five found (a) their vehicle used for target practice, and (b) all their equipment stolen, including the very trousers worn by one of them.

3. Ignore the safety rules of mountaineering, and don't clutter up your team with a physician. The five searchers this summer had no doctor with them (one of them had some kind of certificate in mountain first-aid). Leaving the first-aid man at camp, three of them (a civil-engineering graduate, a Bible-college graduate, and an industrialist with nine children back in the States) climbed to an extremely precarious position on the mountain, got caught in a lightning storm, stayed in the open, were struck by lightning and knocked out, and after partially recovering somehow made their way back to base camp. Had they been permanently injured or killed, the authorities would doubtless have stopped all exploratory work on Ararat for the indefinite future.

4. Rely on your spirituality. When questioned about the wisdom of such activities as the preceding ("shall we sin that grace may the more abound?"), the reply was that they were doing the Lord's will, and were led by his Spirit. The leader of the group constantly talked about his "witnessing to the Turks and Kurds," but I quickly discovered that his knowledge of their languages was so paltry that he could not give the simplest gospel presentation. When will we learn as evangelicals that the Gospel is not our "experience" or our "spirituality," but the message of Scripture that must be conveyed in *words?* And when will we learn that our sanctification can never absolve us from using our heads?

If the Ark is ever to be found, it will require the consistent, long-term planning of a Cape Kennedy operation, not the perspective of a Boy Scout outing. Perhaps the Ark is no more significant than the cradle in which the Saviour lay on the first Christmas, but Luther saw fit to compare that cradle with the Scriptures. The quest for a scriptural artifact demands the clarity of heart of a relic-seeker and the clarity of mind of a scientific investigator.

4

*Science, Satellites, and Noah's Ark**

i. Religion and Science

Three relationships between Religion and Science are logically possible: opposition, indifference, and positive alignment. Since the rise of modern secularism, dating roughly from the 18th century "Enlightenment" and the French Revolution, the first two attitudes have predominated, and in that order.

1.1.—*Religion vs. Science*

With the overthrow of "priestcraft" in the revolutionary Europe of the 18th century, the French *philosophes* and the English deists offered a substitute "Religion of Reason" centering on a God who operated through a perfect scheme of natural laws. For these thinkers, traditional religion had done little more than to impede the rise of scientific attitudes.[1] Thus Thomas Paine, one of the foremost popularizers of the 18th century spirit, devoted one-half of his famous book, *The Age of Reason,* to a criticism of the alleged irrationalities in the Judeo-Christian Bible.

The 19th century, characterized by the progressive idealism of Hegel, the materialism of Marx, and the

---

* Invitational address at the 9th International Symposium on Remote Sensing of Environment, April 16, 1974, conducted at Ann Arbor, Michigan, by the Center for Remote Sensing Information and Analysis, Environmental Research Institute of Michigan (Willow Run Laboratories), in cooperation with the University of Michigan.
1. Roland N. Stromberg, *Religious Liberalism in Eighteenth-Century England* (London: Oxford University Press, 1954), pp. 52-69; Richard S. Westfall, *Science and Religion in Seventeenth-Century England* (New Haven, Conn.: Yale University Press, 1958), pp. 193-220.

positivism of Comte, followed the same path.[2] Great technological advances over previous epochs led to the easy conclusion that Religion had hindered man's upward climb to a scientific millennium. This viewpoint was particularly concretized in Andrew Dickson White's influential work, *A History of the Warfare of Science with Theology in Christendom*.

Today one still occasionally meets with this attitude. Orthodox Marxists must, of course, view Religion as an opiate.[3] Doctrinaire western writers, especially those responsible for sweeping textbook generalizations that are passé before they are recorded, continue to present Religion as an enemy of Science. Thus a recent psychiatry text, containing page after page of half-digested declarations and misstatements such as:

> With the fall of Rome and the failure of the Stoic philosophy of self-sufficiency, the Western world sought some surcease from strife and sorrow in a universal Church, and for the security so promised seemed content to sacrifice its intellectual and personal freedoms to the jealous care of a clerical hierarcy. . . . The priceless library of the Serapeum at Alexandria was ordered destroyed by Bishop Theophilus, and a few generations afterward Pope Gregory the Great (540-604) proscribed as sinful all reading other than the Bible.[4]

In point of fact, "there is not a single writer or authority, good, bad or indifferent, that infers or says that the

2. John Herman Randall, Jr., *The Making of the Modern Mind* (rev. ed.; Boston: Houghton Mifflin, 1940), pp. 458ff.; John Warwick Montgomery, *The Shape of the Past* (Ann Arbor, Mich.: Edwards Brothers, 1963), pp. 70ff.

3. Marcel Cachin: "Religious have always been opposed to the bold flights of philosophers and men of science" (*Science and Religion*, English ed. [New York: International Publishers, 1946], p. 3). Cf. V.I. Lenin, *Religion* (New York: International Publishers, 1933). *passim*.

4. Jules H. Masserman, M.D., *The Practice of Dynamic Psychiatry* (Philadelphia: W. B. Saunders, 1955), p. 369.

Library was destroyed by the Christians,"[5] and "Gregory was himself the author of a considerable series of writings. . . . He may possibly have been the most voluminous author since classic times""[6]! Not only the pressures of historical research, which has shown, for example, that such vital religious movements as the Reformation had the most positive effect on scientific development,[7] but even more especially 20th century holocausts—world wars, genocide, man's appalling inhumanity to man—have burst the bubble of 18th-19th century scientistic perfectionism and left modern man with far less confidence that Science has all the answers and Religion is superfluous. Now the question is often seriously posed as to whether Science and not Religion deserves to be "demythologized."[8]

1.2.—*Science Indifferent to Religion*

More common today than the older and generally discredited view that Religion and Science are polar opposites is the attitude that neither field has anything significantly to do with the other. The relationship is not negative, but it is not positive either; it simply *isn't*. Science deals with one thing, Religion with another; and trouble arises at the exact point where one tries to create interrelationships that do not actually exist.

5. E. A. Parsons, *The Alexandrian Library: Its Rise, Antiquities and Destructions* (Amsterdam, Netherlands: Elsevier, 1952), pp. 353-70; cf. Cambridge Mediaeval History, I, 489-90.

6. George Haven Putnam, *Books and Their Makers during the Middle Ages* (2 vols.: reprint ed.: New York: Hillary House. 1962 [1896-97]). I. 34-35. Cf. also Milkau & Leyh, *Handbuch der Bibliothekswissenschaft*, Bd. III.

7. John Warwick Montgomery, "Lutheran Astrology and Alchemy in the Age of the Reformation," in: (1) *Transactions of the Royal Society of Canada*, 4th ser., I (June, 1963), 251-70: (2) *Ambix: The Journal of the Society for the Study of Alchemy and Early Chemistry*, XI (June, 1963), 65-86; (3) *Revue d'Histoire et de Philosophie Religieuses* (1966), 323-45 (in French); (4) John Warwick Montgomery, *Cross and Crucible* (2 vols.; "International Archives of the History of Ideas," 55: The Hague, Netherlands: Martinus Nijhoff, 1973), I, 1-22.

8. E.g., Anthony Standen, *Science Is a Sacred Cow* (New York: Dutton, 1950).

As this view is usually expressed, Science is supposed to deal strictly with *facts* and their empirical verification, or at least to subject its hypotheses, theories and generalizations to strict factual testing, while Religion is concerned with *values*—with ethical, moral, and societal precepts, and with the problem of acquiring a sense of personal and cosmic worth—none of which can be tested empirically or indeed impinges at all upon the realm of genuine scientific investigation.

Philosophers of the 20th century analytical school have been especially articulate in stating this case. R. M. Hare, for example, has strongly opposed the idea that religions or theological talk about the universe is to be regarded "as some sort of *explanation*, as scientists are accustomed to use the word. As such, it would obviously be ludicrous. We no longer believe in God as an Atlas—*nous n'avons pas besoin de cette hypothèse*."[9] Religious beliefs, unlike scientific propositions, are not subject to judgments of truth or falsity, since they do not really assert any testable state of affairs. Philosopher of science R. B. Braithwaite argues in a similar vein that Religion does not really make cognitive claims, even when the language-game being played seems to be of a factual nature: "A religious assertion, for me, is the assertion of an intention to carry out a certain behavior policy, subsumable under a sufficiently general principle to be a moral one."[10]

The most striking expression of the conviction that religious language is noncognitive is the famous "parable" of analytical philosophers Antony Flew and John Wisdom. In this parable, the two explorers represent a religious believer and an unbeliever; the garden, with ambiguous qualities of order and disorder, is the universe in which we find ourselves; and the gardener is God:

9. R. M. Hare, "Theology and Falsification," in Antony Flew and Alasdair MacIntyre (eds.), *New Essays in Philosophical Theology* (London: SCM Press, 1955), p. 101.

10. R. B. Braithwaite, *An Empiricist View of the Nature of Religious Belief* (Cambridge, Eng.: Cambridge University Press, 1955), p. 32.

Once upon a time two explorers came upon a clearing in the jungle. In the clearing were growing many flowers and many weeds. One explorer says, "Some gardener must tend this plot." The other disagrees, "There is no gardener." So they pitch their tents and set a watch. No gardener is ever seen. "But perhaps he is an invisible gardener." So they set up a barbed-wire fence. They electrify it. They patrol with bloodhounds. (For they remember how H. G. Wells's *The Invisible Man* could be both smelt and touched though he could not be seen.) But no shrieks ever suggest that some intruder has received a shock. No movements of the wire ever betray an invisible climber. The bloodhounds never give cry. Yet still the Believer is not convinced. "But there is a gardener, invisible, intangible, insensible to electric shocks, a gardener who has no scent and makes no sound, a gardener who comes secretly to look after the garden which he loves." At last the Sceptic despairs, "But what remains of your original assertion? Just how does what you call an invisible, intangible, eternally elusive gardener differ from an imaginary gardener or even from no gardener at all?"[11]

The contention of the Flew-Wisdom parable is that religious believers believe in spite of the complete absence of confirming or disconfirming evidence for their beliefs. Their beliefs suffer the "death of a thousand qualifications," being compatible with anything and everything, and therefore really saying nothing. The contrast with the scientific passion for modifying theories to fit the evidence and refusing to entertain untestable vagaries could hardly be stronger.

1.3.—*Christianity and Scientific Verifiability*

To the viewpoint just expressed—that Religion deals

---

11. *New Essays in Philosophical Theology*, p. 96. Cf. John Wisdom, "Gods," in *Logic and Language: First Series*, ed. Antony Flew (Oxford: Blackwell, 1951), pp. 187-206.

not with facts but with "commitment"—one might pose a number of embarrassing questions:[12] Do you seriously mean to say that all religious value-systems are to be allowed to go their way with no factual check upon them? That such diverse and mutually contradictory ultimate commitments as Tantrism, Devil Worship, National Socialism, Islam, and Christianity are to be considered equally satisfactory, because no one of them can say anything of factual significance in its behalf over against the others? And, if all such positions cannot be tolerated, how will the diversity of claims be arbitrated when cognitive facts are not supposed to enter into the religious picture? Finally, can Science itself really operate apart from values, i.e., apart from religious concerns, and if Science thus needs Religion, can it align itself with religious orientations that close the eyes to evidence and refuse all testability?

In point of fact, the general run of belief-systems through history have illustrated the operation of the Flew-Wisdom parable. Commitment has arisen in the absence of evidence, flourished without it, and often revealed in the impossibility of disproving the beliefs in question—in sad unawareness that a belief that cannot even in principle be disproved cannot be proved either, and thus has a status worse than false: it is technically, epistemologically *meaningless*. Examples could be multiplied ad infinitum (and perhaps ad nauseam).[13] Thus Meher Baba, the founder and sage of Sufism, Reorientated, proclaimed "the ten Principal States of God," among which are: God in Beyond-Beyond; God in Beyond (Substates A, B, C); God as Emanator, Sustainer and Dissolver; God as Human Soul in the State of Reincarnation; God as the Divinely Absorbed.[14] One thinks immediately of the current "reve-

---

12. See John Warwick Montgomery (ed.), *Christianity for the Tough-Minded* (Minneapolis: Bethany, 1973), *passim*.
13. For current theological examples, see John Warwick Montgomery, *The Suicide of Christian Theology* (Minneapolis: Bethany, 1970).
14. Meher Baba, *God Speaks* (New York: Dodd, Mead, 1955), pp. 146ff. This book is dedicated "To the Universe—the Illusion that sustains Reality."

lations" of Divine Light by Guru Maharaj Ji. To such effusions one feels compelled to apply the remark the great Wolfgang Pauli jotted on a paper a fellow physicist submitted to him for his perusal: "This isn't right. This isn't even wrong."[15]

Historic Christianity is, however, in an entirely different category. Note the adjective "historic"; it frequently accompanies the noun Christianity, not (obviously) because Christianity appeared as a religion in history (so did all others), but because *Christianity has from the very beginning based its truth-claim on the objective facticity of certain historical events.* The early Christians did not merely make the stupendous claim that God had come to earth in Christ to save the world: "God was in Christ, reconciling the world to himself"[16]; "God so loved the world that he gave his only Son, that whoever believes in him should not perish but have eternal life."[17] They went on to assert the historic facticity of it, based on eyewitness, empirical testimony: "We did not follow cleverly devised myths when we made known to you the power and coming of our Lord Jesus Christ, but we were eyewitnesses of his majesty."[18] And they centered their entire case on the reality of Christ's physical resurrection from the dead as a de facto event, proving that he was the One he claimed to be and capable of conquering death:

I delivered to you as of first importance what I also received, that Christ died for our sins in ac-

---

15. The epistemological nonsensicality of reincarnation has been vigorously demonstrated by philosopher Peter Geach, who also makes an excellent case for the necessity of the Christian concept of the resurrection of the body to keep the very idea of immortality from falling under the same epistemological axe: *God and the Soul* (London: Routledge & Kegan Paul, 1969), pp. 1-29; the author concludes: "There is no reasonable hope of surviving death unless we hold the Jewish and Christian hope of the resurrection of the body" (p. ix).
16. The Bible: II Corinthians 5:19.
17. John 3:16.
18. II Peter 1:16

cordance with the Scriptures, that he was buried, that he was raised on the third day in accordance with the Scriptures, and that he appeared to Peter, then to all the apostles. Then he appeared to more than five hundred brethren at one time, most of whom are still alive. . . . If Christ has not been raised, then our preaching is in vain and your faith is in vain. We are even found to be misrepresenting God, because we testified of God that he raised Christ! . . . If Christ has not been raised, your faith is futile and you are still in your sins. Then those also who have fallen asleep in Christ have perished. If in this life only we have hoped in Christ, we are of all men most to be pitied. But in fact Christ has been raised from the dead.[19]

Note that the Apostle (who wrote this in A.D. 56, putting it in circulation within decades of Christ's death, while hostile witnesses were still alive who could have refuted it if untrue) puts the entire Christian Gospel to the verifiability test of a historical resurrection. No resurrection of Christ, no Gospel and no Christianity. The Christian religious claim is theoretically falsifiable and therefore meaningful.[20]

This approach to truth ramifies through the entire substance of the Christian religion. By subjecting itself to empirical testability, Christianity provided the religious soil in which modern science could grow, once societal conditions allowed for it; disregard of this unique aspect of Christian faith leaves largely unexplained the remarkable fact that scientific advance has

19. I Corinthians 15: see also Luke 24:36-43; John 2:18-22; 20:25-28. In all, there were eleven attested appearance of Christ after his resurrection and before his ascension; see, inter alia, Wilbur M. Smith, *The Supernaturalness of Christ* (Boston: W. A. Wilde, 1940); Merrill C. Tenney, *The Reality of the Resurrection* (New York: Harper, 1963).
20. For the positive historical case confirming Christ's claims, see John Warwick Montgomery, *Where Is History Going?* (Minneapolis: Bethany, 1972), especially chaps. i-iii.

never occurred significantly in a non-western, non-Christian cultural environment.[21]

Christianity thus has a vital stake in scientific episte-mology: its truth depends upon facts, and its doctrines and teachings are subject to factual test. What factual test? As just emphasized, the central facts are those concerned with the historicity of Christ's life, death, and resurrection. But they extend beyond this, as a stone thrown into water forms a whole series of con-centric rings. Jesus, who showed himself to be God-come-to-earth by his resurrection from the dead, stamped with his divine approval certain Scriptures as de facto revelation from God—as having a perfect truth-value comparable to his own teachings and en-tirely compatible with them. Jesus expressly stated that His work was a fulfillment of the Old Testament. "If you believe Moses, you would believe me, for he wrote of me. But if you do not believe his writings, how will you believe my words?"[22] Thus Christianity is con-cerned not only with the historical veracity of Christ's mission, but also with the truth-value of the Old Tes-tament Scriptures. Jesus' imprimatur upon them is lit-erally God's imprimatur, so they become of prime im-portance for understanding God's will for men. Jesus linked his own authority with theirs, so anything that would impugn their value would necessarily reflect upon him.

Is it any wonder, then, that the religion which thor-oughly aligns itself with scientific demands to test as-sertions factually—that alone offers evidence of the Gardener's having actually entered the garden of this world—has a special interest in the historical and ar-cheological investigation of biblical data? Christianity's

21. John Warwick Montgomery, "The Theologian's Craft: A Discus-sion of Theory Formation and Theory Testing in Theology," in: (1) *Concordia Theological Monthly*, February, 1966; (2) *Journal* John Warwick Montgomery, *The Suicide of Christian Theology*, *of the American Scientific Affiliation*, September, 1966; (3) pp. 267-313.
22. John 5:46-47.

concern with cognitive fact translates directly into archeological terms at the point of biblical revelation.

ii. Archeology and the Bible

2.1.—*Revolution in Archeological Perspective*

Modern secular man of the 18th and early 19th centuries was imbued with rationalistic self-confidence. The shackles of supersitition had been thrown off and nothing would now need to be believed which was not "rational" (i.e., conformable to what historian of ideas Carl Becker well termed "the heavenly city of the 18th-century philosophers"). One of the cardinal tenets of that world-view was that the early literature of the race, particularly its religious literature, must no longer be thought to present history, but must rather be seen as the vehicle of poetry and myth. Ironically, however, it was the rationalistic mindset of the early moderns that turned out to be the myth!

First, a non-biblical example. From the rise of modern secularism to the middle of the 19th century, "Homer was conceived to be a mere name, his Ilium an indeterminate, lost world. The great chronicle of the siege of Priam's citadel was deemed by some to be a tale containing a great deal of invention and a few grains of truth. And by others the *Iliad* was relegated entirely to the shadow realm of myth."[23] And then came Heinrich Schliemann, a German amateur archeologist. "Such considerations failed to shake Schliemann's belief, dreamer as he was in Homeric mists. He read Homeric poetry as bare reality. He believed implicitly. This was as true when he was forty-six as it had been when, as a boy, he had been fascinated by the picture of the fleeing Aeneas."[24] And Schliemann found the site of ancient Troy—one of the most impressive

---

23. C. W. Ceram, *Gods, Graves, and Scholars*, trans. E. B. Garside (New York: Knopf, 1951), p. 34.
24. *Ibid*. For selections from Schliemann's own accounts, see C. W. Ceram (ed.), *Hands on the Past* (New York: Knopf, 1966), pp. 51-61.

archeological discoveries in history. How? By taking
the despised, allegedly mythopoeic text of the *Iliad*
and *Odyssey* seriously enough to follow out its historical references and clues. Ironically, the discovery could
as readily have been made by others whose training
and prestige exceeded Schliemann's, and the evolution
of archeological technique would have permitted the
discovery to have been made well before his own generation. Only one thing prevented the great find from
being made by others: their *Weltanschauung* closed
them off from looking; they knew a priori that ancient
literature must not be relied upon as a sound record of
historical fact. But Schliemann "believed implicitly"—
and triumphed.

2.2.—*The Bible As History*

Schliemann's work at Troy is but the extra-biblical
counterpart to an entire movement in biblical archeology that spans the last hundred years. It is, quite literally, the history of a steady retreat by those convinced
of the non-historical character of the biblical narratives, a retreat forced by the constant pressure of one
archeological discovery after the other. In the Introduction to his comprehensive survey of this subject,
from which the title to our present section has been
taken, Werner Keller appropriately writes:

> These breathtaking discoveries, whose signifi-
> cance it is impossible to grasp all at once, make it
> necessary for us to revise our views about the
> bible. Many events that previously passed for
> pious tales must now be judged to be histori-
> cal. . . .
> The opinion has been, and still is, widely held
> that the Bible is nothing but the story of man's
> salvation. . . . Nevertheless, the events themselves
> are historical facts and have been recorded with
> an accuracy that is nothing less than startling. . . .
> In view of the overwhelming mass of authentic
> and well-attested evidence now available, as I

thought of the skeptical criticism which from the eighteenth century onward would fain have demolished the Bible altogether, there kept hammering in my brain this one sentence: "The Bible is right after all!"[25]

These sentiments could be illustrated by the widest range of archeological data. Let us focus, however, just upon the opening portion of the Old Testament—its first five books, Moses' writings, to which Jesus specifically referred in his assertion: "If you do not believe his writings, how will you believe my words?" Professor Gleason Archer has tabulated the four fundamental allegations concerning the Mosaic books which we accepted as rationalistic gospel in the 19th century and which have been destroyed by subsequent archeological research.[26] Here are the claims, and here also, much abbreviated, are the archeological counter-arguments:

19th C. Pentateuchal Criticism	Archeological Refutation
i. Moses could not have written the first five books of the Bible, since writing was almost unknown in Israel before David's time (1000 B.C.).	The Ugaritic or Ras Shamra tablets (1400 B.C.) and the alphabetic inscriptions at the turquoise mines at Dophkah (no later than 1500 B.C.) show that this was not the case. The

---

25. Werner Keller, *The Bible as History,* trans. William Neil (New York: William Morrow, 1956), pp. xxiii-xxv.
26. Gleason L. Archer, Jr., *A Survey of Old Testament Introduction.* (rev. ed.; Chicago: Moody, 1974, pp. 167-76 and citations to monographic and journal literature there given). See also: Oswald T. Allis, *The Five Books of Moses* (2d. ed.: Philadelphia: Presbyterian & Reformed, 1949), Pt. III, chap. ii ("The Pentateuch and Archaeology"), pp. 234-58; and Edwin M. Yamauchi, *The Stonse and the Scriptures* ("Evangelical Perspectives," ed. John Warwick Montgomery; Philadelphia: Lippincott, 1972), especially chap. i. Though dated. Sir Charles Marston's work also deserves mention (*The Bible Is True: The Lessons of the 1925-1934 Excavations in Bible Lands* (London: Eyre & Spottiswoode, 1934); on pp. 265-68 Marston tabulates 24 noteworthy archeological confirmations of Old Testament historically.

Dophkah inscriptions were written by Semitic miners in Egyptian employ; thus even the lower classes among the Semites could read and write in the pre-Mosaic age.

ii. When Genesis describes Abraham's career, it presents mostly fable, not fact; the critic Nöldeke denied that there ever was an Abraham.

The name Abram appears in tablets from the 16th C. B.C.; excavations of Ur, Abraham's home city, show it to have been flourishing just at his time (2000 B.C.); the Mari and Nuzi tablets, together with the Hittite Legal Code confirm names, cities, customs, and transactions mentioned in the biblical narrative of Abraham.

iii. The Mosaic laws are too advanced to have been set forth prior to the 5th C. B.C.

Hammurabi's Code, antedating Moses by centuries, shows close parallels at many points with the legislation in Exodus, Leviticus, and Numbers.

iv. The biblical account of the Israelite conquest of Palestine is hopelessly unhistorical.

Egyptian Execration texts (20th-19th C. B.C.) and the Akkadian Tell el-Amarna tablets (14th C. B.C.) confirm the political situation in Canaan as the Mosaic accounts describe it. The 13th C. B.C. Egyptian Stela of King Merneptah specifically mentions the nation Israel by name, and shows conclu-

sively that the Hebrews
were already in possession
of portions of Palestine by
that time.

Discoveries such as these amply underscore the
soundness of the judgment expressed by Sir Frederic
Kenyon, late Director of the British Museum and one
of the foremost biblical scholars of our century: "The
progress of archeological research will be found to
constitute a steady march in the direction of establishing the essential trustworthiness of the Bible narrative."[27]

iii. Future Possibilities: Remote Sensing—
and Noah's Ark!

3.1.—*Where Do We Go from Here?*

At the close of his helpful little book, *Illustrations
from Biblical Archeology,* D. J. Wiseman observes:
"Let it be remembered that scientific archeological research in Bible lands is a comparatively recent development. Many promising sites are still unsearched and
much remains to be studied and published."[28] Once the
proper perspective has been attained—that the biblical
materials are factually and historically significant and
not pious story-telling—we are in a position to carry
out even more exciting research bearing on the scriptural text.

As Schliemann used the Homeric epics as a map to
direct him to ancient Troy, so one can (with far greater
confidence) employ the Bible as a guidebook to ancient
history. Here the sophisticated techniques of modern

27. Sir Frederic Kenyon, *The Bible and Archaeology* (New York:
Harper, 1940), p. 30.
28. D. J. Wiseman, *Illustrations from Biblical Archaeology* (London:
Tyndale Press, 1958), p. 102. Cf. Kathleen M. Kenyon, *Archaeology in the Holy Land* (2d ed.; London: Methuen, 1965); and
Yohanan Aharoni, *The Land of the Bible: A Historical Geography,* trans. A. F. Rainey (Philadelphia: Westminster Press,
1967).

remote sensing are available to be drawn into the service of theology. Fact-orientated Christianity welcomed such technological advances as printing during the Reformation period; she likewise welcomes comparable scientific developments today.[29]

The fundamental principle of remote sensing is simplicity itself: "Remote sensing embraces any and every qualitative or quantitative process in which the measuring apparatus, or more precisely the sensor of that apparatus, is not in immediate contact with the object to be studied."[30] Photography thus constitutes a variety of remote sensing known to everyone. Indeed, the field originated as an identifiable discipline when, for military purposes, it was desirable to find new photographic and electromagnetic means of effectively scanning terrain under adverse conditions (night, cloud-cover, etc.). As in the case of many other technologies (e.g., controlled atomic energy), what began in war came rapidly and positively to be employed for peace. In medicine, remote sensing devices were developed as substitutes for exploratory surgery and as vital information-gathering aids in brain surgery and other areas of comparable delicacy. Now full-scale remote sensing applications are being pursued across the globe in fields as widely diverse as agriculture, forestry, geology, geography, hydrology, oceanography, and environmental planning.

One of the most exciting new remote sensing techniques involved the use—sometimes alone, but more often in tandem with aerial and ground-based observations—of satellite photography. Particularly well adapted for this purpose has been NASA's Earth Re-

29. Cf. John Warwick Montgomery, *Computers, Cultural Change, and the Christ* [trilingual: English, French, German] (Wayne, N.J.: Christian Research Institute, 1969), and "Mass Communication and Scriptural Proclamation," forthcoming in *The Evangelical Quarterly* [England].

30. R. Tessier & A. Alouges, "Principes généraux," *Principe de la détection à distance et application à l'étude des ressources terrestres* (papers presented at the remote sensing seminar in Paris, November 4-9, 1969, co-sponsored by the Centre National d'Études Spatiales and the University of Michigan), p. 1.

sources Technology Satellite (ERTS), first launched
(ERTS-1) on July 23, 1972. Included among its
operating systems is a multispectral scanner (MSS)
which continually scans an area of the earth's surface
one hundred nautical miles wide along the orbit of the
satellite. The imagery yielded thus covers in each instance 10,000 square nautical miles; it is originally
processed at the Goddard Space Flight Center, NASA
Data Processing Facility, in Maryland. Four MSS wavelength bands are employed to differentiate objects on
the earth's surface, and the four-dimensional data are
then synthesized into a multispectral signature either by
reconstituting a false color image by photographic or
optical means, or by using computer analysis to classify
the data in digital magnetic tape format.

Already ERTS data have been effectively used in archeological work.[31] Particularly as remote sensing systems become capable of finer and finer differentiations
of surface data (some airborne systems now use as
many as twenty-five wavelength bands in obtaining
ground images), the archeological applications will
correspondingly increase. In relation to biblical history,
the possibilities are virtually limitless: locating the sites
of lost biblical cities, uncovering new caches of biblical
manuscripts (the Dead Sea scrolls represent but a small
fragment of the ancient books and parchments buried
and forgotten in the caves and warrens of the Near
East)—perhaps even discovering such sacral objects as
the ark of the covenant, containing the very stone tablets on which the Lord recorded the Law for Moses, a
pot of manna, and Aaron's rod—presumably lost when
the Babylonians destroyed Jerusalem in 587 B.C. and
never seen again!

Too fabulous to deserve attention? Not at all. By
definition, remote sensing, as the French puts it, is
détection à distance ("detects at a distance"). In

---

31. See, for example, Albert E. Belon and John M. Miller, *Remote
Sensing by Satellite: Applications to the Alaskan Environment
and Resources* (Fairbanks: Geophysical Institute of the University of Alaska, 1973), p. [18]. This research was supported by
NASA contract NAS5-21833.

scriptural revelation God has bridged the immense distance between heaven and earth to impart his will to us. Why then should even heavenly truth be too remote for our detection? Let us consider a single, mind-boggling (or, if you will, mind-blowing) example in conclusion.

3.2.—Remote Sensing Noah's Ark

Even in the face of powerful archeological attestations as to the historicity of the first five books of the Bible—even though Moses' writings have proved themselves historically in accord with Jesus' own valuation of them—popular opinion still regards the opening portion of the book of Genesis as religious myth. Prior to Abraham, biblical material remains suspect. In particular, the Genesis account of Noah and the Ark (Genesis 6-9) seems to many to be the archetypical children's story.

Yet one should pause a moment before embracing this commonly held viewpoint. Granted, archeological confirmation of biblical material has not gone much farther back than Abraham (Genesis 11)—but a century ago, as we have seen, Abraham was confidently regarded as myth! From Genesis 11 to Genesis 9 is a very short distance, and scientific biblical archeology has been closing gaps like this steadily for a century. Ought we not perhaps learn from experience?

Moreover, traditions of a universal Flood are worldwide, among peoples as diverse as Laplanders and Fiji islanders, and these traditions very often make mention of a boat by which a few escaped the destructive waters.[32] My interest as a historian in ancient Flood accounts led me to investigate all the documentary records of the actual survival of Noah's vessel, which, according to the book of Genesis, landed "upon the

---

32. Byron C. Nelson, *Deluge Story in Stone* (reprint ed; Minneapolis: Bethany, 1968 [1931]); Frederick A. Filby, *The Flood Reconsidered: A Review of the Evidences of Geology, Archaeology, Ancient Literature and the Bible* (Grand Rapids, Mich.: Zondervan, 1971).

mountains of Ararat" (8:4).[33] The extra-biblical reports commence with the historian Berossus (3d C. B. C.), who states that "of this ship that grounded in Armenia some part still remains in the mountains" and that people removed pitch from it to use for amulets. From Berossus to the 20th century there is a steady stream of such reports of the Ark's survival, almost invariably associated with Greater Ararat (Mount Agri) on the eastern border of present-day Turkey.

Among the most recent testimonies are the following:

Testimony to the Ark's Survival	*Source of the Testimony*
i. Personally seen and climbed upon by a youthful Armenian (1902).	Interview with the Armenian (tape-recorded).
ii. Seen at close hand by a White Russian military patrol (1916-17).	Interviews with members of the families of now-deceased soldiers on the patrol and with officers who knew them (sworn statements).
iii. Explorer Hardwicke Knight comes upon a rectangular wooden framework in the ice on Ararat (1930's).	Knight's sworn statement.
iv. A boat-like form protruding from the ice on Ararat is photographed by engineer George Jefferson Greene from a helicopter (1952).	Drawing by a fellow engineer made on the basis of the deceased Greene's no longer extant photographs.

---

33. See above, the accounts comprising Part Two of this present book.

v. French amateur explor- | Navarra's accounts in his
er Fernand Navarra | two books (*L'Expedition
sees under glacial ice | au Mont Ararat; J'ai
on Ararat a boat- | trouvé l'Arche de Noé*);
shaped form of the bib- | personal interview with
lical dimensions of the | him and examination of
Ark (1952), and later | the wood; wood analysis
(1955) succeeded in | reports from the Forestry
obtaining some of its | Institute of Research and
wood, which is definite- | Experimentation, Madrid,
ly hand-tooled, appar- | Spain, and from the Pre-
ently pitch- (bitumen-) | history Institute of the
impregnated, and at | University of Bordeaux's
least 5,000 years old. | Faculty of Sciences.

Because of the powerful nature of this circumstantial evidence, I myself have been on Mount Ararat four times (August, 1970, 1971, and 1972; April, 1973), ascending to the peak of this exceedingly high (5,165m./16,946 ft.) and treacherous peak on August 17, 1970. Ararat overlooks the Turkish-Russian border and is in a region controlled by the Turkish military; it has therefore been impossible, sad to say, to obtain government permissions to carry out the kind of extensive on-site research required to confirm past testimonies and bring about a firm discovery.

On returning from Turkey to the United States in September of this last year (1973), however, I was contacted by Mr. Thomas B. Turner of McDonnell Douglas Astronautics Company, who had been in touch with M. Delaney of the Earth Resources Observation Satellite Center, Sioux Falls, South Dakota, where ERTS data are stored. While checking ERTS imagery of the Ararat region, Delaney had found a peculiar rectangular shape, apparently foreign to the mountain.[34] Most remarkable was the location of the rectangle: in the very quadrant of the mountain where previous ground sightings had concentrated. Delaney

---

34. "Pattern recognition analysis is based on the fact that many land features have characteristic shapes. Man-made features tend to have geometrical shapes" (Belon & Miller, *op. cit.*, p. 9).

had not known this when he located the strange shape; indeed, he did not read my book collecting past sightings until introduced to it by Turner. (See Figure 14 and Appendix E: "Documents Relative to Satellite Imagery.")

True, the ERTS data are by no means definitive. The overall rectangle is larger than the dimensions of the biblical Ark (there is a smaller, perceptibly whiter area within the total rectangle, but the resolution capabilities of the imagery do not permit determining its size). Jerald Cook's staff at the Center for Remote Sensing of the Environmental Research Institute of Michigan has subjected the imagery to careful scouting and is unable to pronounce upon it with certainty.

But are not the possibilities breathtaking? As Belon and Miller rightly observe: "Satellite remote sensing of the environment must be coupled with data acquired from aircraft as well as with surface observations in order to be completely effective."[35] The use of aircraft in the Ararat region is out of the question because of the military situation, and we have just received word from Ankara that—doubtless because of native Kurdish uprisings in Iraq and Iran near Ararat and the Turkish border[36]—no in-site exploration of Ararat will be permitted this coming summer. The mystery thus remains for a while longer, as it has, in fact, for millennia. But the secret of Noah's Ark seems soon to be unlocked, and when it is, remote sensing may well have played a not insignificant part in showing the essential harmony between observational fact and biblical truth, between Science and Christian Faith.

---

35. *Ibid.*, p. 12.
36. Roger-X. Lantéri, "Kurdes: l'ultimatum," *L'Express* (March 25-31, 1974), pp. 62-63. Cf. the following recent news report (*Christianity Today*, May 24, 1974, pp. 57-58):

"Mount Ararat: Off Limits
The Turkish government last month announced a ban on travel by foreigners to Mount Ararat, which is located in a desolate region close to the Soviet border. All new maps printed by travel agencies are required to indicate Mount Ararat as an off-limits area for foreigners. No detailed explanation was given by authorities; the interior ministry merely cited problems caused by increasing numbers of foreigners wanting to climb the mountain 'under varying

5

The Summer of '74

Political tensions made responsible Ararat exploration impossible in 1973. Though I was able to introduce
an intrepid group of forty tourist friends to the foothills
of the mountain in April, and transport significant
amounts of equipment and gear to the area in July, all
efforts to secure permission for a regular summer expedition failed. California newspaper reports of exploratory activity on Ararat late in the summer were highly
misleading; on December 28, 1973, Semih Günver,
Turkey's Director General for Cultural Affairs, wrote
me from Ankara concerning these reports: "I am aware
of both the article by Nancy R. Willis and the exploits
of Mr. John Willis. For your information please note
that Mr. Willis did not obtain an official permission but
apparently paid a visit to Mt. Ararat without proper
credentials."

As was pointed out in the concluding paragraph and

pretenses.' It did not say what the pretenses were, but a number
of teams of Americans and Europeans have recently climbed Ararat
hoping to find Noah's Ark, which they believe may be buried under
the ice. . . .

Turkey's new head of the interior, Oguz Asiltürk, is a strict
Muslim deputy of the religion-oriented National Salvation party,
which constitutes the lesser right-wing segment of the otherwise leftist
Turkish government. In other recent moves, Asiltürk ordered the
removal of a modern statue of a nude woman in one of the squares
of Instanbul and banned the sale of beer except in licensed taverns.
Observers believe he'll pursue further Islamic-oriented policies.

The intellectuals of the country are unhappy with the right-wing
element of the government, but Prime Minister Bülent Ecevit needs
it in order to govern. Ecevit, the leader of the leftist Republican
People's party emerged from the last election with the highest number
of deputies, but he lacked the absolute majority in the Parliament,
and no party could form a new government for three months. Finally,
Ecevit, whose party adheres to the tenet of a secular state, was compelled to form a strange coalition with the most extreme right-wing
party. This brought a number of embarrassing developments to him
(he's an intellectual who tanslated T. S. Eliot into Turkish). The
members of his cabinet hailing from the National Salvation party
openly court Islamic state precepts in outright defiance of the con-
stitution."

final note of the preceding essay, the chances seemed even less promising to carry on the quest during the summer of 1974. By then I had separated myself from Adventist exploring teams (their vegetarianism and my French cuisine had proved incompatible—and the Sabbath seemed to me to be made for exploration, not exploration for the Sabbath!). In December, 1973, I flew to Paris to seek UNESCO's help on the permissions problem, while simultaneously working through various other high-level channels. A bit of detection revealed that an incredible file had been built up on me in the Turkish Intelligence network—suggesting that I was in league with Armenian nationalists! After convolutions too numerous to describe, we were nonetheless able to return to the mountain in June, 1974, for a brief period of work.

What was accomplished? (1) In the midst of extreme storm conditions, we relocated the site where Navarra found 5,000-year-old, hand-tooled wood almost twenty years before (1955). The cave and the semi-melted ice lake beneath it remain as Navarra found them, but the "object" has evidently sunk farther down. Wet-suit exploration was now mandatory, and one of the members of our team, intrepid advance scout Robert Stuplich, had the experience necessary to do the job. University laboratories at Heidelberg and Cologne were ready to subject to the most searching analysis anything found as a result of such future investigation. (2) We were accompanied on the mountain by expert photo-journalist Brian Bastien and a crack TV documentary team (Jack Dabner of the National Association for Media Evangelism, and Hollywood first cameraman Frank Raymond, who shot the acclaimed film, *His Land);* their photographic coverage provides a record of current Ararat exploration that will soon bring a severe case of "Ark fever" to armchair explorers across the land. (3) On the way home, we were graciously received by Fernand Navarra at his home in Bordeaux. There, Navarra and I discussed the past and present state of the quest for the Ark, and this dialogue-inter-

view was filmed for English dubbing and incorporation
into the projected documentary on the Ark's survival.

The future task? To find more of Navarra's wood;
to identify the site of the "unidentified object" whose
photograph accompanies my essay "Arkeology 1971";
to search out the exact spot on Ararat where the tran-
omaly appears in the ERTS satellite imagery. In the
latter connection, Dr. John M. Miller, a remote sensing
specialist from Fairbanks, Alaska (see notes 31, 34,
and 35 to the preceding essay), is now engaged in the
digital analysis of this imagery. Referring to a more
recent (July, 1973) ERTS image of Ararat, he tantalizingly wrote to me on September 3, 1974: "There
is another spot that could be of greater significance as
a potential anomalous area. It is the somewhat circular,
light-blue region in the northwest quadrant of the snow
field. Such a light blue- gray color tone compared with
more pure white surroundings frequently is indicative
of melting or less thick ice (or snow). This is an effect
that imbedded, dark-colored wood might have in the
summer upon the ice that surrounds it. While the dis-
colored area is much too large for the Ark itself, there
is the possibility that it no longer is intact. If the wood
is broken, deteriorated, and scattered a bit, it might
have an effect over an area much larger than its original
dimensions."

Political conditions, however, continue to worsen.
U.S.-Turkish relations have been severely strained over
Cyprus, and it is anyone's guess as to the immediate
future of the quest for the Ark. But one day Ararat
will yield up her secret, and I for one have little doubt
that it will be still another vindication of the ways of
God to man.

My God, I read this day,
*   That planted Paradise was not so firm*
As was and is Thy Floating Ark, whose stay
And anchor Thou art only, to confirm
*   And strengthen it in every age,*
*   when waves do rise and tempests rage.*

—George Herbert (1593-1632),
English Poems ("Ancient
and Modern Library of Theological
Literature"), p. 83.

Appendices

APPENDIX A

The Muslim Accounts

i. Al-Mas'udi (d. 956)

An Arab geographer of the 10th century, Al-Mas'udi helped to rekindle the scientific spirit that died with Ptolemy. He was a great traveller; most of his life was spent in voyages and travels in various parts of Asia and Africa. "In every region which he visited, he scrutinized available documents and contacted well informed persons of those countries. But, in the description of regions, wherever he depends on hearsay, he somehow errs towards exaggeration and sometimes absurdity. On the other hand when he does not lean on other people's 'opinions' or 'narratives' and is left to his own judgment and observation, he is remarkably accurate and precise."[1] The following account of the Ark on "Al Judi" is taken from Sprenger's English translation of al-Mas'udi's historical encyclopedia, The Meadows of Gold.[2]

In his [Noah's] age corruption and injustice were great on earth. Núh [Noah] rose to be a preacher of

---

[1] S. M. Ali, "Some Geographical Ideas of Al-Mas'udi," in *Al-Mas'udi Millenary Commemoration Volume*, ed. by S. Maqbul Ahmad and A. Rahman (published by the Indian Society for the History of Science and the Institute of Islamic Studies, Aligarh Muslim University, 1960), p. 85. Cf. the article by Mohammad Shafi, "Al-Mas'udi as a Geographer," pp. 72ff. For more information on Al-Mas'udi see the bibliography at the end of this commemorative volume, the article on him by C. Brockelmann in the *Encyclopaedia of Islam,* and Philip K. Hitti's *History of the Arabs* (London, 1958), pp. 391-92.

[2] Aloys Sprenger, trans., *El-Mas'udi's Historical Encyclopaedia, entitled "Meadows of Gold and Mines of Gems"*, I (London: The Oriental Translation Fund of Great Britain and Ireland, 1841), pp. 72-73. We have compared this version with the best modern translation. *Les Prairies d'Or*, trans. by Barbier de Meynard and Pavet de Courteille, ed. by Charles Pellat, I ("Société Asiatique: Collection d'Ouvrages Orientaux"; Paris, 1962), p. 31.

God, but the people were too rebellious and ungodly, so that they would not listen to him. God ordered him to construct a ship; and when he had finished it, the angel Gabriel brought him the coffin of Adam, in which there was his corpse. They went into the ship on Tuesday, the ninth of Adar.[1] Whilst Núh and his family were in the ship, God kept the earth five months[2] under water. Then he ordered the earth to swallow up its waters, and the heaven to withhold its rains,[3] and the ark stood on the mount el-Júdí. El-Júdí is a mountain in the country of Mâsúr, and extends to Jezírah Ibn 'Omar which belongs to the territory of el-Mausil. This mountain is eight farsangs from the Tigris. The place where the ship stopped, which is on the top of this mountain, is still to be seen.[4]

ii. Ibn Haukal (last half of the 10th century)

Though this Arab traveller does not testify to the survival of the Ark, he does offer a bridge between the Muslim accounts and those we have previously cited by placing the Quranic mountain in the vicinity of "Nisibin"—the bishopric of St. Jacob who is said to have ascended Mt. Ararat in the fourth century. Mention must be made of the disputed literary relationship between Ibn Haukal and al-Istakhri which extends to the work from which we quote below. Information on both individuals is available in the Encyclopaedia of Islam; *their critical texts are published by De Geoje in* Bibliotheca Geographorum Arabicorum *(Leyden, 1870ff). The following passage is taken from the translation of*

---

[1] [i.e., Friday, March 19.]
[2] [150 days in Gen. 7-24.]
[3] Koran, Surah xi., verse 46.
[4] [Al-Mas'udi is writing in 332 after the Hegira, or 943 A.D. He died in 956.] El-Kazwini (MS. of the East India House, N. 1377.) informs us that there was still, to the time of the 'Abbasides, a temple on the mount Júdí which was said to have been constructed by Noah, and covered with the planks of the ark. . . . The vicinity of Harrán, which was the seat of learning since Abraham, and the centre of Sabean worship, makes it more than probable that this temple was connected with the Sabean religion.

Ibn Haukal's Oriental Geography by Sir William Ouseley,* who, in the absence of a satisfactory manuscript of the original Arabic, made his version from Persian transcripts which suffer from "obscurities and imperfections."

Joudi is a mountain near Nisibin.[1] It is said that the Ark of Noah (to whom be peace!) rested on the summit of this mountain. At the foot of it there is a village called *Themabin,*[2] and they say that the companions of Noah descended here from the ark, and built this village.

iii. Elmacin (1223-1274)

In his history of the Saracens, extending from the time of Mohammed to the 12th century, George Elmacin (al-Makin or Ibn al-'Amid) makes reference to an ascent of "Al-Judi" by Byzantine emperor Heraclius (ca. 575-642), who wished to see the place where the Ark landed. There is no indication that he saw the Ark. We translate below from Elmacin's Historia Saracenica, Bk. I. p. 17.†

Heraclius departed thence into the region of Themanin[1] (which Noah—may God give him peace!—built after he came forth from the Ark). In order to see the place where the Ark landed,[2] he climbed Mount Judi, which overlooks all the lands thereabout, for it is exceedingly high.

---

* *The Oriental Geography of Ebn Haukal, an Arabian Traveller of the Tenth Century,* trans. (from a manuscript in his own possession, collated with one preserved in the Library of Eton College) by Sir William Ouseley (London: T. Cadell, 1800), p. 60.

[1] [Cf. above, Faustus of Byzantium's account of St. Jacob of Nisibis.]

[2] See note 1 to the account of William of Rubruck in Part Two, section 5.

† George Elmacin, *Historia Saracenica,* ed. and trans. from the Arabic by Thomas Erpenius (Leiden, 1625).

[1] [See note 1 to the account of William of Rubruck in Part Two, section 5.]

[2] [Lat. ut arcae locum videret.]

APPENDIX B

Complete List of the Successful Ascents of Greater Ararat, 1829-1910

(The following list—the most detailed to date—is based upon the following sources: Lynch, *Armenia: Travels and Studies,* I, 199; Louguinoff, "Ascension de l'Ararat," *Bulletin de la Société de Géographie* [Paris], 4th ser., I [1851], 54-55; Freshfield, "Early Ascents of Ararat," *Alpine Journal,* VIII [1877]. 214-16; Rawlinson, in the "Discussion on Mr. Bryce's Paper" [February 25, 1878], *Proceedings of the Royal Geographical Society* [London], XXII [1878], 184; Bryce, *Transcaucasia and Ararat,* pp. 236-38, 247-48; Seylaz, "L'ascension du Mont Ararat," *Tour du Monde,* n.s. XVII/34 [August 26, 1911], 404.)

1. F. Parrot, 1829, Started from the monastery of St. Jacob (Ahora gorge) and made the ascent by the northwestern slope.

2. K. Spasky-Avtonomoff,[1] August 5, 1834. From Ahora. "He is a good friend of mine," wrote Abich, "and his account, given to me on the occasion of my first making his acquaintance, I remember with pleasure. I took great pains to ascertain by a close inquiry into topographical details the accuracy of the narrative. He told me that, being officer of Customs at Nakhitschevan, he felt irresistibly attracted by the sublimity of the silver-headed mountain. His special aim was the desire to know whether it is true that stars of

---

[1] Alternative transliteration of the name: Spasski Aftonomof. On this ascent, see his article in the *Magazin fuer die Litteratur des Auslands,* No. 34 for the year 1835.

the first magnitude are visible from very elevated mountains. It is well known among M. Aftonomoff's friends that, the good man having lately followed the advice of the Vicar of Wakefield, his first son was baptised in water brought by the father from the top of Ararat" (Freshfield, 214).

3. Karl Behrens, July 20 and August 9, 1835. This ascent was attested by the Imperial Russian Geographical Society. Behrens saw the cross planted on the summit by Parrot (Longuinoff, 54).[2]

4. Hermann Abich, 1845. Up the southeastern face from Sardar Bulak, a Cossack station wih a well, located in the middle of the wide semicircular valley or sloping plain between Greater and Lesser Ararat. (Cf. Bryce, 247-48.) He attained the eastern summit, now named for him (this eastern elevation is some thirty feet lower than the western peak, conquered by and now named for Parrot).

5. H. Danby Seymour, 1846.[3] From the present Ahora (?) Longuinoff calls this ascent "une fantaisie de touriste." Seymour himself wrote: "I cannot lay my hands on my notes now. My companions were two Armenians and a Cossack officer. I remember that we slept in a woody dell before commencing the ascent in charge of the Cossack guard. We could obtain no porters, and one of the Armenians served as guide. We had to carry all we wanted for our ascent ourselves. I remember I had chickens, &c., fastened round my waist. At the last moment the Armenian who served as guide refused to come because he had no boots. I had to give him my own boots and wear some Persian slippers. The time we could stay on the summit was very short, as the clouds began to gather round us. We reached the pleateau on the top and descended, I remember, by a different hollow of the mountain to that

---

[2] Behrens' own account appeared in the *Gazette russe de l'Académie*, Nos. 21 and 23 for the year 1838.

[3] Lynch gives the date as 1845 and Longuinoff as 1848; but Sir Henry Rawlinson, Seymour's brother-in-law, establishes the 1846 date, stating that Seymour "wrote a letter from the summit, which was still in the possession of his family [in 1878]."

by which we had ascended, coming down a tremendous snowslide. Our Cossacks lifted a good many cattle on the following day" (Freshfield, 215).

6. J. Khodzko, N.V. Khanikoff, and others, 1850. From Sardar Bulak.

7. R. Stuart and others, 1856. From Dogubayazit and Sardar Bulak. "The Russian Geographical Society knows of no ascents later than 1850 [i.e., from 1850 to 1877]. Herr Abich, however, says: 'In the beginning of 1853 I left the Caucasus for five years. On my return I heard of some ascents of Ararat in the interval. Major Stuart's must have been of the number. From 1860 to 1874 some other ascents were made, but as they had no scientific interest I confess I did not much care about them.' Mr. Bryce, however, doubts whether any ascents were made during this period" (Freshfield, 216).

8. Bryce, 1876. From Sardar Bulak.

9. G. P. Baker, 1878. From Sardar Bulak.

10. Sivoloboff, 1882.

11. E. Markoff, 1888. From Sardar Bulak.[4]

12. Semenoff, 1888(?)

13. Raphalovich and others, 1889. From Sardar Bulak.

14. T. G. Allen and W. L. Sachtleben (1892?). From Dogubayazit.

15. Postukhoff, 1893. From Sardar Bulak.

16. H. B. Lynch. H. F. B. Lynch, and Rudolph Taugwalder, 1893. From Sardar Bulak.

17. A. Oswald, 1897.[5]

18. Ivangouloff, 1902. The purpose of this expedition was to place recording thermometers on the summit (Seylaz, 404).

19. Seylaz, 1910.

---

[4] See E. de Markoff and E. de Kovalewsky, "Expedition scientifique au Caucase," *Bulletin de la Société Royale Belge de Géographie* [Brussels], XII (1888), pp. 577-91.

[5] Oswald, "Eine Besteigung des Ararat," *Jahrbuch schweiz. Alpenclub* (Berne), XXXV (1899-1900), 157-83.

APPENDIX C

The Osnobichine-Cyril Story Exploded: A Dossier of Correspondence

(With the following story-in-letters, see above, Part Two, section 9 ("The Russian Expedition") and Part Four, section 2 ("Arkeology 1971"). The fascination in the quest for the Ark lies not only in the struggles of mountaineering but also in the labyrinths of literary detective work!)

1.

1, rue de Palerme
67 Strasbourg, France
9 April 1970

Le Départment des Manuscrits
Bibliothèque Publique et Universitaire
Jardin des Bastions
Genève-4
SWITZERLAND

Dear Sirs:

Pursuant to my telephone call to your Secretary today, I am enclosing a copy of the correspondence Mme. Arbuthnot of your staff conducted with my associate, Mr. Eryl Cummings.

I cannot tell you how pleased I am that you are granting me special permission to consult the Osnobichine manuscripts Saturday afternoon in the Salle des Lecteurs from 14h00 to 17h00. It is particularly gracious of you to prepare the MS collection in advance for my arrival.

I shall be accompanied on Saturday by Mr. Richard

McCormick, a Russian language specialist on the staff of the U.S. Mission in Geneva, whose services have been obtained through the good offices of Mr. Brian Fitzpatrick, Consul General of the United States in Strasbourg.

Thank you gain for your immediate and most kind service in this matter.

Yours cordially,

(Prof.) John Warwick Montgomery, Ph.D.
Honorary Fellow of Revelle College, 1970

2.

Genève, le May 12, 1966

Mr. Eryl A. Cummings
112 East Broadway
Farmington, New Mexico

Dear Mr. Cummings,

I wish to acknowledge your letter of April 23rd and to answer your question concerning the possible possession by the Bibliothèque Publique et Universitaire in Geneva of documents describing the Russian expedition into Eastern Turkey and the Mt. Ararat region in search of Noah's Ark.

Our library did receive from General d'Osnobichine a portion of his collection but careful examination of the inventories of printed documents now in our possession reveals no material related to the expedition which interests you. We regret our inability to be of service to you.

In a further list of books comprising the library of General d'Osnobichine but which are not in our possession there are two references which might interest you. In 1928 Payot in Paris published in a French translation portions of the secret archives of Nicolas II and also diplomatic documents taken from the archives of the Ministry of foreign affairs. Our library does not have either of these books but the exact references are as follows:

Archives secrètes de l'empereur Nicolas II. Traduit du russe et annoté par Vladimir Lazarevski. —Paris, Payot, éditeur, 1928. In-8, 251 p. (Collection de mémories, études et documents pour servir à l'histoire de la Guerre Mondiale.)

Documents diplomatiques secrets russes (1914-1917), d'après les Archives du ministère des affaires étrangères à Petrograd. Traduit du russe par J. Polonsky. Paris, Payot, éditeur, 1928. In-8, 333 p. (Collection de mémoires, études et documents pour servir à l'histoire de la Guerre Mondiale.)

If you have not already consulted these books access to them might be possible by interlibrary loan through your local library.

Sincerely yours,
(Mrs.) Eugenie H. Arbuthnot
Assistante bibliothécaire

3.

[TRANSLATION OF THE RELEVANT PARA-GRAPHS]

Geneva, April 15, 1970

Dear Professor:

We have received your letter of the 9th in which you apprise us of your coming visit to our Reading Room on Saturday, April 18, to consult the Osnobichine manuscripts. However, we regret to have to inform you of what we found in our attempt to prepare these manuscripts for you in advance. In point of fact, the [University of Geneva] Library does not own and has never owned any Osnobichine manuscripts whatever, contrary to what you were led to believe on the basis of the letter of May 12, 1966, a copy of which you sent us. . . .

If, nonetheless, you still wish to come to the Reading Room Saturday afternoon, the attendant will make available to you two items concerning Osnobichine: a catalog of his personal library (2 typewritten notebooks), and some photographs related to the General. . . . The catalog comprises a handwritten list of 48 printed works which Osnobichine gave to our Library in 1947; 35 of these are in Russian and on Russia. . . .

Paul Waeber
Librarian

4.

1, rue de Palerme
67 Strasbourg, France
16 April 1970

M. Paul Waeber, Bibliothécaire
Bibliothéque Publique et Universitaire
Jardin des Bastions
Genève-4
SWITZERLAND

Dear Mr. Waeber:

Again let me thank you for your graciousness in making special arrangements for my research. As indicated in our telephone conversation this afternoon, Mr. R. McCormick of the U.S. Mission will arrive with me at the Salle des Lecteurs at 18 h 00 on Monday to check the Russian printed books given to the Library by General Osnobichine. If the books have been brought together in the Salle des Lecteurs, together with MSS Av 3 and Ys 39, prior to our arrival, I am reasonably sure that we can go through them to see if they contain the desired information prior to the time the Library closes for the night.

I myself plan to be at the Library early that same afternoon to examine the 13 non-Russian books in the General's collection (this will leave the 35 Russian

items for Mr. McCormick and me in the evening).
There is also the possibility that Mr. McCormick may
come alone to the Library to make a preliminary examination of the collection before we meet there on
Monday evening. Thus it will be especially advantageous if the books are brought together in the Salle des
Lecteurs as soon as this can be done conveniently by
your staff.

Perhaps I should give you some background on this
research. In 1953, an article was published by a reputable (and now deceased) writer which stated: "Information relating to the existence of remains of the ark
. . . is contained in documents presented to the library
of the University of Geneva by Gen. Dmitri Osnobichine, an aide to the Grand Duke Cyril in Czarist days.
According to the document, a Russian aviator, Vladimir Roskovitsky, who flew over Mount Ararat in 1916,
saw the timbers of a boat in one of the mountain valleys. . . . According to the Geneva library documents, a
detachment of 200 men climbed the mountain, found
remains of huge timbers which they measured and
photographed and forwarded to the grand duke. Before
any further action could be taken, the Red revolution
broke out. Grand Duke Cyril salvaged some of the reports, including the statement by Roskovitsky" [here
follows, in translation, some direct quotations from the
report]. Now it seems highly unlikely that this is a fabrication, since the names connected with the narrative
—especially Osnobichine—are genuine persons, and
Osnobichine did in fact give books to the University of
Geneva Library.

My supposition is that the above-mentioned reports
are contained in one or more of the printed books in
General gave to the Library (thus my forthcoming visit
to check the books). But there are other possibilities,
and I would much appreciate your giving me your
opinion and advice on them when I come to the Library Monday afternoon:

(1) Could the article have mistakenly referred to
the University Library when in fact another Library in
the city received Osnobichine MSS? Is there a "White

Russian refugees or expatriates library" in the city? In
Mme Arbuthnot's letter of 12-5-66, she says that your
Library received only "a portion" of the General's collection; where did the rest go? perhaps to another library in Geneva? Any checking along this line for me
would be an invaluable asset.

(2) Is it possible that the University of Geneva also
received papers and materials from Duke Cyril or from
aviator Vladimir Roskovitsky? Perhaps a mistake has
been made in restricting the search to Osnobichine's
collection, and the desired documents appear under one
of these two other names? Could this be checked out
for me prior to my arrival? If there is any subject-
indexing of the Library's Russian materials, there is always the chance that something might turn up under
the three proper names in question or even under the
rubrics "Ararat" or "Ark of Noah."

Your help in these respects is inestimable. The success of the endeavor to trace all reputable reports of
"sightings" on Ararat during the last hundred years and
the expedition to the mountain in August will doubtless
be directly dependent on the aid received from you and
your kind staff.

Yours very truly,

(Prof. Dr.) John Warwick Montgomery

5.

*This booklet was uncovered in the University of
Geneva Library during my research there on Monday,
April 20, 1970. It is a laudatory tribute to Grand Duke
Cyril by the White Russian Monarchists Union, which
still hoped in 1922 to restore the imperial family to the
throne, and was pinning its hopes on the Grand Duke.
The pamphlet was published in 1922 at Munich, Germany—but in French, not in German. The paragraphs
translated below led me to believe that Cyril's son
Vladimir, or other members of the family, might still
be living on the French Riviera, in the area of Nice. I*

therefore made contact with the American Consulate at Nice, and had the incredible good fortune to encounter Mme Silatiess, a Russian-French lady who had been a member of the Consulate staff for years. She had known the Osnobichine family and put me in touch with M. Iserguine of Nice, who acts as a secretary to Vladimir in France.

The news of the Tsar's abdication arrived shortly thereafter [in March, 1917] and immediately the Grand Duke [Cyril] served notice of his demission.

He resided for a time in St. Petersburg. In June, 1917, His Imperial Highness departed with his family for Finland. . . .

From the marriage of the Grand Duke and the Grand Duchess these children were born: on February 2, 1907, Princess Mary . . .; on May 9, 1909, Princess Kyra . . .; and on August 30, 1917, at Borgo [Finland], Prince Vladimir Kirillovitch. . . .

. . . The Grand Duke and his wife stayed three years in Finland. . . .

After a year in Switzerland, the Grand Duke and his family took up residence in the Midi region of France, where they live now, passing their time between Brittany and Nice.

6.

Address for reply:
1, rue de Palerme
67 Strasbourg, France
4 May 1970

M. Iserguine
3, rue Père Valencin
06 Nice

Dear Mr. Iserguine,

Enclosed is a copy of the letter which I sent today to His Imperial Highness, The Grand Duke Vladimir. Thank you so much for giving his Madrid address to

Mme Silatiess of the American Consulate so that I could contact him.

As you will see from the letter, I made an effort to find the documents concerning Ararat and the Noah's Ark expedition in the books General Osnobichine gave to the University of Geneva Library. However, if these documents were in the possession of the General, he almost certainly did not give them to the Geneva Library.

I was unsuccessful while in Geneva in my efforts to determine what has happened to the rest of the General's personal library. When I telephoned the Eglise Orthodoxe Russe, rue Toepffer, I was told that no one there had known General Osnobichine personally. The antiquarian bookseller Slatkine said that his father had known the General, but his father was now dead—and so was everybody who had been intimate with the General. According to the bookseller, the General died in the 1950s and did not leave any surviving relatives, at least in Geneva. He had lived with a housekeeper at the time of his death.

Do you have any information that might be of help to me? Do you know of relatives or friends of General Osnobichine who might have information as to the ultimate disposition of his personal library and papers? I am naturally hopeful that Grand Duke Vladimir will be able to supply me with direct information on the Ararat expedition from his father's papers or from conversations Grand Duke Cyril had about this with members of his immediate family; but there is still the possibility that General Osnobichines' papers might yield the required information. Any help you can render will be greatly appreciated. You may of course reply in French.

Yours sincerely and cordially,

(Rev. Prof. Dr.) John Warwick Montgomery

7.

Address for reply:
1, rue de Palerme
67 Strasbourg, France
4 May 1970

His Imperial Highness,
    The Grand Duke Vladimir of Russia
Guisando, 13
Ciudad Puerte de Hierro
Madrid 20
ESPANA

Sire,

I am engaged in a very important research project concerning the possible remains of the Ark of Noah on Mt. Ararat in Turkey. All reliable reports of sightings in modern times are presently being checked, and an expedition is scheduled for this summer to determine whether archeological evidence of the Ark still remains on the mountain. One of the reported sightings relates to your father, His Imperial Highness, The Grand Duke Cyril; and I am therefore writing to you in the hopes that you may be able to shed further light on the subject. M. Iserguine of Nice was kind enough to supply me with your address, through the good offices of Mme Silatiess of the American Consulate there. I hope that you will pardon the intrusion of this letter for the sake of the vital importance of the research project—which could uncover the most significant ancient artifact of all time and could do much to support common Christian faith over against the atheistic forces that removed your distinguished family from the throne of Russia.

In 1953, an article was published by a reputable (and now deceased) writer which stated: "Information relating to the existence of remains of the ark . . . is contained in documents presented to the library of the University of Geneva by Gen. Dmitri Osnobichine, an aide to the Grand Duke Cyril in Czarist days. Accord-

ing to the document, a Russian aviator, Vladimir Roskovitsky, who flew over Mount Ararat in 1916, saw the
timbers of a boat in one of the mountain valleys. . . .
According to the Geneva library documents, a detachment of 200 men climbed the mountain, found remains
of huge timbers which they measured and photographed and forwarded to the grand duke. Before any further action could be taken, the Red Revolution broke
out. Grand Duke Cyril salvaged some of the reports,
including the statement by Roskovitsky."

I have myself gone to the University of Geneva Library during the last month, and though General Osnobichine did give a part of his large library to the
University, no report of the Ararat discovery is contained in his donation. I have been unable to determine
what became of the rest of the General's personal library, but it is clear from the above quoted article that
your esteemed father was the direct recipient of the reports of the expedition and would therefore have had
much fuller knowledge of them than ever General Osnobichine.

It will interest you to know that the above article is
by no means the only confirmation of the White Russian expedition to Ararat in 1916. In February, just
before I left for Europe to carry out research on the
project here, I spent an afternoon with Mr. Alexander
A. Koor, former colonel and chief-in-command of the
19th Petropaulovsky regiment, who now lives at an advanced age in Menlo Park, California. Colonel Koor
has stated: "About July or August, 1921, I and Lt.
Leslin met 1st Lt. Rujansky in Harbin [Manchuria,
where they had escaped from the Bolsheviks]. During
one of our conversations, 1st Lt. Rujansky told me
about the discovery of Noah's Ark. He didn't know
about the details because he was wounded, and was
sent to Russia, but he knew because his brother Boris
Vasilivich Rujansky, Sergeant of the Military Railroad
Battalion, was a member of the investigating party
which was sent to Mount Ararat to corrobrate the discovery of Noah's Ark. . . . Lt. Leslin admitted he had
also heard about the discovery of Noah's Ark, not as a

rumor, but as news, from the Senior Adjutant of his Division, who had told him that Noah's Ark was found in the saddle of two peaks of Mount Ararat." Moreover, we have testimony from the families of two now-deceased soldiers who were on the Ararat expedition to the effect that remains of the Ark were discovered.

Thus the expedition was no "myth." However, we have not been able to locate the actual reports, photographs, or other detailed information that could conceivably aid in the rediscovery of the remains of the Ark this summer. This is why we turn to you.

Did your esteemed father tell the family about the expedition? Were the reports of the expedition perhaps retained by your father and passed on to you in the family library? Do you know certainly that General Osnobichine served as an aide to your father? Have you any idea where the General's papers may be today (the papers and books he did not donate to the University of Geneva Library)?

Even if all you have heard about this is in the nature of oral remarks made by your father, I would consider it a great privilege to converse with you on the subject. The most minute amount of additional information could have the greatest concrete value. I should be most happy to fly to Madrid to talk with you at your earliest convenience. I speak English and French fluently, and I could certainly have a Spanish translator with me if you wish to use that language. (Naturally, you may reply to this letter in Spanish, French, or English, as you wish.)

To give you further information on myself, I am enclosing a detailed biographical dossier. If you wish further verification of my qualifications, you can consult my notices in *Who's Who in America, Who's Who in France, The Dictionary of International Biography,* etc. etc. It may also interest you to know that I am one of the three Montgomerys included in *The Royal Blue Book* (1968); our family traces its ancestry from Comte Roger de Montgomery, one of the associates of William the Conqueror in the Norman invasion of England in 1066.

Please accept my humblest thanks in advance for your attention to this letter. Any help you can render will be most deeply appreciated, and, as mentioned above, could provide direct aid in the uncovering of the greatest archeological support of all time for the truth of our Holy Christian Faith.

Respectfully yours,

(Rev. Prof. Dr.) John Warwick Montgomery

8.

Madrid
11th May 70

Dear Dr. Montgomery,

Thank you for your letter of May 4th.

Unfortunately I can be of very little help to you, as I have never come across the report in question among my father's archives. I most certainly should have noticed any such document because I am, and have always been, extremely interested in this and similar subjects.

I shall try to get information concerning the whereabouts of Gen. Osnobichine's papers, and let you know as soon as possible.

Best regards,

Yours sincerely,

Wladimir
Grand Duke of Russia

9.

Rev. Dr. J. W. Montgomery
1 Rue de Palerme,
67-Strasbourg
FRANCIA

6-VII-70

Thank you for your letter of June 29th.

I got an answer from a friend of Gen. Osnobichine, now in Brasil, but unfortunately he does not know what became of his archives. The general had but one heir, a nephew, but I've not yet been able to locate him. My secretary will continue investigating and also write to Bishop Antony.

Best regards,

Wladimir
GD of R.

10.

[TRANSLATION OF THE RELEVANT PARA-GRAPHS]

Brussels, February 14, 1971

Sir:

Following the instructions of His Imperial Highness Grand Duke Vladimir of Russia, I am honored to inform you that General Osnobichine's nephew and heir, Alessandro Iordanov, died some years ago, but his widow and daughter still live in Rome. . . . Perhaps these ladies would have something relevant to the Noah's Ark documents which interest you.

Further, His Imperial Highess is of the opinion that, along the same line, you might find it useful to contact the Rev. Father and Archpriest Stephan Lyashevsky. . . .

N. de Wouytch

11.

March 23, 1971

Mr. N. de Wouytch
Av. des Sept Bonniers 130
B-1190 Brussels
BELGIUM

Dear Mr. de Wouytch:

I can't tell you how much I appreciated receiving your note of February 14, which just reached me at my U.S. address.

I have today written both to Mrs. Iordanov and to Father Lyashevsky. I shall most certainly keep you posted, if their replies yield significant information.

If other research possibilities occur to you, please do not hesitate to write. In the absence of the expedition report, we are concerned to contact any of the surviving soldiers who took part in the expedition or persons who had direct contact with them.

Thank you again for your efforts in our behalf.

Yours most cordially,

John Warwick Montgomery

cc:
Grand Duque Wladimir
Guisando 13
Madrid-20
SPAIN

12.

March 23, 1971

The Rev. Father Stephan Lyashevsky
Route 2, Box 196
Valrico, Florida 33594

Dear Father Lyshevsky:

The enclosed materials should be self-explanatory. As you will see, I am sending them to you on the strong recommendation of His Imperial Majesty, Grand Duke Wladimir.

You should regard this material as confidential, but at the same time you should feel personally free to show it to any trusted person who might be able to shed light on the missing Ararat expedition report which presumably was once in the hands of General Osnobichine and Grand Duke Cyril.

I should much appreciate hearing your reactions to all of this—particularly any suggestions you may have concerning avenues that have not yet been pursued which might yield the missing documents or primary testimony from persons who participated in the expedition or who had direct contact with those who did.

I shall be delighted to hear from you. As I indicated to Mrs. Iordanov, a reply should be sent to my Strasbourg address (marked NE PAS FAIRE SUIVRE):

> 1, rue de Palerme
> *67 Strasbourg*
> FRANCE

Yours most cordially,
John Warwick Montgomery

Enclosures

13.

March 25, 1971

Dear Mr. Montgomery,

In today's mail I received your letter plus information regarding the Mt. Ararat Expedition.

Are you familiar with Mr. Fernand Navarra? If so, he will be able to assist you. Probably, he even was a member of your planned expedition of last year? The reason I am referring to Mr. Navarra is because you have not mentioned his name in your letter to me.

All the information that I have, has come from Mr. Navarra's book, printed in 1956 in the French language in France. The name of the book is *I Did Find Noah's Ark. J'ai trouvé l'Arche de Noé.* There are many plans, maps, photos and laboratory tests of the piece of timber which he has cut from the Ark. The laboratory tests shows the timber's age to be 5,000 years old.

I received from Mr. Navarra his book and a tiny piece of the timber from the Ark. Mr. Navarra told me—it is impossible to purchase this book because all editions are sold out. However, if you are interested in seeing the piece of timber plus the book, it will be necessary for you to come to Florida, because I am afraid to mail it, lest it be lost somehow. Should you be interested you must fly to Tampa and take a taxi to my home. Kindly telephone from Tampa or better from Illinois, to be sure we are at home for your visit.

Yours in Christ,

Stephan Lyashevsky

14.

March 23, 1971

Mme. Vve Allesandro Iordanov
112, via del Plebiscito
Rome
ITALY

Dear Madam:

The enclosed correspondence will inform you of the vitally important search in which we are presently engaged. In brief, there is every reason to believe that General Osnobichine possessed a report of a White Russian expedition which successfully verified the report of a Russian flyer in 1916, identifying the extant remains of Noah's Ark on Great Ararat.

You will note that I have been in correspondence with Grand Duke Wladimir, son of Grand Duke Cyril, who also allegedly had contact with the expedition report. Grand Duke Wladimir has graciously been endeavoring to determine the disposition of General Osnobichine's papers; it was a result of Wladimir's correspondence with M. de Wouytch (copy of note enclosed) that I am writing you.

It is plain that the General's personal papers were not donated to the University of Geneva library along with his books, for I examined the situation at the University of Geneva library in considerable detail myself.

Is there any chance that, as the wife of the General's nephew and heir, you may personally be in possession of the desired material? The expedition report could well have been incorporated into the General's personal files and thus have been lost to view. It does not seem possible that the General would have left Russia without taking the report with him; its importance and the entire lack of sympathy of Marxists toward such a report would have assured his retention of it.

Our exploratory work on Ararat continues this summer, and we need every scrap of datum concerning the survival of Noah's vessel. It is therefore of greatest importance that you communicate with me concerning the above-mentioned documents. As I wrote to Grand Duke Wladimir: "I hope that you will pardon the intrusion of this letter for the sake of the vital importance of the research project—which could uncover the most significant ancient artifact of all time and could do much to support our common Christian faith over against the atheistic forces that removed your distinguished family from the throne of Russia."

Please feel free to reply in English, French, or Italian. The following address should be used for reply, since I shall be at my Strasbourg address by April 7 (please mark the envelope NE PAS FAIRE SUIVRE to insure that the letter will remain there for my arrival):

> 1, rue de Palerme
> *67 Strasbourg*
> FRANCE

If you should wish to phone, my Strasbourg number is (88) 36-49-14. I speak English and French fluently; however, I read Italian, but do not speak it. If the needed documents are in your possession, I should be most happy to come to Rome and discuss them with you. We do not need the originals, if you wish to retain them for sentimental reasons, but we desperately need to obtain photocopies.

Thank you in advance for your willingness to read

the enclosed materials and to work with us on this exceedingly important project.

Yours appreciatively,

John Warwick Montgomery

Enclosures

15.

April 17th 1971

Dr. John Warwick Montgomery
1 rue de Palerme
67 Strasbourg, France.

Dear Sir,

I received your letter of March 23rd last a few days ago. I regret that all I can do to clarify your problem is to correct the statements concerning my husband's uncle, General Dimitri Osnobichine, made in the article of 1953, quoted in your letter to the Grand Duke Vladimir of May 4th 1970, paragraph 2.

1) There is no report, no document or notes concerning the search for remains of the Ark on Mount Ararat, either amongst the gifts of General Osnobichine to the Bibliothèque Universitaire de Genève, or amongst the personal or family papers that came to my husband after the General's death in 1956.

2) It is true that the General as a young man served in the Caucasus, but this was from 1892 until 1894, when he entered the Staff College. In 1900 he served in China throughout the Boxer campaign. Shortly after his return to Europe, in 1902 or 1903, he was appointed aide-de-camp to H.I.H. the Duke of Leuchtenberg, who resided in Paris. From that time until the Second World War, my uncle made his home in Paris. He never had the honour of being aide-de-camp to H.I.H. the Grand Duke Cyril.

I am afraid that the inaccurate statements made in

this article of 1953 have led you to believe that my uncle had some connection with the attempts made in 1916 or later to discover the remains of the Ark, or at least that official reports of a military expedition sent to Mount Ararat for this purpose could have passed through his hands. I can assure you that this was not the case. In the years that the General lived with us, and later, during our frequent visits to Geneva, he would speak of his service in the Caucasus as a young officer, and of the picturesque peoples and legends of that region; as he told delightful stories of events he had witnessed and people he had met in the course of a long and interesting life. But he never mentioned an expedition in the last years of the Empire (or at any other time) to Mount Ararat.

I return the photocopies enclosed in your letter, and sincerely regret that I cannot help.

Yours very truly,

Phyllis Iordanow-Osnobichine.

APPENDIX D

Addendum: Correspondence and Documents Relative to ERTS Imagery of What May Be the Remains of Noah's Ark on Mount Ararat.

1.

12250 Corrida Court
Maryland Heights, Mo 63043
September 23, 1973

Dr. John W. Montgomery
Trinity Seminary College
Deerfield, Illinois 60015

Dear Dr. Montgomery:

In my role as Manager, Market Analysis, McDonnell Douglas Astronautics Company, St. Louis, I have occasion to keep in touch with most of the developments in the U.S. Space Program. Recently, one of the staff of the Earth Resources Observation Satellite Center at Sioux Falls, South Dakota, called to tell me that he had just been made aware of the importance of a particular bit of data that he had uncovered in January 1973. The staff member, a Mr. Mike Delaney, whose background included attending Concordia Seminary, Springfield, Illinois, had been playing around with the satellite imagery when it was first delivered to the Center in January 1973 to determine ways and means that the Center could service the public's interest in remote sensing by satellites. His theological interests led him to study the photography of the Middle East and to home in on Mt. Ararat in Turkey which had particularly good cloud free coverage. Mr. Delaney put the imagery through the high resolution devices at the Center and found that a foreign object appeared on the mountain—in a decidedly rectangular shape, quite long, and three-quarters of the way up the mountain. This all occurred in January, 1973. Then, in August, 1973, a Lt. Col. Brown from the U.S. Air Force Academy visited the Center with the purpose of seeing whether there might not be some imagery of Mt. Ararat which would highlight the location of Noah's Ark, which was reputed to still be on the mountain. Mr. Delaney told Col. Brown about his own discovery and Col. Brown bought copies of that imagery to study.

Mary Crain, assistant to the Administrator of the McDonnell Douglas Astronautics Company, whose office is across the hall from my own, heard me discussing this with Mr. Delaney when he called in early September 1973. She came right over after the conversation to tell me that she had just read a book on the subject which I should see. It was called, "In Quest of Noah's Ark," by John Warwick Montgomery. Mrs. Crain brought in the book the next day and, after reading it, I called Mr. Delaney. Without giving details, I asked him whether he had read the book. He had not. I asked him whether he knew any facts describing the size of Noah's Ark, where it might be located on the mountain and in what sort of terrain it supposedly rested. He told me that he knew that the ark was supposed to be 300 cubits by 50 cubits from Biblical accounts and that this would come out to be around 500-600 feet by 75-100 feet—dimensions which seemed to jibe with the foreign object appearing on the mountain. When asked about those aspects about which he had not read, namely, position and location, Mr. Delaney said that the object appeared to be resting in a ravine and covered by an ice sheet and that it was on the north side of the mountain three quarters of the way up (which according to my calculations would place it at or about 14,000 feet). All of this corroborated facts oulined in the Montgomery book. Mr. Delaney and I then agreed that I should contact Dr. Montgomery and tell him that there were objective means of substantiating details in his book by means of the remote sensing data. This was the occasion of my original call to you during the week of September 16, 1973.

This is, to the best of my knowledge, the manner in which this whole matter came to my attention and my role in it. It is my understanding that Mr. Delaney originally located the object on the imagery of Mt. Ararat in January 1973, and that Lt. Col. Brown impressed him with the importance of the potentials of this discovery.

With all best wishes for your work, I remain,

Faithfully yours

Thomas B. Turner

2.

Environmental Research Institute of Michigan
Ann Arbor, Michigan

December 4, 1973

Mr. Semih Günver
Ambassadeur
Directeur Général des Affaires Culturelles
Ministère des Affaires Étrangères
Ataturk Blvd. 140
Ankara
TURKEY

Dear Mr. Günver:

On 27 November, 1973 Dr. John Warwick Montgomery of Trinity Seminary, Deerfield, Illinois, U.S.A. visited our Institute to discuss data which, in his opinion, could bear importantly on his research into cultural and historical legends relating to the Mt. Ararat region. The nature of these data was a frame of spacecraft imagery obtained with sensors on-board the U.S. Earth Resources Technology Satellite (ERTS-1). Specifically Dr. Montgomery, and others viewing this imagery, have located an interesting feature, part-way up the mountain, in an area which generally coincides with independently derived theories as to the potential location of the legendary Ark of Noah.

Experts, on our staff here at the Institute, have made a cursory examination of this imagery with Dr. Montgomery and have discussed with him the capabilities and limitations of modern spaceborne sensors related to an object of the size generally attributed to the Ark. While we cannot support the hypothesis that this imagery represents any definitive data on either the legend, or even man-made artifact on the mountain, we can definitely state that a tonal change does exist at the point of interest and that the spacecraft sensor resolution is not sufficient to define the exact nature of the source of this tonal contrast.

At this time it is not possible to speculate beyond this point as to the potential usefulness of this information or its possible cultural or historical importance. It is quite possible that the higher resolution imagery or on-the-ground inspection will be necessary to gain any additional information on this unidentified feature.

If I can be of any assistance to you or to Dr. Montgomery please do not hesitate to contact me.

Sincerely,
Jerald J. Cook

Center for Remote Sensing
Information and Analysis

cc: J.W. Montgomery
    T.B. Turner

3.

Environmental Research Institute of Michigan
Ann Arbor, Michigan

8 February 1974

Dr. John W. Montgomery
Trinity Seminary College
Deerfield, Illinois 60015

Dear Dr. Montgomery:

Enclosed are transparencies of the Ararat region provided to us by Mike Delaney. Several of our people have examined each band, enlarged to 28.5 times, and remain unable to draw any definitive conclusions regarding the anomalous rectangular pattern observed by Mr. Delaney. I have personally spent several hours studying the imagery in connection with several illustrations and the topographic map made by the Archaeological Research Foundation, as contained in your book.

The anomalous rectangular pattern is most easily seen in band 7, while band 5 provides more detail in the surrounding shadowed area. This pattern is apparently caused by sunlight striking the terrain in an area otherwise shadowed by the ridge (or glacial ice) to the east. This, in turn, can be considered as due to a rectangular object or ridge projecting upward out of the shadowed area or as due to a notch or break in the ridge of ice to the east causing this peculiar shadow on otherwise smooth terrain.

Several of the Research Foundation illustrations in your book appear to show the area in question (e.g. Photographs A and B, p. 234 and D and E, p. 235) but unfortunately, none indicate a clear source of this anomalous pattern in the terrain and ice conditions existing in 1966. Regrettably the ERTS imagery enclosed herewith raise the question of the origin of this pattern, but do little to answer same.

I hope your contact with the UN officials in Paris was successful and that our modest endorsement was beneficial. I would personally have been somewhat more positive in that regard, but was superseded by a more conservative viewpoint.

I have certainly enjoyed reading your book and learning much about the history of Ararat and the search for the ark. However, I remain pessimistic. Perhaps hearing your talk on the subject will do more to convince me. I am looking forward to an enjoyable discussion with you, now that I am somewhat more familiar with the fact and history of the "quest."

Sincerely,
Jerald J. Cook

CC: Mike Delaney

4.

NEWS Senator Frank E. Moss

FOR RELEASE:

February 21, 1974

SATELLITE PHOTOS MAY PINPOINT NOAH'S ARK

In a speech in Salt Lake City today Utah Senator Frank E. (Ted) Moss said a professor of theology and education who has been studying Earth Resources Technology Satellite photos believes some of the pictures corroborate evidence that the remains of Noah's Ark may be found on Mount Ararat.

Speaking to the Utah Section of the American Congress on Surveying and Mapping, Moss said Dr. John Montgomery, who has led an expedition on Mount Ararat, is currently seeking permission to take an expedition to the site of a "formation" found in recent ERTS photos.

Moss, who is chairman of the Senate Aeronautical and Space Sciences Committee, said photos of the Ararat area from Skylab are expected to improve on the ERTS pictures.

"ERTS photographs taken from 450 miles above the earth show a formation at the lower end of the satellite's resolution capability which appears to be foreign to other materials found on the mountain," said Moss.

"It's about the right size and shape to be the Ark . . . The location of the object in question is at about 14,000 feet in the northeast quadrant of the mountain in a canyon filled with ice. It is consistent with the other sightings mentioned earlier. Obviously, the significance of this finding, if it can be verified, can hardly be overemphasized."

Montgomery has been investigating the possibility that the remains of the Ark (described in Genesis 8:4) are on Ararat. Montgomery has seven earned degrees including a Ph.D. from the University of Chicago. He teaches half of each year at Trinity Divinity School in Deerfield, Illnois, and the other half in France where he is Trinity's director of the European Program at the Faculté de Théologie Protestante de l'Université de Strasbourg.

Dr. Montgomery is the author of 14 books. He is a Phi Beta Kappa and is listed in Who's Who in America, Who's Who in France, Who's Who in Europe and other biographical directories.

Mount Ararat is located in eastern Turkey near the borders of Russia and Iran.

APPENDIX E

Maps of the Ararat Region

SCALE: 1 INCH=1.58 MILES OR 1 MILE=5/8 INCH

Ahura

TAKALTI Da Takatu

Gomik

Serdarbulak

KÜCÜKAGRI

Biçare

2750

3925

JOYS

Bibliography

Abich, O. W. H. von "Hauteurs absolues du système de l'Ararat et des pays environnants," *Bulletin de la Société de Géographie* [Paris], 4th ser., I (1851), 66-73.

Abich, O. W. H. von "Notice explicative d'une vue du cône de l'Ararat," *Bulletin de la Société de Géographie* [Paris] 4th ser., I (1851), 515-25, 556; simultaneously published in the *Bulletin de la Société Géologique de France*, 2d ser., VIII (1850-1851), 265-71.

Adams, H. C. *The Wonder Book of Travellers' Tales.* New York: Liveright Publishing Corp., 1936.

Adelsen, Charles. "Land of Great Ararat: Turkey's Forbidden Territory," *Geograph. Magazine* [London], XLII/3 (1969), 188-93.

Ali, S. M. "Some Geographical Ideas of Al-Mas'udi." In *Al-Mas'udi Millenary Commemoration Volume.* Edited by S. Maqbul Ahmad and A. Rahman. Published by the Indian Society for the History of Science and the Institute of Islamic Studies, Aligarh Muslim University, 1960.

Allen, Don Cameron. *The Legend of Noah: Renaissance Rationalism in Art, Science and Letters.* Illini Books. Reprint edition. Urbana: University of Illinois Press, 1963 [1949].

Al-Mas'udi. *Ed-Mas'udi's Historical Encyclopaedia, entitled* "Meadows of Gold and Mines of Gems." Translated by Aloys Sprenger. Volume I. London: The Oriental Translation Fund of Great Britain and Ireland, 1841.

Al-Mas'udi. *Les Prairies d'Or.* Translated by Barbier de Meynard and Pavet de Courteille. Edited by Charles Pellat. Volume I. "Société Asiatique: Collection d'Ouvrages Orientaux." Paris, 1962.

Altink, I. E., Pamir, H. N., and Erentöz, C. (compilers) *Turkiye Jeoloji Haritasi 1-500,000. Geological map of Turkey, sheet Van, with explanatory text.* Ankara, 1964.

Alzog, Dr. *Manuel de Patrologie.* Translated by L'Abbé P. Bélet. Paris: Gaume Frères et J. Duprey, 1867.

Andree, Richard. *Die Flutensagen, ethnologisch betrachtet.* Germany: Viehweg und Sohn, 1891.

Andres, Stefan. *Noah und seine Kinder* (Mit sechzehn Holzschnitten von Hansen-Bahia). Munich: R. Piper, 1968.

Backer, Louis de. *L'extrême orient au moyen âge*. Paris: Ernest Leroux, 1877. For negative criticisms of this work, see Sir Henry Yule's review in *The Athenaeum*, August 11, 1877, and Henri Cordier's evaluation in *Revue Critique*, May 19, 1877. It remains, however, a basic source for Haithon.

Baring-Gould, Rev. S. *Legends of the Patriarchs and Prophets and other Old Testament Characters from various sources*. New York: Hurst & Co., Publishers, n.d.

Barrows, John Henry. *Christianity the World Religion*. Chicago: A. C. McClurg, 1897.

Barrows, John Henry. *A World-Pilgrimage*. Edited by Mary Eleanor Barrows. Chicago: A. C. McClurg, 1897.

Beazley, C. Raymond. *The Dawn of Modern Geography. A History of Exploration and Geographical Science*. 3 volumes. London: John Murray; Oxford: Clarendon Press, 1897-1906. (From *ca.* A.D. 300 to *ca.* 1420.)

Bedin, Auguste. *Les traditions messianiques, ou Démonstration de la divinité du Christianisme par le témoignage de tous les peuples de la terre*. Lyon: C. Couvat, 1851.

Bernos de Gasztold, Carmen. *The Creatures' Choir*. Translated by Rumer Godden. Illustrated by Jean Primrose. New York: The Viking Press, 1965.

Bernos de Gasztold, Carmen. *Prayers from the Ark*. Translated by Rumer Godden. Illustrated by Jean Primrose. London: Macmillan, 1966.

Bessière, Paul. *L'Alpinisme*. "Que sais-je?" No. 1255. Paris: Presses Universitaires de France, 1967.

Bisaccia, Mario, et al. *Alpinisme Moderne*. Edited and translated by Félix Germain. Paris: B. Arthaud, 1971.

Blumenthal, M. "Der Vulkan Ararat und die Berge seiner Sedimenterung," *Revue de la Faculté de Sciences* [Université Istanbul], Ser. B. XXIII/3-4 (1958), 177-327.

Blumenthal, M. "Die Vergletscherung des Ararat," *Geographica Helvetica*, IV (1956).

Blumenthal M. *Verhandl. d. Schweizer, naturf. Ges.* Basel, 1956.

Bochart, Samuel. *Geographia sacra, seu Phaleg et Canaan*. 4th edition. Edited by Peter de Villemandy. Lugduni Batavorum. [Leiden]: Boutesteyn & Luchtmans, 1707. (This is Vol. I of Bochart's *Opera omnia*.)

Bourgeat, M. L'Abbé J.-B. *Études sur Vincent de Beau-*

vais, théologien, philosophe, encyclopédiste. Paris: Auguste Durand, 1856.

Bréhaut, Ernest, *An Encyclopedist of the Dark Ages: Isidore of Seville.* Studies in History, Economics and Public Law. Edited by the Faculty of Political Science of Columbia University. Volume XLVIII/1, Whole No. 120. New York: Columbia University, 1912; reprint edition in "Burt Franklin Research & Source Work Series 107." New York: Burt Franklin, n.d.

Bretschneider, E. *Mediaeval Researches from Eastern Asiatic Sources.* 2 volumes. London: Kegan Paul, Trench, Trubner, 1910.

Bright, John. "Has Archaeology Found Evidence of the Flood?" *The Biblical Archaeologist,* V/4 (December, 1942), 55-62.

Brinton, Daniel G. *The Myths of the New World: A Treatise on the Symbolism and Mythology of the Red Race of America.* New York: Leypoldt & Holt, 1868.

Broydé, Issac. "Zacuto Abraham ben Samuel." *The Jewish Encyclopedia.* Edited by Isidore Singer. Volume XII. P. 627.

Bruyn, Cornelius de (1652-1726/7). *Voyages . . . par la Moscovie, en Perse, et aux Indes Orientales . . . Et quelques remarques contre Mrs. Chardin & Kempfer. Avec une lettre écrite à la* [sic] *auteur, sur ce sujet . . . .* 2 volumes. Amsterdam: Freres Wetstein, 1718. Translation of his *Reizen over Moskovie . . .* (1711). Eng. trans. (of French), 1737. This critique deals only with Chardin's remarks on the ruins of the "ancient temple of Persepolis," and does not impugn his general integrity.

Bryant, Jacob. *Of the Deluge in Ancient Mythology.* London, 1775. Bryant (1715-1804) was a fellow of King's College, Cambridge, and a learned if eccentric Christian apologist (cf. his *Treatise upon the Authenticity of the Scriptures and the Truth of the Christian Religion* [1792]). For biographical data, see the article devoted to him in the *Dictionary of National Biography.*

Bryce, James. "The Ascent of Ararat," *Alpine Journal* [London], VIII (May, 1877), 208 ff.

Bryce, James. "On Armenia and Mount Ararat," *Proceedings of the Royal Geographical Society* [London], XXII (May 9, 1878), 169-86.

Bryce, James. *Transcaucasia and Ararat: being notes of a vacation tour in the Autumn of 1876.* London: Macmillan, 1877. A "fourth edition revised with a supplementary chapter on the recent history of the Armenian question" was published at London in 1896; our citations, however, are in every case to the first edition.

Burdick, Clifford L. "Geological Reconnaissance of the Anatolia and the Ararat Area." In *The Geological, Glaciological and Botanical Reports Taken During the 1964 and 1966 Expeditions to Eastern Turkey and Mount Ararat.* Edited by Lawrence Hewitt. New York: The Archaeological Research Foundation (51 Madison Ave., New York 10010), [1967].

Calmet, Augustin. *Dictionnaire historique . . . de la Bible.* 2 volumes. Paris: Emery [*et al.*], 1722.

Cassuto, U. *A Commentary on the Book of Genesis.* Translated by Israel Abrahams. 2 volumes. Jerusalem: Magnes Press, 1961-1964. (Pt. I: "From Adam to Noah," Gen. 1:1-6:8; Pt. II: "From Noah to Abraham," Gen. 6:9-11:32.)

Catcott, A. *A Treatise on the Deluge.* London, 1761.

Chardin, Jean (Sir John). *Travels in Persia.* Edited by Sir Percy Sykes. London: The Argonaut Press, 1927. Reprint of a practically unknown, two-volume edition of Chardin's *Voyages* which is useful for its Introduction.

Chardin, Jean (Sir John). *Voyages . . . en Perse, et autres lieux de l'Orient.* Volume II, Part 2. Amsterdam: Jean Louis de Lorme, 1711. The first complete edition of Chardin's travels. Some volumes of this edition carry the title, *Journal du voyage . . . .*

Coan, Frederick G. *Yesterdays in Persia and Kurdistan.* Claremont, Calif.: Saunders Studio Press, 1939.

Codrington, R. H. *The Melanesians: Studies in their Anthropology and Folk-Lore.* Oxford: Clarendon Press, 1891.

Crosby, Oliver S. "Demavend and Ararat, 1951," *The American Alpine Journal,* IX/1 (1954), 76-87.

Cyril of Alexandria. "Contra Julianum." *In:* J.-P. Migne (ed.), *Patrologiae cursus completus . . . series graeca.* Volume LXXVI. Paris, 1859. Columns 513-16.

DeBeer, Sir Gavin. *Early Travellers in the Alps.* Reprint edition. New York: October House, 1966 [1930].

Desbarreaux-Bernard, Dr. *Étude Bibliographique sur L'Édition du* Speculum Quadruplex *de Vincent de Beauvais.* Paris: Léon Techener, 1872.

Elmacin, George. *Historia Saracenica.* Edited and translated by Thomas Erpenius, Leiden, 1625.

Epiphanius, *Panaria.* Edited by Franz Oehler. Volume I,

Part I. "Corpus Haereseologicum." volume 2. Berlin: A. Asher, 1859.

Eusebius of Caesarea. *Praeparatio Evangelica.* Edited by E. H. Gifford. 4 volumes. Oxford: Oxford University Press, 1903.

Fabricius, Jo. A. *Codicis Pseudepigraphi Veteris Testamenti, Volumen Alterum. Accedit Josephi Veteris Christiani Scriptoris Hypomnesticon in Lucem Editum cum Versione ac Notis.* Editio Altera. Hamburg: Felgineriam et Bohnium, 1741.

Filby, Frederick A. *The Flood Reconsidered: A review of the evidences of geology, archaeology, ancient literature and the Bible.* "Contemporary Evangelical Perspectives." Grand Rapids, Mich.: Zondervan Publishing House, 1971.

Fink, Josef. *Noe der Gerechte in der Frühchristlichen Kunst.* Edited by Herbert Grundmann and Fritz Wagner. "Beihefte zum Archive für Kulturgeschichte," volume 4, Münster/Köln: Böhlau-Verlag, 1955.

Freshfield, Douglas W. "Early Ascents of Ararat," *Alpine Journal* [London], VIII (May, 1877), 214-16.

Freshfield, Douglas W. *Travels in the Central Caucasus and Bashan including Visits to Ararat and Tabreez and Ascents of Kazbek and Elbruz.* London: Longmans, Green, 1869.

Freygang, Frederika (Kudriaskaia) von. *Letters from the Causasus and Georgia; to which are added, the Account of A Journey into Persia in 1812 and An Unabridged History of Persia since the time of Nadir Shah.* London: John Murray, 1823.

Garnett, David. *Two by Two: A Story of Survival.* New York: Atheneum, 1964.

Gautrat, Jacques. *Dictionnaire de la Montagne.* Paris: Éditions du Seuil, 1970.

Gemelli-Careri, Giovanni Francesco. *Voyage du tour du monde.* Translated by M.L.N. 2d edition. Volume I. Paris: Étienne Ganeau, 1727. This translation was based on the latest Italian edition.

Gillispie, Charles Coulston. *Genesis and Geology: A Study in the Relations of Scientific Thought, Natural Theology, and Social Opinion in Great Britain, 1790-1850.* Harper Torchbooks. New York: Harper & Row, Publishers, 1959 [1951].

Gonzalez de Clavijo, Ruy. *Narrative of the Embassy of Ruy de Gonzalez de Clavijo to the Court of Timour, at*

Samarcand, A.D. 1403-6. Edited and translated by Clements R. Markham. Hakluyt Society, 1859.

Hakluyt, Richard. *The Tudor Venturers.* Edited by John Hampden. London. The Folio Society, 1970.

Hanauer, J. E. *Folk-lore of the Holy Land, Moslem, Christian and Jewish.* New edition. London: The Sheldon Press, 1935.

Heidel, Alexander. *The Gilgamesh Epic and Old Testament Parallels.* 2d edition. Chicago: University of Chicago Press, 1949.

Herzog, Maurice. *Annapurna.* New York: Popular Library, 1952.

Hewitt, Lawrence B., *et al. The Geological Glaciological and Botanical Reports Taken During the 1964 and 1966 Expeditions to Eastern Turkey and Mount Ararat.* New York: Archaeological Research Foundation (51 Madison Ave., New York 10010), [1967]. (Includes: "Geological Report" by Clifford L. Burdick; "Glaciological Report" by N. A. Van Arkel, etc.)

Holl, Karl. *Die Handscriftliche Überlieferung des Epiphanius.* Leipzig: J. C. Hinrich'sche Buchhandlung, 1910.

The Holy Qur-án. Containing the Arabic Text with English Translation and Commentary by Maulvi Muhammad Ali. 3d edition. Lahore, Punjab, India: Ahmadiyya Anjuman-I-Isháat-I-Islam, 1935.

Horne, Thomas Hartwell. *An Introduction to the Critical Study and Knowledge of the Holy Scriptures.* 7th edition. Volume III. London: T. Cadell, 1834.

Hunt, John. *The Ascent of Everest.* London: Hodder and Stoughton, 1953.

Ibn Haukal. *Configuration de la terre (Kitab Surat Al-Ard).* Edited and translated by J. H. Kramers and G. Wiet. Volume I. "Collection UNESCO d'Oeuvres Représentatives: Série arake." Paris: Editions G.-P. Maissoneuve & Larose, 1964.

Ibn Haukal. *The Oriental Geography of Ebn Haukal, an Arabian Traveler of the Tenth Century.* Translated by Sir William Ouseley. London: T. Cadell, 1800.

Imhof, E. "Der Ararat," *Die Alpen* [Berne], XXXII (1956), 1-14.

Isidore of Seville. *Etymologiarium sive Originum.* Book XX. Edited by W. M. Lindsay. "Scriptorum Classicorum Bibliotheca Oxoniensis," volume 2. Oxford: Clarendon Press, 1911.

Jacoby, Felix (ed.). *Die Fragmente der Grieschischen His-*

toriker (FGR HIST). Volume II/A. Berlin: Weidmann, 1926. (90 F, Nicolas of Damascus); Volume III/C. Leiden: E. J. Brill, 1958. (685F, Abydenos; 787F, Hieronymos the Egyptian).

Jordanus, Friar. *Mirabilia Descripta. The Wonders of the East, by Friar Jordanus of the order of the preachers and bishop of Columbum in India the Greater (circa 1330).* Edited by Sir Henry Yule. Hakluyt Society, series 1, volume XXXI. London: Printed for the Hakluyt Society, 1863. Translated from the Latin original, this edition was first published at Paris in 1839 in the Society of Geography's *Recueil de voyages et de mémoires,* volume IV, pp. 1-68.

Josephus, Flavius. *Josephus with an English Translation.* Edited and translated by Henry St. John Thackeray, Ralph Marcus, and Louis H. Feldman. 9 volumes. "Loeb Classical Library." Cambridge, Mass.: Harvard University Press, 1926-1955.

Keller, Werner. *The Bible as History: A Confirmation of the Book of Books.* Translated by William Neil. New York: William Morrow and Co., 1956.

Kircher, Athanasius. *Arca Noe in tres libros digesta, sive de rebus ante diluvium, de diluvio et re rebus post diluvium a Noeme getis.* Amsterdam, 1675.

Komroff, Manuel, editor. "The Travels of Rabbi Benjamin of Tudela, 1160-1173." In *Contemporaries of Marco Polo.* New York: Liveright, 1928.

Langlois, Victor. *Collection des historiens anciens et modernes de l'Arménie.* Volume I ("Première Période—Historiens Grecs et Syriens traduit anciennement en Arménien"). Paris: Firmin-Didot, 1881.

Lenormant, François. *The Beginning of History according to the Bible and the Traditions of Oriental Peoples.* Translated by Francis Brown. New York: Charles Scribner's Sons, 1882.

LePelletier, Jean. *Dissertations sur l'Arche de Noé. . . .* Rouen: Jean B. Besongne, 1700. One of the older classic treatments. Detailed (520 pp.) discussion of the size, arrangement, construction, and logistics of the Ark. Apologetic refutation of objections to the historicity of the flood and the Noahic voyage. Author holds to a universal deluge.

Lessing, Erich. *Die Arche Noah in Bildern.* Zurich: Verlag Fritz Molden, 1968.

Lewis, C. Day. "Noah and the Waters." *A Time to Dance, Noah and the Waters, and Other Poems.* New York: Random House, 1936.

Lewis, Jack P. *A Study of the Interpretation of Noah and the Flood in Jewish and Christian Literature*. Leiden, The Netherlands: E. J. Brill, 1968.

Longuinoff. D. "Ascension de l'Ararat," *Bulletin de la Sociéte de Géographie* [Paris], 4th ser., I (1851), 52-65.

Lynch, H. F. B. *Armenia: Travels and Studies*. 2 volumes. London, 1901.

Manuel D'Alpinisme. Zurich: Club Alpin Suisse, 1943.

Markoff, E. de, and Kovalewsky, E. de. "Expédition scientifique au Caucase." *Bulletin de la Société Royale Belge de Géographie* [Brussels], XII (1888), 577-91.

Massian. Michel. *Les Explorateurs*. "Encyclopédie Essentielle" (Série Histoire No. 10). Paris: Robert Delpire, 1965.

Meisner, Balthasar. *Orationes duae, prior de Arca Noachi, cum qua comparatur Academia . . . .* Wittenberg: Matthew Henckel, 1677. A public lecture (1615) by the great orthodox Lutheran theologian (1587-1626) on the occasion of his retirement as rector of Wittenberg University. Meisner presents his conception of the ideal Christian university by analogy with Noah's Ark!

Michael, M. A. *Traveller's Quest: Original Contributions to a Philosophy of Travel*. London: William Hodge and Co., 1950.

Miller, Hugh. *The Testimony of the Rocks; or, Geology in its Bearings on the Two Theologies, Natural and Revealed*. Edinburgh: Thomas Constable & Co.; Shepherd & Elliot, 1857.

Moïse de Corène (Chorene, Khorene). *Géographie . . . d'apres Ptolémée*. Translated by Le P. Arsène Soukry. Venise: Imprimerie Armènienne, 1881.

Moïse de Corène. *Historie d'Arménie*. Translated by P. E. Le Vaillant de Florival. 2 volumes. Venise: Saint-Lazare, 1841.

Montgomery, John Warwick. "The Apologetic Approach of Muhammad Ali and its Implications for Christian Apologetics," *Muslim World*. LI (April, 1961), 111-22. (See author's "Corrigendum" in the July, 1961 issue.)

Navarra, Fernand. *The Forbidden Mountain*. Translated by Michael Legat. London: Macdonald, 1956.

Navarra, Fernand. *J'ai trouvé l'arche de Noé*. Paris: Éditions France-Empire, 1956.

Nelson, Byron C. *The Deluge Story in Stone: A History of the Flood Theory of Geology*. Reprint edition. Minneapolis: Bethany Fellowship Publishers, 1968 [1931].

"Noah's Ark?" *Life*, XLIX (Sept. 5, 1960), 112, 114.

Noyce, Wilfrid. *Scholar Mountaineers: Pioneers of Parnassus.* London: Dennis Dobson, 1950.

Obey, Andre. *Noah: A Play.* New York: Samuel French, 1935.

Olaguë, Ignacio, editor. *Journal de Bord de Jean de la Cosa, Seconde Christophe Colomb.* Paris: Éditions de Paris, 1957.

Olearius [Oelschlager], Adam. *The Travels of Olearius in Seventeenth-Century Russia.* Edited and translated by Samuel H. Baron. Stanford, Calif.: Stanford University Press, 1967. "The present edition contains slightly more than half of Olearius's 1656 edition. Essentially I have translated only the portion of the account that deals with Russia" (p. x). The translation does not include Olearius' passage concerning Noah's Ark on Ararat. The value of Baron's edition for us lies in his excellent editorial introduction. We take this opportunity to thank Professor Samuel H. Baron, of the Department of History, University of California at San Diego, who corresponded with us on the problems of locating the Olearius passage on the Ark.

Olearius [Oelschlager], Adam. *The Voyages and Travels of the Ambassador Sent by Frederick Duke of Holstein, to the Great Duke of Muscovy, and the King of Persia.* Translated by John Davies. London, 1662.

Parrot, Dr. J. J. Friedrich. *Journey to Ararat.* Translated by W. D. Cooley. London: Longman, Brown, Green, and Longmans, 1845.

Paust, Ingerose. *Der Berg Ararat.* Berlin: Evangelische Verlagsanstalt Gmb H., 1969.

Peake, Harold. *The Flood: New Light on an Old Story.* London: Kegan Paul, Trench, Trubner & Co., 1930.

Peeters, P. "La légende de saint Jacques de Nisibe," *Analecta Bollandiana.* XXXVIII (1920), 285-373.

Pegna, Mario Lopes. "L'Arca di Noè e la Torre de Babele: Miti e Realtà nella Tradizione Biblica," *Universo* [Florence], XXXIV (1954), 701-710.

Poljak, Željko. "Ararat (5165)"; Aleksic, Nikola, "Za one, koji će na Ararat." *Naše Planine* ["Our Mountains"], XII (November-December, 1970), 273-79, 280-83 respectively. (In Yugoslavian; illustrated. Account of the 1970 Yugoslavian expedition to the summit of Greater Ararat.)

Porter, Sir Robert Ken. *Travels in Georgia, Persia, Armenia, Ancient Babylonia, &c. &c. during the years 1817,*

1818, 1819, and 1820. 2 volumes. London: Longman, Hurst, Rees, Orme, and Brown, 1821-1822.

Pritchard, James B., editor. *Ancient Near Eastern Texts Relating to the Old Testament*. Princeton, N.J.: Princeton University Press, 1950.

Quasten, Johannes, *Patrology*. 3 volumes. Westminster, Md.: Newman Press, 1950-1960.

Räcke, Horst, illustrator. *Gehört und Gesehen: Hundert Bilder zur Bibel*. East Berlin: Evangelische Haupt-Bibelgesellschaft, 1969.

Rehwinkel, Alfred M. *The Flood in the Light of the Bible, Geology, and Archaeology*. St. Louis, Mo.: Concordia Publishing House, 1951.

Rich, Claudius James. *Narrative of a Residence in Koordistan and on the Site of Ancient Ninevah; with Journal of a Voyage Down the Tigris to Bagdad and an Account of a Visit to Shirauz and Persepolis*. 2 volumes. London: James Duncan, 1836.

Riquier, J.-A. de. "Le Pays d'Ararat," *Acta Geographica* [Paris], XXI/1 (1957), 5-8.

Schloessinger, Max. "Joseph ben Gorion (Josephus Gorionides)." *The Jewish Encyclopedia*. Edited by Isidore Singer. Volume VII. Pp. 259-60.

Seylaz, Louis. "L'ascension du Mont Ararat," *Le Tour du Monde*, n.s., XVII/34 (August 26, 1911), 397-408.

Shafi, Mohammad. "Al-Mas'udi as a Geographer." In *Al-Mas'udi Millenary Commemoration Volume*. Edited by S. Maqbul Ahmad and A. Rahman. Published by the Indian Society for the History of Science and the Institute of Islamic Studies, Aligarh Muslim University, 1960.

Smith, A. E. Wilder. *Man's Origin, Man's Destiny*. Wheaton, Ill.: Harold Shaw, 1968.

Smith, Eli. *Researches of the Rev. E. Smith and Rev. H.G.O. Dwight in Armenia; Including a Journey through Asia Minor, and into Georgia and Persia, with a Visit to the Nestorian and Chaldean Christians of Oormaih and Salmas*. 2 volumes. Boston: Crocker and Brewster, 1833.

Smith, George Adam. *The Historical Geography of the Holy Land*. 4th edition. London: Hodder and Stoughton, n.d.

Smith, George Alan. *Introduction to Mountaineering*. Revised edition. New York: A. S. Barnes and Co., 1967.

Stephens, James. *The Crock of Gold*. New York: The Macmillan Co., 1940.

Struys, Jean. *Les Voyages de Jean Struys en Moscovie, en*

Tartarie, en Perse, aux Indes, & en plusieurs autres Pays étrangers. Volume II. Lyon: Plaignard & Guillimin, 1684. This translation was made by Glanius from the original Dutch edition in 1677 and was first published at Amsterdam in 1681.

Stuart, Major Robert. "The Ascent of Mount Ararat in 1856," *Proceedings of the Royal Geographical Society* [London], XXI/1 (January, 1877), 77-92.

Styles, Showell. *The Arrow Book of Climbing.* London: Arrow Books, 1966.

Sussman, Aaron and Goode, Ruth. *The Magic of Walking.* New York: Simon and Schuster, 1969.

Tavernier, Jean-Baptiste. *Travels in India. . . .* Edited and translated by V. Ball. Edited by William Crooke. 2d Edition. 2 volumes. London: Humphrey Milford, 1925. This volume was translated from the original French edition of 1676.

Turkish Fairy Tales. Mount Vernon, N.Y.: Peter Pauper Press, 1964.

Turquie. "Les Guides Modernes Fodor." Paris: Éditions Vilo, 1968.

Ullendorff, Edward. "The Construction of Noah's Ark," *Vetus Testamentum,* IV (1954), 95-96.

Van Arkel, Nicolaas A. "1966 Archaeological Research Foundation Expedition to Mt. Ararat, Eastern Turkey Glaciological Report." In *The Geological, Glaciological and Botanical Reports Taken During the 1964 and 1966 Expeditions to Eastern Turkey and Mount Ararat.* Edited by Lawrence Hewitt. New York The Archaeological Research Foundation (51 Madison Ave., New York 10010), [1967].

Vincent of Beauvais. *Speculum quadruplex: naturale, doctrinale, morale, historiale.* Duaci [Douai]: B. Beller, 1624. On the fraudulent "morale" section of this work, see Gabriel, p. 10.

Wales, Henry. "Relics of Noah's Ark." *Chicago Sunday Tribune,* March 29, 1953.

Walker, Warren S. and Uysal, Ahmet E. *Tales Alive in Turkey.* Cambridge, Mass.: Harvard University Press, 1966.

Wells, Carveth. *Kapoot: The Narrative of a Journey from Leningrad to Mount Ararat in Search of Noah's Ark.* London: Jarrold Publishers, 1934.

Whitcomb, John C., Jr. and Morris, Henry M. *The Genesis Flood.* Philadelphia: The Presbyterian and Reformed Publishing Company, 1961.

White, Andrew Dickson. *A History of the Warfare of*

Science with Theology in Christendom. Reprint edition. 2 volumes. New York: Dover Publications, 1960 [1896].

White, Frederic R., editor. *Famous Utopias of the Renaissance.* New York: Hendricks House, 1946.

Whittingham, William R. "Essay on the Life and Writings of Samuel Bochart." In *Essays and Dissertations in Biblical Literature.* New York: G. & C. & H. Carvill, 1829.

William of Rubruck. *The Journey of William of Rubruck to the Eastern Parts of the World, 1253-1255, as narrated by himself, with two accounts of the earlier journey of John of Pian de Caprine. Edited and translated by William Woodville Rockhill.* Hakluyt Society, series 2, volume IV. London: Printed for the Hakluyt Society, 1900.

Woolley, Sir Leonard. *Excavations at Ur.* London: Ernest Benn, 1954.

Wright Thomas, editor. *Early Travels in Palestine, comprising the narratives of Areulf, Willibald, Bernard, Saewulf, Sigurd, Benjamin of Tudela, Sir John Mandeville, de la Brocquière, and Maundrell.* London: Henry G. Bohn, 1848.

Yamauchi, Edwin M. *The Stones and the Scriptures.* "Evangelical Perspectives," edited by John Warwick Montgomery. Philadelphia: Lippincott, 1972.

Yule, Colonel Sir Henry, editor and translator and Cordier, Henry, editor. *Cathay and the Way Thither.* Hakluyt Society, series 2, volume XXXIII. Revised edition. London: Printed for the Hakluyt Society, 1913. (Vol. II—"Odoric of Pordenone.")

Yule, Colonel Sir Henry, editor and translator and Cordier, Henri, editor. *Cathay and the Way Thither.* Hakluyt Society, series 2, volume XXXVII. Revised edition. London: Printed for the Hakluyt Society, 1914. (Vol. III—"Missionary Friars—Rashíduddín—Pegolotti—Marignolli.")

Zurcher, F. and Margollé, E. *Les ascensions célèbres aux plus hautes montagnes du globe.* "Bibliotheque des Merveilles." 2d edition. Paris: L. Hachette, 1869.

Index of Names

This index contains: the names of all personal entities mentioned in the book, real or fictitous, individual or corporate; the names of all places, regional, national, territorial, civil, and local; and the names of local institutions, monuments, and sites.